THE
FATEFUL
PEBBLE

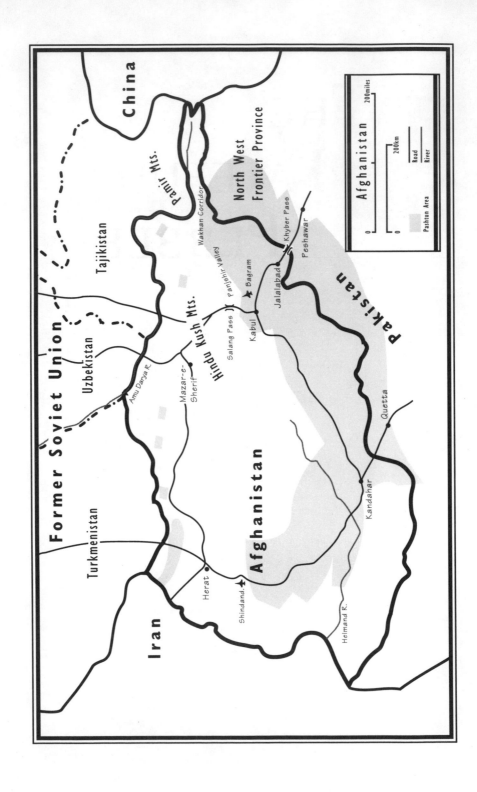

THE
FATEFUL
PEBBLE

Afghanistan's Role in the Fall
of the Soviet Empire

ANTHONY ARNOLD

With a Foreword by Theodore L. Eliot, Jr.
U.S. Ambassador to Afghanistan, 1973–78

★

PRESIDIO

To the Afghans and the "afgantsy"

May you be granted, en-shallah, *the will, tolerance, and forgiveness to build a peaceful future for your countries.*

It's harder than war.

Published by Presidio Press
505 B San Marin Dr., Suite 300
Novato, CA 94945-1340

Library of Congress Cataloging-in-Publication Data

Arnold, Anthony.
    The fateful pebble : Afghanistan's role in the fall of the Soviet Empire / Anthony Arnold ; with a foreword by Theodore L. Eliot, Jr.
      p.   cm.
    Includes bibliographical references (p. 211-219) and index.
    ISBN 0-89141-461-4
    1. Soviet Union—Foreign relations—Afghanistan. 2. Afghanistan—Foreign relations—Soviet Union. 3. Soviet Union—Foreign relations—1945-4. Afghanistan—History—Soviet occupation.
1979–1989. I. Title
PK67.7.A3A76 1993
327.470581—dc20   92-27948
                                                                   CIP

Typography and map by ProImage
Printed in the United States of America

CONTENTS

ACKNOWLEDGMENTS

Thanks go to the many direct and indirect contributors to this book including:

—William F. Whitmore, whose perusal and clipping of the domestic and British press were a godsend; Mary Ann Siegfried of the *Afghanistan Forum*, who supplied the latest news releases from Kabul; librarians at Berkeley, Stanford, and the Hoover Institution, but especially Edith Malamud and Lone Beeson of the San Francisco World Affairs Council library;

—Margit Grigory of the Hoover Institution for taking time off her busy schedule for so many scholarly favors;

—Bob Kane of Presidio Press for taking a chance with an unfamiliar author and subject;

—my wife Ruth, who did so much of the research, tracked down innumerable misplaced references ("that should be easy—it's on a piece of paper"), and deftly trod the diplomatic minefield of creative editing for a curmudgeonly author;

—a nameless individual who implied that the Soviet-Afghan war had about as much historical significance as the War of Jenkins's Ear, a comment whose recall regularly provoked new heights of outrage and industry whenever my energies flagged.

FOREWORD

When a future historian tackles the question of "The Decline and Fall of the Russian Empire," Anthony Arnold's book will be an important source. His is the first comprehensive analysis of the effects of the Soviet invasion of Afghanistan and the ensuing war for Afghan independence on the Soviet Russian imperial system. He clearly and succinctly demonstrates that the Afghan war was one of the key factors in causing the disintegration of the Soviet Union.

Arnold is well qualified to undertake this analysis. He has been a lifelong student of the Soviet Union. In the 1970s he lived for two years in Afghanistan and became intimately acquainted with its culture and intricate tribally-based politics. He has published two books on aspects of Soviet-Afghan relations. I know of no other writer who has such deep knowledge of both countries. Although many experienced observers of the Soviet Union and Afghanistan engaged in wishful thinking from the onset of the Soviet invasion in 1979 that the Afghans might win the war, Arnold was the only one I know who never wavered in his conviction that the Afghans would win.

History is full of interesting parallels. Some observers have compared the Soviet-Afghan War with the American experience in Vietnam. Aside from many similarities, however, and despite the severe (and continuing) effects on American politics and economics of the Vietnam War, the United States continues to survive as a prosperous democracy.

Another parallel is with the British experience in Afghanistan, including two signal setbacks in the nineteenth century. As was the case with the Russian Empire, the British Empire in Asia reached its zenith in Afghanistan. But British institutions proved far more stable than those of the Soviet Union in the 1980s, and the British Empire survived its setbacks in Afghanistan for almost another century.

Still another set of parallels, and Arnold describes these in this book, is with past Russian military setbacks—in the Crimean, Russo-Japanese, and First World wars—and their effects on the internal stability of the empire. In every case, the imperial system was severely strained; and in one, 1917–18, the imperial leaders were replaced. The Afghan War's effects were similar to those of past defeats; but in this case, as Arnold points out, due in large measure to the improvements in education and communications within the Soviet Russian Empire, defeat led to the rapid collapse of a five-hundred-year-old system.

So the last great European empire has come to an end, and a new era of history has arrived. There are many heroes of this historic dénouement, Afghans and Russians foremost but also their supporters in other countries. Critically important was the steadfastness of the western world in giving moral and material support to the Afghans who fought for their country's independence against enormous odds and in standing up to Soviet imperial designs on a global basis.

Who will be the heroes of the reconstruction of Afghanistan, of the development of the new nations that have emerged from the Soviet Empire, of the efforts to establish global peace and security in a post–Cold-War era? I look forward to Arnold's views on these matters.

Theodore L. Eliot, Jr.
U.S. Ambassador to Afghanistan, 1973–78

PREFACE

A dead-tired man may stumble over a pebble and fall; but his weariness, rather than the pebble, is the cause.

George Stewart, *Storm*

Stewart may have been right, but he fails to give the pebble its due. How much farther might that dead-tired man have staggered on before collapsing of his weariness alone? How much more serious might the consequences of his fall have been after his last reserves of strength had been exhausted, and he was unable to cushion his fall?

In this book, I submit that the Soviet Union, beset with a myriad of economic, social, and political problems in the waning years of Leonid Brezhnev's reign, was analogous to the weary traveler, and Afghanistan to the pebble that brought him down.

If it had not been for the Soviet setback in Afghanistan the next challenge to Moscow's hegemony almost surely would have been met with the same resort to arms. That challenge (from Poland, later in 1980) in fact very nearly did trigger an invasion, first in early 1981 and again in December that year; a Soviet general has stated that his troops were ready to occupy the entire country "within one day or at most two," and Polish Communist leaders have generally contended that only General Jaruzelski's imposition of martial law stayed the Soviet hand at the last moment.* Surely, however, another major element in the Kremlin's decision not to intervene must have been the embarrassment they were suffering in Afghanistan.

What the international repercussions of a Soviet invasion of Poland might have been can only be conjectured. Even without that fateful step, however, it is arguable that a quick victory in Afghanistan might have meant that: the Communist party of the Soviet Union (CPSU) traditional apparat would still be in full command of the USSR; its

---

San Francisco Examiner, March 15, 1992, p. A-4 (AP, Warsaw).

general secretary would be someone a good bit more intransigent than Mikhail Gorbachev; the military budgets of both the United States and the USSR would be continuing their mad expansions of the 1970s and 1980s; active Soviet involvement in Africa, Asia, and Latin America would still be the order of the day; the reform movements that have exploded throughout the Marxist-Leninist world would be the stuff of dreams; and international tensions would be at an all-time, virtually unbearable high.

This suggested alternative to today's reality, although impossible to prove or disprove, is but a logical extension of old Soviet policies whose single virtue was—until Afghanistan—demonstrable success. Since World War II, at tremendous cost to the Soviet people, Moscow's export of Marxism-Leninism had been pushed relentlessly, if not always successfully, throughout the world and had sparked equally costly defensive moves from the West. Meanwhile, in areas already won to Moscow's side, opposition had been suppressed by ruthless police action or, when necessary, by force of Soviet arms (East Germany in 1953, Hungary in 1956, Czechoslovakia in 1968), thus increasing Western concerns still further.

Ultimately, the inherent weaknesses of the old Soviet system were bound to cause a major reform movement, but as long as the empire could be perceived as successfully expanding, the Kremlin leaders had few incentives for changing their policies. Despite a falling standard of living, even the common Soviet citizen would probably have been prepared to accept many more years of privation for the greater glory of the realm. There doubtless would have been some popular grumbling about conditions, but the three basic pillars of Soviet society—the party, the military, and the KGB—would have continued to suppress dissent and enforce discipline. It was only when the corrosive effects of the unwinnable war ate into each of those pillars that the empire they supported began to come apart.

Many books have been written about the fate of empires. Most fail to touch on one vital politico-psychological aspect: the perception of imperial failure, both within and without the empire. Regardless of how much economic progress is being sacrificed to military needs, the problem only becomes acute when it becomes self-evident. In this respect, the war in Afghanistan occurred concurrently with a world revolution in communications, a revolution wherein the old Soviet system of information control simply broke down. When Soviet dissidents could simply fax their works to the West by telephone, censorship became a largely outmoded tool.

A third factor that undermined the old Soviet system was the U.S. hard-line response to Soviet military muscle flexing and its willingness to go head-to-head with the USSR in an arms race. The critical element here was the fulfillment of a pledge in the late 1970s to deploy ground-launched cruise missiles (GLCMs) and Pershing II ballistic missiles in NATO countries if the Soviets proceeded with deployment of SS-20 missiles aimed at Western Europe. The Soviet response was to ignore the warning, proceed with deployment, and pull out all the stops in a massive overt and covert political action campaign to prevent the U.S. countermove. This campaign failed. The United State deployed its missiles in the early 1980s, and the USSR wound up in worse strategic shape than before.

Although this drama unfolded far away from Afghanistan, it is arguable that both the U.S. firmness and the failure of the Soviet campaign were results of the December 1979 invasion, which the West accepted as a more convincing demonstration of basically aggressive and expansionist Soviet intentions than any propaganda could negate.

Although all three factors were important in triggering the collapse of the Soviet empire, a key element was the erosion of public support for the Kremlin's aggressive policies. Popular perceptions are difficult to analyze in a society where until recently the legal media have been entirely government controlled, political nonconformity has been treated as a criminal offense, and the image of public support for Kremlin policies has been foisted on both domestic and foreign audiences.

Afghans who know of this book have no quarrel with its basic thesis, which they already accept as axiomatic. Most other nationalities I have interviewed, however, had not considered the Afghan dimension of the Soviet collapse. The most curious reaction, however, was encountered among Russians, almost all of whom instantly rejected the concept when it was first presented, yet on reconsideration—usually a day later—would volunteer their basic agreement with it.

This book, then, seeks to analyze how the Afghan war exacerbated the process of alienation among the regime's main pillars of support and between those pillars and the people. In focusing on the Afghan dimension, I ask the reader's forgiveness for not exploring more deeply the other factors that contributed to the Soviet collapse. Those must be the subjects for others' books.

In Lieu of an Introduction

(This anonymous article appeared in the underground Russian journal *Referendum* [No. 1, December 1987. Publisher: Lev Timofeyev] in 1987 and was reprinted in the Russian-language émigré monthly periodical *Possev* of February 1988. Translation by the author.)

Will Gorbachev Die in Afghanistan?

We are in a war. But how many people in our country know it? The soldiers know it. The wounded know it. The families of those who died know it . . . But do the rest of us think much about it?

Why are we in the war? Whom are we fighting? For what? That's the main thing—for what? And also, when you get down to it, who is doing the fighting?

Remember [World War II]? "This is a just war, a holy war." And the war for us was in fact just that—both a people's and a holy war—but this one? Who's fighting? Our whole people? Well, the government is fighting, using its "limited contingent" of troops—but society? Society is quietly burying its dead, healing its wounded, sheltering its invalids—and that's all. And how about public opinion—where is there room for public opinion in the Afghan problem?

Soviet forces went into Afghanistan at the very end of 1979. Our country said nothing. Nobody asked us whether to start the war. As a matter of fact, nobody told us that they'd started it. They did not find that necessary.

Now they say that the Afghan government is supposed to have asked us some thirteen times to bring in our troops. (Which Afghan government? Surely not the one that was shot as soon as Soviet troops entered Kabul?) But if it was a case of measuring thirteen times before cutting once, then why didn't [the Soviet government] ask, why didn't it say one word, just once, to the people, to society? Do you know the reason? [Because] the country is silent—and will continue to be silent—just as the government had known it would be. Afghanistan from the outset was our societal humiliation.

But the country was silent not only and not so much because there was no public opinion, but mainly because there was no information that could have nurtured such an opinion. In the simplest terms, they were hiding from society the most elemental fact— that the government was waging a war.

We well remember the early stage, the first two or even three years that passed without the slightest word in Soviet newspapers or journals. The war was there, but here at home all was peace and quiet. We knew nothing. Peacetime. And our children left to serve in a peacetime army. And didn't come back. Zinc coffins came back.

We didn't actually know anything about the war until we heard rumors of the dead and the crippled. ("They say the hospitals are full over in the next county." "Building new convalescent homes for the wounded, too.") In short, we learned about the war in Afghanistan only after the problem of the wounded and the crippled became a social problem, a problem that was dumped in society's lap because the government couldn't handle it. And so it became clear that the government, having started the war without asking society, was now showing itself incapable of solving the war's growing problems without the help of society.

The war in Afghanistan began under the Brezhnev government. It is supposed to be clear that the Afghanistan problem is a product of those times, the times called either stagnant or crisis-ridden. Afghanistan is a terrible symbol of the morals of those times. But the symbol of whose morality? Of society's? Or of the government's? Today they swear from the highest tribunal that those days have gone forever. But what has really gone—has the moral outlook of the government changed?

But the war in Afghanistan continues. This is not merely the statement of political or military fact. Doesn't the continuation of the war mean that there have in fact been no serious moral changes in the country? One thing is clear: the war in Afghanistan means that society still has no possibility of affecting government policies. And how could it? To have an effect, you have to know what is going on. And knowledge is just what we do not have.

How many have died in Afghanistan since the start of the war? Silence.

How much money does each day of the eight-year-long (and no end in sight) war cost the people? Silence.

Is there any popular judgment about the war other than that which favors the presence of Soviet troops on foreign soil? Silence.

(But we know that there is such an opinion. After all, it was for just that opinion that Academician Sakharov was exiled to Gorky. Now that they have let him come back, why don't they publish his opinion? And of those few [other] timid opinions that have been published, where is the resounding condemnation of "expansionist geopolitical thinking"?)

One of the Soviet journalists who writes about Afghanistan has said that the war will have its Bykovs and Balklanovs [Soviet equivalents of Ernie Pyle in World War II—TRANS.]. It will? No way. Here the mood of public opinion is quite different from the Great Fatherland War: then it was, "Your motherland calls." Now it's an incomprehensible "international duty." No wonder it's such a murky slogan—you can't be precise when you start with a lie. Society builds its legends on the basis of its own fate—you don't create legends on lies.

Now they are talking of withdrawing the troops. Any old day now. Maybe. And why are they withdrawing them? Why, in fact, is it now possible (if indeed it is possible) to withdraw troops from Afghanistan when for eight years it was not possible? What has changed? What is the situation now? What is this, a collapse of policy? Or a victory? We know that in Spain there was a defeat of the International Brigade. In the Great Fatherland War, a people's victory. But here? Victory or defeat?

We know nothing.

CHAPTER 1

THE CULTURAL GULF

I will lift up mine eyes unto the hills
From whence cometh my salvation.
121st Psalm*

Father Vasily, a native of the central Russian
plain, . . . complain[ed] during a visit to the spectacular
Caucasus range that there was "no scenery" . . .
the mountains got in the way.
Ronald Hingley, *The Russian Mind*

————————

In this age of racial sensitivity, it is uncomfortable to generalize on "national characteristics" for fear of somehow endorsing prejudice or discrimination. It can also be misleading, for labels that are more or less typical for populations as a whole cannot and should not be automatically pasted on individuals. There are, for example, Russians who love to be alone in the mountains, and presumably there is such a thing as an Afghan who finds mountains confining, though that would be rarer.

Comparing "Russians" and "Afghans" is also misleading, because when we speak of the former we often have in mind all Soviet citizens, about half of whom are not Russian at all. Similarly, the typical "Afghan" traits apply mostly to the dominant Pashtuns, less so to Tajiks, Uzbeks, and other ethnic groups that make up half of all Afghans.

————————

*I have been told that today's biblical scholars place a period after the first line, a question mark after the second. Perhaps that makes sense—to a flatlander.

1

Nevertheless, there can be little doubt that it is *Russian* thinking that has dominated Soviet policy, just as it is *Pashtun* values that have dominated Afghan policy. Moreover, the thinking of each has been profoundly affected by the cultural and physical environments in which each set of people has been raised. Between the two psychologies there lies the age-old gulf between the plainsman and the hill man.

In its sense of mass, space, and timelessness, Afghan geography has a unique grandeur. The country is only the size of Texas, but its altitudes dwarf ours, ranging up to twenty-two thousand feet, with knife-edge ridges and plunging chasms isolating its small communities from each other. There are vast flatlands as well, but one is almost never out of sight of mountains, even if they are only far-off, shimmering mirages. The horizons have boundaries.

We in the United States get something of the same effect in the high plateaus of southwestern Wyoming, the basin-and-range district of Nevada and Utah, and the craggier regions of the Rocky and Sierra Nevada mountains. Travel an interstate westward from the Mississippi Valley, and you will—unless you are totally insensitive to your surroundings—feel both bigger and smaller than you did in the more comprehensible, domesticated East. The desolate masses of rock that jut from the desert are not softened by distance; the air is so dry that objects twenty miles away look close at hand. It calls for rare human conceit not to feel personally shrunken by the surrounding infinities of land and sky.

But there is also a sense of liberation and exultation in these same vast distances. If you, personally, are insignificant, so is every other living thing, and you feel able to expand spiritually, almost physically, from the lack of crowding. It is an environment that suited and even helped mold the individualism that lay at the heart of our pioneer forefathers' philosophy.

Afghan geography is like that, and in the Afghan character we find many of the traits associated with our pioneering days, before the social blender of modern communications, the luxuries of a fat economy, and the relentless quest for "progress" began to collectivize and homogenize us.

Take the stereotype of the Montana cowboy of yore: a straightforward, unsophisticated, tough character, violent when offended but generally hospitable and helpful even to total strangers, if only because the harshness of frontier life demanded these qualities for human survival.

He had an abiding contempt for authority, and he customarily went armed as a way of showing his independence. He was self-sufficient and usually possessed an innate self-respect that let him relate to others according to his own personal set of values. He ignored class distinctions, scorned grovelers, rebelled against domination, and abhorred organization. Afghans are like that.

To this somewhat idealized portrait we must, unfortunately, add a few warts. The real-life cowboy was often a snaggle-toothed, illiterate, shambling roustabout, was secretly leery of the strangers he hosted, and had a broad thieving streak. When it came to violence, he would usually ambush an opponent rather than go for any of that fast-draw nonsense (Why take unnecessary risks?), and his self-respect could easily spill over into braggadocio and arrogance. So also the Afghan.

Probably the cowboy had fewer antiorganizational feelings than the Afghan—certainly than the Pashtun—whose avoidance of group thinking is almost compulsive. Whether Communist or non-Communist, a Pashtun's loyalties tend to be fierce, personal, unbending, and very local. There is little or no concept of nationalism, patriotism, or vested loyalty to whatever government reigns in Kabul. Unity with other Afghans may be voiced as an ideal, but if it involves an ounce of compromise or loss of prestige, he will reject it. (Tajiks and some other Afghan ethnic groups are more amenable to cooperation than Pashtuns, but none could be termed collectivist.)

For example, the Homeland party (HP—until April 1992 the pro-Soviet ruling party in Kabul) is riven into two main factions, Parcham and Khalq, each of which has subfactions loyal to particular leaders. The six-party Afghan Interim Government (AIG) based in Peshawar, Pakistan, is no less splintered but, fortunately for it, is less ideologically committed to the unity principle. For both, however, the inability to command organizational loyalty has proven to be a dangerous weakness.

To get a better, if still rough, idea of the Afghan national character we must add four other dimensions to simple rugged individualism: an intense family orientation, a specific code of personal behavior, an immense patience, and a fervent dedication to religion. Traditionally, each of these characteristics has outweighed in importance any governmental authority; should an executive edict contradict any one of them, so much the worse for the edict. It is in this relative contempt for government authority that one of the main differences between the Afghan and the Russian can be found.

Family Unlike the industrialized world, with its multiple nation-wide organizations and restless individual mobility, Afghanistan until the most recent times relied on the family as its basic social unit. Insofar as broader organizations existed at all, they commanded relatively little loyalty. The family was the cement of society, the fundamental building block that offered each of its members protection against a hostile outside world (as often as not represented by another family with which the first was feuding), and demanded in return some strict obligations. The family very often maintained its unity by having first cousins marry each other, so that sometimes entire generations shared only one set of grandparents or even great-grandparents. Paradoxically, the tightness of the family connection did not necessarily imply close intrafamily harmony ("I hate him like a cousin" expresses the ultimate in Afghan hostility), but the cement of family was supposed to withstand even the fiercest of rivalries among blood relatives.

Presently, one important unknown is how much the huge social upheavals that have wracked Afghanistan since 1978 and led to the dislocation of about half its population will weaken the family role. Many individuals have become permanently estranged, physically separated, or simply orphaned from family groups, whereas others have bonded more intimately to resistance groups and relate more firmly to their commanders than to family patriarchs. Nevertheless, the family role will probably reestablish itself to some degree after the foreign exiles return; there are still no clear-cut, proven alternatives to it.

Behavior Code For the Pashtuns, behavior is supposed to be regulated by the *Pashtunwali,* an unchanging set of rules that each succeeding generation is required to learn by heart while still in childhood. The rules provide lifelong guidelines for what to do under most of life's important situations. It says something for Afghan values that detailed instructions on the proper conduct of feuds heads the list, followed by the obligations of hospitality and asylum, including the right of anyone to demand—and receive—asylum from his worst enemy under certain specified conditions.

A fugitive from other enemies, if successful in crossing the threshold of a blood foe, can demand asylum from his unwilling host, who for three days is required to shelter, feed, and defend to the death his unwelcome guest. (By the end of the third day, however, it behooves the refugee to have found a discreet way of slipping away.) It is interesting that during the Soviet occupation, for the first known time in Afghan history, the right of asylum was specifically denied Soviet citizens serving in the country.

Patience The Afghans have a sense of time that is profoundly different from ours. They rarely feel our compulsion for speed, dynamism, and deadlines. Their capacity for patience probably comes from having lived in a stable social environment for centuries. Although they have been periodically invaded by outsiders, those invasions have not occurred very often, historically speaking, and they have left few permanent marks. Even the two British invasions of the nineteenth century (1839 and 1878) resulted only in partial, short-term occupations, and most Afghans remained completely unaffected by them. Unlike the British, the Soviets were in the country for nearly the entire decade of the 1980s; to find anything similar to their occupation, one would have to go all the way back to the time of Tamerlane, in the fourteenth century. But ten years to an Afghan means very little, and in the end it is unlikely that Moscow's various attempts to Sovietize Afghanistan will have much lasting effect. "The Afghan waited a hundred years to take his vengeance," goes an old Pashtun saying, "and cursed himself for his impatience."

Islam The last distinguishing factor, religion, plays a vital role in society. Brought to the country by Arabs in the seventh century, Islam remained as a permanent legacy after the Afghans had chased its purveyors back into the western deserts whence they had come. Particularly the Sunni branch of Islam, with its absence of hierarchy, its egalitarianism, and its belief in individual responsibility, suited native Afghan values. Today, even with the secularization of society in the latter half of this century, most Afghans are still devout believers. Most of them, also, are Sunnis; only about 15 percent of them, mainly the Hazaras, belong to the Shia branch of Islam, with its more rigid, hierarchical organization.

Islam affects virtually all Afghans every day of their lives. The devout heed all five calls to prayer daily, and even Westernized Afghans often break from secular activity to pray. It is not merely social pressure, such as one finds in some Christian churchgoers, that motivates this behavior. Miles from the nearest habitation, oblivious of any chance witnesses, the Afghan herdsman will lay out his prayer rug at the proper time and make his obligatory bows to Allah. It is an *inner* discipline that drives him, not fear of public censure.

Aside from his own communing with Allah, the Afghan encounters Islam in education and in settling local legal or social problems. The village mullah, in addition to handling ecclesiastical affairs, is also the local judge and, as he is often the only literate person around, the village teacher as well. He is responsible for settling all manner of disputes among his flock, basing his decisions on local precedent and the Koran. He teaches children the rudiments of the alphabet and readings from Mohammed that they must memorize.

Unlike the Shia clergy, Sunni mullahs are virtually independent. They are elected locally by members of the community and are not subordinate to any higher secular or ecclesiastical authority. As a group, they represent a true separation of judicial from legislative and executive power. Because they can declare any given government edict or activity contrary to Islamic law, they ensure against possible attempts by would-be dictators to impose totalitarian rule on the country.

This juridical function is based on a commonly accepted code of Islamic law, the *shariat*, which outweighs secular authority. Although harsh in some of its formal provisions, the *shariat,* like Western law, is open to interpretation on a case-by-case basis, and it recognizes both personal freedom and limits on the despotic powers of government. Most basically of all, it rests on the concept of a society ruled by law, with the law itself subject to consensus.

This is not to say, however, that the mullahs—or even Islam itself—represent a politically cohesive force in Afghan society. If the traditional basic social unit is the family, the basic political unit has always been the village, some twenty thousand to twenty-five thousand of which held about 85 percent of the Afghan population before the Soviet invasion. Another 10 percent were nomads, and the remainder of the people lived in fewer than a dozen major towns and cities.

In politics, as in psychology, geography again plays an important role in Afghan life. With the poor communications of a mountainous, economically undeveloped, and sparsely populated land, Afghanistan has been less a nation than an agglomeration of largely self-sufficient village-states, each independent of—and not infrequently hostile toward—its nearest neighbors. Insofar as representatives of the central government in Kabul used to be tolerated in the villages, they lived apart, dressed differently, spoke with a different accent, and were provided with one village-designated contact, usually the village headman, or *malik*. There was usually a relationship of "profound and mutual contempt" between the villagers and the lonely government man, who understandably fled to the nearest urban center whenever possible.[1] Since the invasion, and especially since the Soviet withdrawal, the government representative became an endangered species and has vanished from most villages.

Administration of village life is shared basically by the elected *malik* (often the wealthiest landowner of the community), the mullah, and usually a *mirab*, who is responsible for allocating the ever-scarce water resources. Proposals of villagewide consequence are submitted to a *jirga*, or town meeting of adult males, for consideration, argument, and decision by open vote. Although only males cast the votes, all such issues are first debated within the village families, where women exert influence to the extent of their own personal power within the family. There is open, brisk debate before a question is decided, but once the decision is taken, all are supposed to be bound by it.*

Small-town life in Western society usually implies a measure of intimidating social pressure on each member of the community. The same constraints could be found in the traditional Afghan village, but they were always weaker than in many other societies for the reasons we have cited: the diffusion of power at the top, the egalitarianism of Sunni Islam, the town-meeting atmosphere of the *jirga*, and the peculiar individualism that mountain men everywhere seem to share. Furthermore, there was always the option of leaving the village if the atmosphere got too stifling. During peacetime this was a relatively rare phenomenon, for quitting the village usually also implied abandoning the security of the family and all that was familiar. For the past decade of war, however, the pressure to conform and remain in the village had to contend with the dream of becoming a jihad (holy war) hero, a battle for loyalties that the village rarely won.

---

*I have been assured by Afghans that the only brake on women's participation in the pre*jirga* debates is one that applies equally to men; each may argue the issues with any other family member, with one exception—his/her spouse. Not a bad rule.

Thus, just as the war has weakened the social cement of the Afghan family, so has it undermined the basic political unit, the village. In many areas of Afghanistan today, it is the regional resistance commander who has the most political authority. Like it or not, the Afghan is becoming a bit more cosmopolitan.

But the mystique of the country remains. Foreigners of widely differing (and often mutually antagonistic) cultures, such as Yugoslavs, French, Germans, Americans, and even Soviet Russians, find a common ground in admiring Afghanistan and its people. Friendly without being obsequious, apparently oblivious to the outer trappings of wealth or title, the Afghan has an inner dignity that is almost universally attractive. A stranger feels that he is being judged more as an individual than as a representative of some group, and that the Afghan expects to be treated the same way. Outsiders who depend on group association for their authority find this attitude unnerving, especially when trying to impose their will on these hardy individualists.

One does not "command" the respect of an Afghan. One earns it.

Turning now to the Russian, we find at least one common denominator with the Afghan: the influence of immense space on Russian psychology. For some poets and philosophers, the country's vast reaches are a key factor in what they perceive as Russia's special destiny: "The landscape of the Russian soul corresponds to the landscape of Russia, the same boundlessness, formlessness, reaching out into infinity, breadth," rhapsodized the Russian philosopher Nikolay Berdyayev in 1937. And according to the nineteenth-century poet-philosopher Tyutchev (this author's translation): "The measure of Russia / No brain can conceive. / In infinite Russia / One can only—believe."[2]

The psychological impact of that spaciousness translates into something we might liken to a Texas personality, with a penchant for the extravagant gesture, a bigness of heart, and open generosity—and also the occasional tornado of rage—to match the environment. The Russian makes friends quickly, and with them he will share virtually everything he owns, but until that breakthrough has been achieved, suspicion and rudeness are often the order of the day. Historical experience has taught the Russian some bitter lessons about strangers on the open prairie, and, unlike the Afghan, he has never had a reliable sanctuary.

Where the Afghan's horizon is bounded by his friendly mountains, his ultimate refuge from invaders, the Russian horizon offers no such comfort. It goes on forever, and out of its reaches, throughout history, have come successive waves of pitiless invaders: Attila the Hun, Genghis Khan, Napoleon Bonaparte, and Adolf Hitler, to name just a few. The steppe, observes Tibor Szamuely, was for centuries a "source of constant menace, a land of terror, death, destruction, and degradation."[3]*

The vulnerability to alien invasion is probably the single most important stimulus to the Russian reliance on collective behavior. In the mountains, a man may escape enemies on his own, but on the open plains the individual is helpless. His only salvation from an onrushing sweep of massed cavalry or armor lies in communal defense, and it should be no surprise to find the herding instinct running strong in Russians.

Walk down a sidewalk with your Moscow friend, and you will often find yourself edged slowly toward the road or the flanking buildings. Switch sides with him, and he will edge you the other way. This is not because he is pushy, but because physical contact is instinctively right in his society and instinctively intrusive in ours. He keeps politely trying to touch, you keep politely trying to give him room. Or take him shopping where there is an infinite variety of goods to choose from, and you will find that he is interested only in what every other Russian is seeking at that time. In fact the very idea of choice tends to be rather unsettling for him, the concept of originality almost sinful.

"Set a collection of Russians down in a street, tell them to start walking in the same direction, and in no time they will all be singing together and smiling," says the English Russian scholar Hingley, and whether tongue-in-cheek or not, the comment is believable.[4] The subtle aspect of this saying is the implied necessity for someone to do the setting down and telling. (A collection of Afghans faced with the same instruction certainly would neither smile nor sing, and probably would show their independence by dispersing to all points of the compass.)

And yet the Russian, too, has a strong streak of anarchism in him, a trait which he tries to overcome and in which he takes a kind of gloomy, perverse pride. The story is apocryphal, but the first ruler of old Russia,

---

*The plainsman of our Old West had a different philosophy only because he was the consistent winner, not the loser, in confrontations with Native Americans. He himself did not suffer an alien occupation—he *was* the occupation.

the Swede Rurik, is supposed to have accepted the figurative crown in A.D. 963 in response to a plea from the elders of Novgorod: "Please come and rule over us; it is a rich land, but there is no order." One could scarcely conceive of an Afghan making such a request, even in fable.

In many respects the millenium of Russian history that followed Rurik was one long, largely fruitless search for order. Traditionally, the Russian respected firm rule as a way to keep him from giving in to his worst instincts, which, he was sure, would be unleashed as soon as the reins were loosened. So ingrained has been the sense of collectivity and the wish for imposed order that for many Russians the Western distinction between state and society has been an alien concept: the state *is* society, and vice versa. (Note that the Russian, unlike the Afghan, did not believe in overlapping cultural, religious, and social authorities; there was only one authority, the state, to which the individual was supposed to subordinate himself.)

This brief excursion into Russian psychology finds some confirmation in the Russian language. Regarding the quest for order, the Russian word for order, a neutral or perhaps slightly negative term for us, is *poryadok,* which in Russian carries very positive connotations. One adjective that derives from this word, *poryadochnyy,* is translated as "decent, honest" in most Russian-English dictionaries. In a Russian-Russian dictionary, however, it is defined as "honest, *corresponding to accepted rules of conduct,*" in other words, behaving oneself according to rules set by some higher authority and not by one's inner self (emphasis added).[5]

The reverse of *poryadochnyy* is *stikhiynyy,* meaning *natural, spontaneous.* These are both usually positive terms for us, but for the Russian they are defined as bad concepts: "1. called forth by the forces of nature, not subjected to the will or influence of man, as in *natural disaster . . .* 2. *fig.* unorganized, without proper organization or direction."[6]

Russians also love show and pageantry, to the point that the border between the real world and make-believe is sometimes blurred for them. False boasting, such as that seen in Soviet propaganda of the pre*glasnost* era, is no new invention but has been an accepted part of Russian society for centuries. For example, in the late 1700s Catherine the Great's adviser-lover, Count Potemkin, built false-front villages to impress his empress and foreigners with the prosperity of Russian peasants, even though no one—perhaps least of all Catherine—really believed in them.

The yearning for directed order and the devotion to show are an unusual combination, but the link has its own peculiar logic. Russian rulers have traditionally borrowed doctrines from abroad to inflict on their people but have partially made up for them with various glittering façades. To the sovereign, the underlying ideals of the doctrine he imposed counted for little; what mattered to him was the doctrine's practical application in forcing his subjects into orderly obedience, even though (or perhaps just because) the demanded behavior had only disciplinary, not practical, value. But the doctrines were always enshrined in gilded constructions, such as the church towers in Moscow's Red Square, unreal in their fairy-tale splendor.

From the Kievan St. Vladimir, who brought Christianity to Russia in A.D. 988 by forcibly baptizing his subjects en masse in the Dnepr River, to Peter the Great, who made his nobles shave off their beards and adopt Western table manners in the early 1700s, to Lenin, who imposed the communist creed on a population of whom most had never even heard of the German Karl Marx, the pattern of autocratic rule via alien doctrine runs like a thread through Russian history. For the Russian masses, security from repression has traditionally lain in fervent belief in the creed of the day and in strict adherence to its rituals, for to behave otherwise was to defy the ruler and to suffer accordingly.

And this devotion to ritual was not always merely protective coloration; when the Orthodox church made some minute changes in the church service in the seventeenth century, literally thousands of Russians (the Old Believers) burned themselves to death in their own churches rather than change their ways.

The disciplinary, rote aspect of religion is also revealed in the language, where the student at a Russian Orthodox seminary is called a *poslushnik*, from the word meaning to listen, to obey.

Rule and obedience may be the root reasons for adopting foreign doctrines, but such crass considerations are concealed by the luxuriant foliage of the outer image. The ritual and ornate beauty of the Russian church, its icons and architecture, its choral liturgies (perhaps the most beautiful in the world) are deeply moving, even to those who do not subscribe to the faith. The congregation looks on, rarely called on to contribute, as the service unfolds. Behind the altar, only partially visible through open screens, are glittering, gilded inner sancta, places that only the priests may enter.

(These mystical, shining, forbidden zones, where the annointed carry out their mysterious duties, have their parallels in secular life. The best example is the Kremlin itself, where until recently only occasional, tantalizing glimpses of the political maneuvering that determines the country's fate were visible from the outside.)

For the Russian believer, the holy imagery is not only beautiful in itself but is part of the mysticism in which he wraps his religion. But the abstract ideas that spawned the faith, if known to him at all, will remain something apart from the service, whose concrete imagery (icons, candles, choir, incense, the formal and barely comprehensible words) are the most vital part of his religious experience.

Let us again turn to the Russian language for confirmation, if only negative, in a term that is translated into English as "1. ugliness, hideousness, deformity. 2. disgraceful occurrence. 3. *exclam.* Outrageous! . . ." That word is *bezobraziye,* literally "without image."[7]

Although the foregoing has emphasized the example of the church, the Leninist application of Marxist thought to the Soviet people follows the same pattern, except that the beautiful has remained mostly in the realm of promise rather than fulfillment, and the doctrine is purely secular. In the dry words of George Kennan as quoted by Professor Hingley, the main difference between Orthodoxy and Marxism is the latter's "attempt to remove from the next world to this both the promise of heaven and the reality of hell."[8]

There is another, darker side to traditional Russian psychology, one that is connected to the Russian imperial dream. Just as there has been little distinction between state and society, so the Russian concepts of nation and empire have also been blurred. In part, this is because there was no physical separation of the two; unlike classic European empires, the Russian colonies were not overseas but were contiguous to Russia, in fact part of it. While the colonies remained colonies, this eased imperial administration, but now, as the minority peoples have achieved independence, there are immense complications in dismantling the empire. The Russians, unlike the French, English, Dutch, and Portuguese, cannot simply sail away from their former responsibilities.

But more important than the administrative problems in dissolving the empire is doing away with the Russian imperial psychology that was part of it. In the words of one Soviet Russian scholar, Evgenii Anisimov, this has led to a "wrenching identity crisis" for Russia, a "colossal, rapid change in Russian national mentality and the formation of a genuinely new Russian national consciousness." In his description of the old "imperial consciousness," he touches on many views long associated with the former European colonial powers (and not, unfortunately, put entirely to rest yet either in Europe or the United States): smugness at their own perceived national superiority and sinless virtue, outrage at the colonial peoples' ingratitude, and a firm belief in their self-appointed mission of enlightening and civilizing the backward heathen.[9]

Some other aspects of the Russian imperial consciousness identified by Anisimov seemed to go further than the typical European model: the "inalienable right" of Russia to interfere in the internal affairs of its neighbors; exploitation of the Pan-Slavic ideal to justify the Russian domination of all Slavs; the creation and propagation of the theme of some outside "great enemy" to justify sacrifices and explain away failings; and the propagation of the equally false theme that the colonies had voluntarily and gladly accepted Russian rule. The last illusion, in particular, has led Russian rulers down to and including President Gorbachev to brand as "treason" or "thievery" attempts by minority nationalists to assert their independence.[10]*

With such comfortable assumptions, Russians have long awaited the day when the right blend of leadership and system would allow Moscow to fulfill her destiny of becoming the third (and last) Rome, the final and everlasting spiritual and secular center of the world. Despite today's painfully apparent Russian failures on the secular side, it was quite clear until at least August 1991 that many Soviet policymakers still had such aspirations. Even today, many who have despaired of catching up with the West materially still expect some kind of spiri-

---

*Gorbachev used the term *thievery* in relation to the Lithuanian declaration of independence in 1990. Did this represent a deliberate falsification or an honest belief that most of the republic's inhabitants preferred Moscow's rule? We cannot quite rule out the latter possibility; even émigré nationalists seem to have been surprised by the strength of nationalist fervor that boiled up back home as soon as the restraints on free speech were lifted.

tual renaissance that will see Russia emerge at some future date as the moral leader of the world. It is the occasional glimpse of such messianic ambitions, secular as well as spiritual, that has disquieted some outside observers of the Russian scene for generations. This messianism, implicitly confirmed by such philosophers as Nikolay Berdyayev and examined in detail by historian James Billington, is heatedly denied by others.[11]

To sum up, the basic Afghan values stem from the overlapping imperatives of several institutions that are independent of the government: the family, the *Pashtunwali* code of behavior, and Islamic law. Each of these is strong in its own right, and though differing in detail they tend to reinforce each other. Nevertheless, when they conflict it is the individual who in the end must choose which of the three guides his actions and must take responsibility for those actions.

Soviet Russian values in the past derived from a single authority, that of the party and its various state organs. Behavior was monitored and controlled not just by state organs but by a natural, native Russian sense of collectivity, which the state fostered at every opportunity. These unitary command and collective enforcement systems left the individual with no responsibility beyond following orders. As long as the whole massive apparatus worked, it was frighteningly efficient in mobilizing human endeavor toward this or that goal. Although it had suffered setbacks and temporary failures, there was reason to fear (as an embassy colleague of mine, Graham Fuller, did in 1976) that before the year 2000 we would see democracy reduced to small islands of beleaguered rich states in a broad sea of quasi-Marxist despotism. History, however, decreed otherwise.

At its very roots, the war in Afghanistan was less a matter of military capability or topography or economics or formal ideology—though all of these played important roles—than it was the clash between responsible individualism and obedient collectivity. And when obedient collectivity lost, it lost globally.

NOTES

1. Roy, *Islam and Resistance,* 10.
2. Berdyayev, *Origins of Russian Communism,* 9; Billington, *Ikon and Axe,* 732.
3. Szamuely, *Russian Tradition,* 25.
4. Hingley, *Russian Mind,* 75.
5. Daglish, *Russko-angliyskiy sloar,* 653; Ozhegov, *Slovar russkogo yazyka,* 520.
6. Ozhegov, 706.
7. Daglish, 37.
8. Hingley, 113.
9. Kennan Institute, *Meeting Report* (Leningrad Academy of Sciences senior researcher Evgenii Anisimov), May 14, 1991.
10. *Ibid.*
11. See Billington, 48–49; Berdyayev, 10ff. For a spirited opposing view, see Karpovich, "Russian Imperialism or Communist Aggression?"

CHAPTER 2

WAR AND REFORM IN RUSSIAN HISTORY

Of all the burdens Russia has had to bear, the heaviest and most relentless of all has been the weight of her past.
Tibor Szamuely, *The Russian Tradition*

Russia came late to Europe. Under the heel of the Golden Horde of Genghis Khan and his descendants, the country missed out on the age of inventive nation building in the West and arrived on the scene only in time to inherit the finished product, including the developed nation-state's unfortunate penchant for swallowing weakly defended neighbors. Seen from the outside, sixteenth-century Europe offered Russia little more than clear proof of the dictum that might makes right.

In their wholesale adoption of this foreign doctrine and their preoccupation with its surface features, the Russians were only repeating what they had already done with the Christian religion and would do again with communism. The same pattern would also be repeated to some degree in other fields, including culture, economics, military science, and technology. In all of them, Russians enthusiastically copied the concrete results they could observe, but investigated only later— or ignored—the basic ideas that underlay them. The Russian copy was usually successful and sometimes was even an improvement on the Western original, but almost never did it serve as the solid foundation for some radically new *Russian* development. Sometimes the modifications were embarrassing failures, especially when overdoing the Russian "bigger-is-better" philosophy. (Within the Kremlin walls today are two seventeenth-century relics that illustrate the point: a bell so huge it could never be hung, and a cannon too large to be fired.)

Down through succeeding centuries, the most active Russian attempts at sociopolitical reform were always based on the increasingly democratic Western model, most noticeably stimulated whenever war forced close contact with Westerners. It is intriguing, though perhaps not too surprising, that as a general rule losing wars impelled Russian leaders to impose reform from above (so as to do better in the next war), whereas winning wars resulted in a reactionary, don't-fix-it-if-it-isn't-broken approach by the rulers. Reform movements in the latter case had to come from lower-ranking elements, whose occupation of Western territories gave them firsthand exposure to Western life.

Whether reform attempts came after a winning or a losing war, however, they have always been destabilizing and have prompted an eventual reaction from above. The rulers, relying for support on the popular fear of anarchy, have reimposed a more-or-less despotic system, which they have perceived as the only cement strong enough to hold the empire together. The dilemma, notes Adam Ulam, has always lain in loosening autocracy without imperiling Russia's unity and greatness. That dilemma was as sharp at the end of the twentieth century as it was at the beginning of the nineteenth.[1]

The real fault, however, lies in the failure of any autocratic system to be sensitive and responsive enough to public opinion to head off problems before they develop into either-or confrontations. Since the end of Peter the Great's reign, the consistent lesson from Russian history is that reforms have always been either a sham or too little and too late, or both.

Peter the Great

In Stockholm, one of the main streets is Narvavägen, named for the site of Swedish king Charles XII's victory over Peter the Great of Russia in 1700. Though only twenty-eight years old at the time, Peter was a graybeard compared to Charles, who was only eighteen. Peter's forces vastly outnumbered Charles's, but the young Swede's troops, gallantly led by the monarch himself, knifed through the Russian lines in a November snowstorm, diced the Russian forces into isolated, manageable pieces, and leisurely annihilated them, one by one. It was a humiliating experience for Peter, one he would never forget.

There is nothing like an unsuccessful war to focus the mind of the loser on his nation's weaknesses, and Peter promptly accelerated the reforms that he had already set in train before the battle. The Petrine reforms covered a good deal more than just the military, but all of them—as virtually everything else that Peter turned his hand to—grew out of the needs of his army and his desire to expand the empire. It is a measure of his forty-three-year reign that during only two of those years was Russia at peace.

A giant in many respects, the six-foot-seven Peter was intensely energetic, bright, willful, ruthless. Like subsequent ambitious Moscow rulers, his main goal was to make his backward country competitive with technologically advanced Europe; also like his successors, he found perhaps his worst enemy in the immense lethargy of the Russian people. To overcome this, he mobilized the country under his personal command and forced change by his own furious energy, his implacable willpower, and the application of brute force. By personal example, by rewarding the obedient, and by swiftly punishing those who ignored or opposed him, Peter dragged Russia forward almost single-handedly. "The quiet man," notes the historian Bernard Pares, "was everywhere affronted," but by the end of Peter's reign his Russia had won Europe's fear if not its respect.[2]

Peter's reforms touched all parts of Russian society. He subordinated the Orthodox church to state power by putting it under a Holy Synod (one of whose members was a layman unofficially designated as the "tsar's eye"), after which the church never regained its former independence and prestige. He rudely shook up the landed gentry by obliging all of them to be on call as full-time servants of the state, and by assigning them ranks on the basis not of their family lineage but of how well they were serving tsar and country. In compensation for their sacrifices, he gave them practically slaveholder powers over their peasants. In many respects, Peter was a prototype of twentieth-century totalitarian dictators.

Whereas the army had formerly been a ragtag militia, conscripted for a given war or operation, Peter gave it Western uniforms and turned it into a semiprofessional force. He made individual provinces responsible (at huge expense to them) for recruiting, paying, feeding, and quartering these new, full-time units, whose command rested not with the province but with the tsar and his military staff. So burdensome were the provincial and federal taxes imposed to support the army that many common men were driven into armed opposition. Robber bands achieved a size and power that only the army itself could oppose effectively. The military thus gained a responsibility for maintaining domestic public order, a responsibility that it never lost.

Peter strove mightily but ineffectually to overcome corruption in the land. To this end he set up a vast network of *fiscals,* government agents whose task was to detect financial abuses. These in turn solicited information from volunteer informers, who were encouraged by rewards of a quarter of the property—and sometimes the domains, rank, and legal status—of their victims. The guilty, who included such notables as the governor of Siberia and, eventually, the chief *fiscal* himself, were promptly executed. There was no penalty for false accusations, and there were few restraints on unscrupulous or embittered citizens who wished to advance at the expense of their enemies. The result was a demoralized society, infested with spies yet no less burdened with corruption than before. Prince Dolgoruky put it succinctly to Peter: "In the long run you will have no subjects at all, for we are all thieving."[3] (Two hundred years later, Stalin's secret police would follow in the *fiscals'* footsteps, with no less negative results on society.)

Nine years after Narva, long before his reforms were complete, Peter decisively defeated Charles at the battle of Poltava, a conflict that signaled the beginning of the end of Sweden as a great power. The basic goal of Peter's reforms—establishment of Russia as a power center in the civilized world of the day—was thus achieved, but at a cost that has plagued Moscow's rulers ever since. Many of his despotic means, themselves a natural outgrowth of Russian history before his time, were applied by later Moscow leaders. They, like Peter, have failed to see the connection between those very means and the human failings they were trying to correct: corruption, laziness, lack of initiative, disorder, indiscipline, irresponsibility—all attributes of the unfree man. Local initiative, though seen as necessary and encouraged in theory, was stifled in practice by the absolute power of the tsar. The Russian philosopher-historian Klyuchevskiy summarized the paradox best: "He [Peter] wanted the slave, while remaining a slave, to act consciously and freely."[4]

Catherine the Great

The next forceful personality and reformer to sit on Russia's throne was one of the most remarkable sovereigns of all time, Catherine the Great, who reigned from 1762 to 1796. Catherine's wars were mainly with Turkey, not the West, but the unreal, theatrical nature of much of her administration—and especially of her reforms—was typically Russian and deserves our brief attention.

Sexually active by nature and upbringing—she and her mother were almost deported from Russia to their native Germany for the mother's indiscretions when Catherine was only fourteen—Catherine was betrothed to the Russian crown prince in 1744, shortly after she turned fifteen, and married to him in 1745. Her husband, Peter III, was a cruel, brainless incompetent who became tsar in 1761 but reigned only a few months. Catherine saw to that, and it was probably with her foreknowledge—if not on her orders—that Peter, shortly after being deposed, met a sudden, violent death while drunkenly carousing with Catherine's palace guards.* Catherine consoled herself in her widowhood with a succession of lovers who ranged from junior noblemen pets to the leading Russian statesmen of her day.

Even without ill-fated European wars, Catherine had more than her share of troubles with peasant rebellions at home. After Peter the Great's day, the gentry were gradually liberated from obligatory state service, but their rights over the impoverished and sometimes starving serfs increased to include not only beatings but Siberian exile. Leaving their estates in the hands of overseers, the landlords gravitated toward Moscow and St. Petersburg, where they heatedly argued the latest liberal philosophies of France. Again, there was no Russian development of these theories, much less any effort to practice on their own lands what they argued so passionately and persuasively in the salons of the big cities.

Catherine herself led the way. Her *Instruction* (*Nakaz*) of 1766 to a national commission for establishing a new legal code was based on Italian and French progressive writings and was so shockingly liberal that its publication was forbidden in France itself. But it had absolutely nothing to do with the real administration of justice in Russia, either before or after its publication. Like Potemkin's false-front villages, it served only to point up the contrast between glistening ideal and sordid reality in a Russia that Catherine herself predicted might undergo

---

*The official announcement of the tsar's death claimed that he had died of "hemorrhoidal colic." When Catherine later asked a French intellectual to come grace her court, he refused on the grounds that hemorrhoids, to which he also was prone, were bad enough in France but "too serious in that country [Russia]." (Troyat, 159.)

a huge upheaval if it did not reform. Nevertheless, following the al-
most-successful Pugachev peasant rebellion of 1773–75, she ignored
her own warnings, and the remaining twenty-one years of her reign
were increasingly reactionary.

Alexander I

After Catherine died (of natural causes) in 1796, her son Paul took
over and so mismanaged Russia that he was murdered in 1801. Alexander
I then mounted the throne at the age of twenty-three. The liberal French
tutors who raised him, however, did not succeed in exorcising his autocratic
instincts and heritage. Like his grandmother, he talked a good game
of liberalism, but after some promising youthful experiments, he did
not practice it. (No less than commoners, tsars always became more
conservative as they grew older; where they differed from their subjects was in their power to impose their views on others.)

It was under Alexander I that Russia scored its most signal military victory of the nineteenth century, the defeat of Napoleon in 1814.
But with military victory came ideological subversion, as the young
officers on occupation duty in Paris saw firsthand the contrast between
the enlightened West and murky Russia. On their return, they (like many
Soviet soldiers returning from Germany after World War II) expected
a political thaw—and like their descendants were met with a stone wall
of reaction.

In response, a few of the officers formed a secret society whose misty,
unstructured program was to bring some form of democracy to Russia. In their idealistic enthusiasm, they foresaw a reborn nation that
would borrow the best from the West and then go on to forge a whole
new, advanced society that would leave the formerly scornful Europeans in openmouthed admiration and clambering to catch up.

Their chance for action came when Alexander died prematurely just
after he turned forty-eight, in December 1825. But the conspirators,
thereafter to be known as the Decembrists, suffered from irresolution
and were swiftly put down. Their five leaders were hanged, and several hundred others were publicly humiliated and sent off to permanent Siberian exile. Both their unrealistically high ambitions and low
capabilities, however, served as object lessons for succeeding generations
of Russian revolutionaries, whose ultimate triumph was to come in 1917.
(But seventy-four years after that the lesson had been forgotten: the

August 1991 coup attempt by reactionary descendants of the victorious 1917 rebels would suffer defeat from the same disastrous indecisiveness that had cursed the Decembrists.)

Nicholas I

The failure of the Decembrists ushered in a period of reaction under Nicholas I, whose reign (1825–55) spanned the famous era of revolution in Europe. Where other monarchies tottered or fell, Russia remained a bastion of autocracy, the leader of a dwindling host of old-style regimes. After the revolutions that swept Europe in 1848, repression in Russia intensified. The tsar's secret police, a direct ancestor of today's KGB called the Third Department, was responsible not only for security but for stamping out nonconformity of any kind. Private travel abroad was prohibited. Censorship reached such paranoid extremes that even a reactionary former minister of public instruction, Count Uvarov, found that the word *demos* (the root of that satanic term *democracy*) had been excised in his book on Greek antiquities, and that Roman emperors he had listed as "killed" turned out only to have "died."[5] (The old Russian custom of liquidating unwanted leaders, it appeared, was not to be encouraged in any way.)

The reactionary regime found its philosophical base in Slavophilism, the belief that Russia had no need to borrow from the West in order to make her mark on the world, as the Decembrists had argued. She was already innately superior to all other countries, insisted the Slavophiles, and if she had not yet asserted her birthright of leading the world, it was only because of the corrupting influence of the chaotic, secular, decadent West. Denying the superiority of democracy, they preached that Russia was uniquely capable of an orderly, benevolent despotism rooted in the Orthodox church. This smug doctrine was rudely shaken when Nicholas I died and was replaced by Alexander II, the most radically reforming tsar since Peter the Great.

Alexander II

Nothing in Alexander II's background suggested even remotely that his would be the role of the "tsar liberator," the man who, over a thirteen-year span starting in 1857, would oversee the abolition of serfdom in Russia. The freeing of the serfs has often been compared to the American abolition of slavery that was going on at the same time, but in fact the Russian reform was far more basic and socially destabilizing. There were only about three million slaves in the United States in 1860, roughly 10 percent of the population. In Russia there were forty-three million serfs out of a total population of about sixty million, nearly *three-quarters* of the population. The serfs were divided about equally between those who served some thirty thousand private owners and those belonging to the state and the tsar himself.

With Nicholas I for a father, it is not surprising that Alexander II was brought up to be an old-school despot. Nothing in the record indicates that he was averse to this role; in fact, as he prepared to inherit the crown, he worked directly with the censors and was more supportive of the rights of the gentry than the tsar himself. But a funny thing happened on the way to the throne.

From the 1830s until 1854, Russia's prestige both abroad and at home rested almost totally on its armed forces. The Europe of 1850, like the Europe of 1980, saw in Moscow's immense military establishment and obviously expansionist designs a menace that not even a defensive alliance could be sure of defeating. Despised for its political, cultural, social, and economic backwardness, Russia was still given cautious respect because of its military might and presumed sinister intentions. Russian intellectuals in both eras mirrored these views: ashamed of the nation's many civilian shortcomings, they took quiet pride in its ruinously expensive but awesome military establishment.

All this changed in 1854, when England and France took up arms against Russia—one imagines with considerable trepidation—to prevent Russian expansion into Turkey. The Anglo-French invasion of the Crimea that followed showed just how poorly prepared the vaunted Russian war machine really was, and by early 1855 Moscow was facing disastrous defeat. Some troops fought bravely, but a combination of rampant corruption among civilian contractors, a wholly inadequate transportation system for supplying the front, and a conscript peasant army that had little stomach for dying to defend an iniquitous system revealed the military giant's feet of clay. For true national security, the Russians learned, a modern army was not enough—it had to be supported by a reliable, respectable civilian infrastructure.

It was at this point, with his army largely defeated, that Nicholas I conveniently died (some say by his own hand), and Alexander II took over. It was clear to the young tsar that the empire was doomed unless drastic reforms were undertaken immediately. He promptly released the surviving Decembrists from Siberian exile (although they still were not permitted to live in Moscow or St. Petersburg), eased censorship, and began laying the groundwork for his greatest contribution, the abolition of serfdom. Further reforms followed, including promulgation of rules for the first independent judiciary in Russia's history.

But in spite of these breathtaking moves, Alexander II held onto his own absolute power, he kept intact the infamous Third Department and the mechanism for censorship, and he flatly refused to give Russia a constitution. In the end, he was opposed as much by the proserfdom Slavophiles as he was by the Westernizers, who came to believe most of his reforms were a sham. Ironically, in his benign despotism Alexander II was probably as close to the ideal Slavophile tsar as any person who has ever ruled from Moscow, and in his liberal reforms he moved Russia further toward Western values than any other, but that did not spare him the wrath of both sets of dissidents. In 1881, in the last of several attempts on his life, a terrorist's bomb put an end to his reign.

Nicholas II

Alexander II's son, Alexander III, was a forthright reactionary. A man of limited intellect, he bludgeoned his way through a fourteen-year tour on the throne and died in bed, to be succeeded in 1895 by Nicholas II, the last tsar.

Under Nicholas II, the old pattern of reform developing from a losing war was to be repeated, not once but twice. At first, like Catherine, Nicholas II went to war in Asia, not Europe. Unlike Catherine, he was not very good at it, and there were some unique other circumstances. For one thing, the war itself (with Japan—1904–1905) was viewed as a way of taking the minds of the tsar's restive subjects off their own difficulties. If Russia had any ambitions in the West, they were blocked by the combined might of Europe's modern armies, first and foremost by powerful imperial Germany; Asia, however, provided the apparent potential for large gains at low cost.

So Nicholas turned eastward in the expectation that a small, successful war in that region would not only satisfy territorial aims but kindle enough patriotic fervor to overcome the deteriorating loyalty of an increasingly unhappy public. What better way to deflect attention from the pains of industrialization, from the still unresolved inequities left over from serfdom, and most of all from the indecisive tsar and his all-too-decisive German wife, than for the glorious Russian army and navy to thrash the upstart Japanese?

What better way indeed? But the Japanese proved uncooperative, winning the war they were supposed to lose. Instead of solidifying public opinion behind the Russian throne, the unsuccessful conflict only inflamed the unrest it was supposed to mollify. Waves of spontaneous strikes paralyzed the economy, and demonstrations surged through the streets of major cities. It had been a losing war, but this time reform was not initiated from above. The people preempted that choice, and the monarch, though issuing the reforming decrees, did so only to save his throne. Even so, if there had been any unifying organization bent on destroying tsardom in 1905, Nicholas II's reign would have ended a dozen years earlier than it did.

Nicholas held on, but he was forced to retreat, step by grudging step, before popular demands for democracy. A consultative parliament, the Duma, was set up in May 1906, and though it lacked any real political power it managed to embarrass the government by exposing the incompetence of its court-appointed ministers. After only two months, a new prime minister, Pyotr Stolypin, dissolved the first Duma by decree. Although he set the next (second) session for March 1907—within the legal time limit—the break gave him a temporary opportunity to rule arbitrarily and without criticism.

Stolypin made the most of his chances, employing both carrot and stick to defuse the revolutionary tide that was building. He freed large government tracts of land for sale to the peasants, he liberated peasants from their obligation to stay within their communes, and he made them full-fledged citizens, eligible for any office. He also, however, dealt harshly with revolutionaries. Field courts-martial freely dispensed summary justice, with an average trial length of four days and a customary sentence of death, which was carried out in many hundreds of cases.*

By the time the Duma reconvened, the situation in the country had eased, and the tsar began to reverse some of the protodemocratic steps

---

*Pares (*History of Russia*, p. 439) puts the number of executions at 600, whereas Ulam (*Russia's Failed Revolutions*, p. 196) refers to 1,042 death sentences. Either way, the hangman's noose became known as the "Stolypin necktie."

he had been forced to accept. Elections became more controlled, the Duma waned in potency and respectability, and political twilight again settled over the land. For better or worse, this period coincided with an economic boom (the equivalent of a winning war?), and the impetus for reform dropped. Under these circumstances, Stolypin became something of a political embarrassment, disliked by the reactionaries for having given the peasants more than they believed he had to, by the liberals for his no-holds-barred executive actions, and by Nicholas for being so obviously much more effective than the tsar himself. When an assassin's bullet finally killed Stolypin in 1911, all three heaved sighs of more or less open relief, some of the last such sighs many of them would enjoy. Six years later, after the disastrous defeats of World War I, the power to reform was permanently removed from the Romanov dynasty's hands as Nicholas was first forced to abdicate and then, with his entire immediate family, was slaughtered by the victorious Communists. Most of the anti-Stolypin reactionaries shared their fate, and the turn of the liberals would come shortly.

Lenin and Stalin

Neither the February Revolution that overthrew the monarchy, the Communist coup of October (which swiftly arrogated to itself the title of The Revolution), the bloody civil war that followed, nor the imposition of Communist rule by mass terror can be treated under the gentle term *reform*. Only after the violence had subsided did something approaching reform occur in Lenin's New Economic Policy of the 1920s, a reversion to semicapitalism that he grudgingly accepted as the only way to revive a land devastated by nine years of war, civil war, terror, and famine.

At the end of the 1920s, however, the contradiction between limited economic reform and continued political absolutism would see the total defeat of the former as Stalin launched his twin drives of industrialization and collectivization. Again, *reform* is too gentle a term for the catastrophic upheavals that these programs brought to the country, and for the wholesale horrors (tortures, executions, labor camps, induced starvation) that the dictator then visited on the Soviet peoples.[6]

Stalin's punishment for these excesses came in the opening months of the USSR's involvement in World War II, when masses of Soviet troops and civilians greeted the advancing Nazis as liberators. Only

the immensity of the area open for retreat, the huge reserves of man-
power, and the dawning realization by the Soviet population that the
Nazis were just as capable of atrocities as Stalin's secret police saved
the regime.

As his armies crumpled, Stalin reacted like his tsar predecessors under
the same kind of circumstance, but with much more alacrity. In his
first wartime speech, he addressed the nation as "brothers and sisters,"
not "comrades." The fight became one to save Holy Russia from the
barbarian invader, not one to save socialism. The remnants of the Orthodox
clergy, decimated by massive repression and execution in the 1920s
and 1930s, suddenly became state-approved ministers to the troops.

Reform was in the air—until the Germans began to retreat, where-
upon Stalin reverted to type. Was he mindful of the Decembrists' dreams
of revolution from below, or was he merely instinctively aware that
he had to deal with ideological contamination from the West? For the
victims, it made little difference, but the postwar repression was massive.
The Germans had captured millions of Soviet troops and had seized
and deported to Germany large numbers of involuntary civilian laborers
from occupied Soviet territories. Stalin considered all of these cap-
tives as traitors, and those repatriated at the war's end suffered his wrath.
In addition, those unwise enough to believe that the political relaxation at the beginning of the war signaled a real change of policy found
themselves sharing the same fate.*

As a winning war, World War II had the predictable effect of rein-
forcing reaction and absolutism in the USSR. Even to suggest such
an aftereffect would have been extremely rash in Stalin's day, however, and the lesson of history remained unlearned. In fact, as late as
1990 there was strong resistance to acknowledging the effect, as shown
by the following extract of an article by Soviet Col. S. Kulichkin bitterly
attacking a liberal journalist for his antimilitary posture: "A. Borovik
allies himself with a general-scholar with whom he became friends in

---

*Among those swept up in the postwar purge was a young artillery officer who had
written some politically rash letters to a personal friend while the war was still going on. Sent to a forced labor camp, Capt. Alexander Solzhenitsyn began collecting
detailed information for what was to be the ultimate and definitive indictment of the
labor camp system: *The Gulag Archipelago*. (New York: Harper & Row, 1973, 1974,
and 1978.)

Afghanistan. 'All victorious wars waged by Russia have led to a strengthening of totalitarianism in the country,' said the general to the journalist, 'and all unsuccessful ones have led to democracy . . .' A strange
interpretation of history, is it not? It turns out that . . . Borodino [a pyrrhic
victory for Napoleon], Shipka [a battle in an 1870s war with Turkey,
after which Alexander II dealt sternly with all oppositionists], and even
the Great Patriotic War [i.e., World War II] only impeded the development of democracy in our country."[7] (Indeed, every one of those
wars had precisely that effect.)

Almost exactly a generation would pass after the end of World War
II before Moscow again committed a significant number of troops to
combat. This time the results would be the reverse—both the military
result and its impact on Russian politics.

Gorbachev's Inheritance

When Soviet troops invaded Afghanistan in the waning days of 1979,
few people outside Afghanistan itself believed that the small country
could offer successful resistance. Probably even fewer believed in the
possibility of an internally generated, thoroughgoing reform of the Soviet
system. When the occupation forces were compelled to withdraw, more
than nine years later, their own society was undergoing the initial stages
of the most tumultuous reform-from-above since the reign of Alexander
II. Looking back at our brief historical overview, we can see a number of parallels in various eras.

Soviet society on the eve of the invasion was as afflicted with
corruption, indiscipline, irresponsibility, and grass-roots apathy as Peter
the Great's society had been, and for the same basic reason: the rotting
effect of centralized, autocratic power on the national psychology.

As was the case under Catherine the Great, the obvious failings of
Soviet society were concealed under a blanket of false propaganda that
echoed Catherine's *Nakaz* and the Potemkin villages. The difference
was that at the start of the Afghan war Soviet propaganda was far more
effective in hiding defects than Catherine's, whereas by the war's end
Soviet propaganda was discredited almost everywhere.

In attacking a supposedly weaker Asian adversary, Moscow repeated
the error of Nicholas II and his war against Japan. In the present era,
however, expressions of public dissent were fewer than under Nicholas, because until near the end of hostilities the Soviet state could still

stifle adverse news from the battlefront and suppress demonstrations. Nevertheless, there are strong indications, as we shall see, that public opinion did play a role in inducing the USSR to quit the war.

The closest parallel with the present day, however, is that of Russia 130 years ago, when, after an unsuccessful war, a despotically educated and despotically inclined ruler was forced to abandon his own convictions and reform a society that otherwise threatened to come down around his ears. Like Alexander II, Gorbachev appeared to betray his ideological birthright by liberalizing a society whose hallmark had always been autocratic rule. No less than Alexander's, Gorbachev's reforms shook the empire to its roots; there was even a parallel with the freeing of the serfs, as Gorbachev hesitantly tried to turn away from collectivized agriculture by offering peasants long-term leases of state land. Just as then, censorship was relaxed, and a breath of freedom spread through the land. Judicial reform under Gorbachev paralleled that under Alexander.

But also like Alexander, Gorbachev sought to preserve and even to increase his personal power and to maintain the organs of suppression that were so carefully nurtured by his predecessors. Like the tsar-liberator, Gorbachev began with an immense reservoir of goodwill at home and abroad, goodwill that over time gave way to disenchantment because of his uncertain concessions, now to reformers, now to reactionaries. Like Alexander, he "merely succeeded in proving that a pseudoliberal autocrat is an unhappy hybrid unlikely to achieve political success . . . He was a disappointing liberal and (worse) an inefficient autocrat."[8] And in the end, like Alexander, he would be removed from power by shortsighted conspirators.

An assassin's bomb killed Alexander II, and popular revulsion overwhelmed the revolutionary perpetrators. In August 1991, Gorbachev suffered only political assassination as the reactionary communist regime he was trying to reform (but above all to preserve) turned on him, and in so doing buried both itself and him.

NOTES

1. Ulam, *Russia's Failed Revolutions*, 123.
2. Pares, *History of Russia*, 211.
3. *Ibid.*, 208.
4. Szamuely, *Russian Tradition*, 104.
5. Pares, 336.
6. See Conquest, *Great Terror* and *Harvest of Sorrow*.
7. Kulichkin, "Desecration of Banners," 8.
8. Mosse, *Alexander II*, 149.

CHAPTER 3

AFGHANISTAN AND THE GREAT POWERS, 1839–1965

If we knew beforehand where we were going to fall,
we could lay down a carpet.
Old Russian proverb

Imperial Britain's Costly Lessons

Russian ambitions in Afghanistan go back a long way. In the nineteenth century, it was just such ambitions that induced England to launch her own two wars in Afghanistan to block Russia's slow march south and east through central Asia, perceived in London as the prelude to an invasion of India.

Technically, the English were winners over the Afghans in both wars, but at a cost that has never been properly calculated. When the invaders occupied Kabul in 1839, no significant body of British troops had ever been defeated by an Asian adversary. Not quite three years after this "victory," in January 1842, the last European survivor of a mixed British-Indian garrison in Kabul that had numbered 16,500 (including 12,000 dependents and camp followers) reached the fort at Jalalabad on a stumbling pony. Most of the rest had been slaughtered along the retreat route, with only a few taken prisoner. The British stormed back that same year to take the capital, but shortly thereafter withdrew to the lowlands, to what is now Pakistan.

Fifteen years later, the Indian subcontinent erupted in a bloody mutiny that very nearly spelled the end of the British presence in the region. No history book explores in depth the probable connection between

these two events, but it is hard to believe that without the Afghan example
the Indian revolutionaries would have been as ready to take up arms
against the main superpower of the nineteenth century. It is worth noting,
however, that when the Indians asked for Afghan help in throwing off
the British yoke, they were rebuffed. Kabul's response was that India's
war with England was India's, not Afghanistan's.

The next British invasion, late in 1878, also motivated by fear of a
Russian encroachment, gave another bloody nose to the empire (again
after victory supposedly had been achieved), this time as a regiment-
sized force was cut to ribbons near Kandahar in July 1880. This time,
after exacting vengeance, the English avoided any 1842-style unpleas-
antness by quickly pulling out their occupation forces in April 1881.
They would never return.

Aside from some minor but strategic territorial acquisitions in the
east (including control of the famous Khyber Pass), the major British
gain from the second Anglo-Afghan war was a treaty that left Afghan
foreign policy in their hands and a permanent British representative
in Kabul. In return for this, they pledged to pay the Afghans sixty thousand
pounds a year.

Anglo-Russian Negotiations

Friction between the Russian Empire encroaching from the north
and the British Empire from the southeast was inevitable, and it very
nearly led to war over Afghanistan in the 1880s. Late in the decade
and on into the 1890s, however, a series of conferences and border
commissions established Afghanistan's national frontiers, and the Russians
reaffirmed that Afghanistan lay outside their sphere of political influence.

In the course of these negotiations—in which the wishes of the Afghans
were not considered worth soliciting, much less heeding—the British
and Russians recognized that a common boundary between the two empires
would itself be a dangerous source of friction, and that beyond clari-
fying the formerly fuzzy borders of Afghanistan, they should expand
its borders to create a further buffer zone. This was the origin of the
Wakhan Corridor, the long tongue of Afghan land that now extends
northeast to the Chinese border.

The territorial generosity of the empires was as unprecedented as
the reaction to it of the beneficiary. Abdur Rahman Khan, the "iron
amir" who ruled in Kabul at the time and who was trying to weld his
fractious peoples into a single country, had enough headaches with-

out taking on the wild Kirghiz tribesmen of the high Pamir Mountains. He so informed London and St. Petersburg but was ignored.

Another result of the border demarcation was the arbitrary splitting of the Pashtun people living in Afghanistan's eastern regions between those on the British and those on the Afghan side of the line. Sir Mortimer Durand, the British official in charge of establishing the line, led a survey party through the mountainous Pashtun areas in 1893, leaving in his wake a trail that cut through tribes and even families.*

The Durand line remains the official but disputed border between Pakistan and Afghanistan to this day. It has given rise to what has been known since World War II as the Pashtunistan issue, the question of who, if anyone, should administer the Pashtun regions of Pakistan. Afghan governments from monarchist to Communist have maintained that this area should be independent, though they have clearly made the unspoken assumption that it would cleave to Afghanistan if freed from Pakistani control. For their part, the Pakistanis point to a 1946 referendum in which Pashtun voters were given a choice between rule by fellow Moslems in Pakistan or Hindus in New Delhi. Not surprisingly, the Pashtuns chose the Islamic option. The Pakistanis rarely mention that no other choices were given the voters. In fact, however, neither in historic nor in present-day circumstances has any outside authority exerted more than partial and temporary control over the area, which runs its own affairs according to local custom.

Nevertheless, in the name of Pashtunistan the Pakistanis and Afghans have imposed trade sanctions, closed their borders, ruptured diplomatic relations, engaged in subversive operations, and even fought some armed skirmishes against each other. Through it all, the residents of the disputed area have happily welcomed the opportunity to hone their fighting, negotiating, and double-dealing skills against both sets of would-be patrons. The Anglo-Russian agreements of the 1890s may have temporarily removed the threat of a Great-Power war fought on Afghan territory, but they scarcely brought permanent peace or stability to the region.

---

*An ardent hunter, Sir Mortimer reputedly meandered his way from covey to covey of upland birds in pursuit of each day's sport and a just international boundary, in that order.

Efforts to Exploit Afghan Anglophobia

But in the early twentieth century other players began to be felt on the world scene, including the Central Powers (Germany, Austria-Hungary, and Turkey) that were gearing up to fight Russia and the western Europeans in World War I. The Afghans had a natural feeling of kinship for their fellow Moslems in Turkey, the most advanced Islamic nation of the time. Nevertheless, Turkish efforts to induce the Afghans to launch a jihad against the British in India's (now Pakistan's) Northwest Frontier Province, and thus to ease Allied pressure on the Central Powers in Europe, came to nothing. As in the case of the Indian rebels sixty years before, the Afghans drew back from involvement with outside powers.

In the wake of World War I came the third and last Anglo-Afghan war, this one instigated in 1919 by the Afghans themselves, which resulted in the country's complete independence. England, exhausted from World War I and already engaged in helping the losing side in the emerging Russian civil war, had no stomach for yet another land invasion of Afghanistan. After successfully turning back a series of unprovoked Afghan armed raids into India and launching a less-than-massive air assault on Kabul (one creaky Handley-Page biplane, four bombs on the royal palace), the British induced the new amir, Amanullah, to sue for peace. They then foreswore any further responsibility for the mountain kingdom's affairs.

There are grounds for suspicion that the Soviets may have had a role in the 1919 assassination of Amanullah's father and predecessor, Habibullah, who was much more in sympathy with the British than his Anglophobe son.[1] If so, one must also suspect that it was at least with Soviet encouragement that Amanullah, as one of his first acts on the throne, proclaimed Afghanistan's complete independence, and when this failed to provoke any British reaction, followed up with his probes into the lowlands. While the war was in progress, the new Communist government in Moscow was the first to give diplomatic recognition to Kabul, a matter of great pride and pompous propaganda among Soviets and their Afghan sympathizers then and ever since. Lenin also made points for his new regime by loudly proclaiming support for national self-determination by peoples under foreign domination.

But the swiftness with which Amanullah abandoned his military campaign after the token bombing of his palace is not in the Afghan tradition, and one wonders to what extent Amanullah's belligerency against the British was merely technical fulfillment of his debt of gratitude to the Soviets. If so, then Amanullah was probably happily surprised (and Lenin almost certainly keenly disappointed) when the outcome of Afghan negotiations with the British in the summer of 1919 was a quick peace with honor rather than a protracted war.

Whether or not the Soviets were involved in the Habibullah assassination and the Anglo-Afghan war that followed, they certainly used their favored position in Kabul afterward to exploit Afghanistan as a launching pad for subversive operations against British India. Still fighting a civil war in which the British were openly supporting its opponents, Moscow saw a golden opportunity for such a diversionary move, which would cost it little and the British much. Unlike preceding and succeeding Afghan rulers, Amanullah was willing to help out, though probably not as wholeheartedly as the Soviets might have wished. In agreeing to let Indian subversives trained in the USSR transit Afghan territory, for example, Amanullah insisted that their weapons travel separately and under Afghan control.[2] Even after the civil war's end and a 1921 Anglo-Soviet treaty that forbade further Moscow meddling in India or Afghanistan was signed, in 1923 London had to threaten an economic boycott to stop Soviet aid to Pashtun rebels in the Northwest Frontier Province.[3]

The Soviets paid for this favored position, not only by diplomatic recognition and the endorsement of national self-determination, but by the promise in 1920 to give the Afghans one million gold rubles annually to make up for the loss of the pre-1919 British subsidy. Thanks to all these moves, the Afghans began their life as a fully independent nation with an immense store of goodwill toward their northern neighbor. As the 1920s rolled on, however, problems began to arise. The promised million-ruble subsidy failed to materialize until 1924, and Kabul's ambitions to become the center of a central Asian confederation ran head-on into Soviet plans to annex the same territories.

Soviet Central Asian Annexation

In this connection, the Afghans were upset that Moscow's national self-determination policy appeared to apply only to other powers' colonies and not to those that had broken free from the old tsarist empire or had been directly inherited by the tsar's communist heirs. Among those who had liberated themselves were the central Asian khanates, for-

merly under loose imperial control from St. Petersburg, the prerevolutionary Russian capital. One by one, the khanates fell to the Red
Army, and puppet leaders were set up in place of the deposed leaders. One puppet, the Bukharan party chief, proved unreliable, and to
justify the armed intervention needed to reimpose Soviet rule, it was
necessary to create an invitation: "The Russian Red Army came to Bukhara
not on its own initiative . . . but . . . at the request of the Bukharan People's
Soviet Republic, to liberate its territory and downtrodden people from
the ongoing *Basmachi* Movement," a Soviet book was still solemnly
stating a half century later.[4] The identical excuse would later serve to
justify Moscow's invasions of Hungary (1956), Czechoslovakia (1968),
and Afghanistan (1979).

Basmachi (literally "robbers") would also be the word used by Soviet propagandists for the anticommunist Afghan resistance after the
Communists took over in 1978, but to Afghans it was not a negative
term. The *basmachi* (another definition is "the barefooted") were regarded, from the 1920s onward, as dedicated fighters for Islam and
independence, people deserving of popular support and asylum between
raids on the infidel foreigners and their puppets in central Asia.

Despite popular Afghan sympathy for the *basmachi*, Kabul's official relations with Moscow remained good during the 1920s. The Kremlin
accepted Amanullah's claim that he had little practical ability to curb
the *basmachi's* influential and largely independent supporters in the
northern provinces. At the end of the decade, when Amanullah was
overthrown for having tried to move his nation away from traditional
Islamic practices too rapidly, it was with obvious Soviet connivance
that a force of "Afghan volunteers" moved in from the north to try to
help him. Before the expeditionary force could affect events, however,
Amanullah formally abdicated, and a British-sponsored Pashtun, Nader
Shah, seized the throne from the illiterate Tajik Bacha-e-Saqao (literally "water-carrier's son") who meanwhile had taken power in Kabul.*

---

*The force, led by a former Soviet military attaché to Kabul, one Primakov, and by
the Afghan ambassador to Moscow, Ghulam Nabi, included air and artillery arms,
weapons with which the Afghans in the 1920s were not familiar, and which probably were officered (if not totally manned) by Red Army personnel. Ghulam Nabi,
possibly relying on his Soviet connections for protection, later made the error of being
insolent to Nader Shah, who had him shot out of hand.

Amanullah had been an unusual Afghan monarch. Unlike most of his predecessors and successors, he seemed to enjoy dabbling in international intrigue. Aside from quietly assisting the Soviet-sponsored Indian revolutionaries, he may also have sanctioned British undercover operations to aid the *basmachi*. His removal from the scene did not seem to have much effect on the formally good relations between Kabul and Moscow, which persisted after he gave up the throne. Popular opinion, however, particularly in the north, did not shift in favor of the Communists. In the 1930s, Stalin's agricultural collectivization program and the purges of "bourgeois nationalists" resulted in thousands of refugees, who fled across the border with firsthand accounts of the successive waves of terror unleashed in the north.

World War II and Postwar Problems

Unlike Amanullah, Nader Shah pursued a policy of strict neutrality. He drove out the *basmachi* and closed the border against their return, but he also put an end to Afghan connivance in helping Indian revolutionaries. After the assassination of Nader Shah in 1933, his son Zahir Shah pursued the same policies. During this latter interwar period, Afghanistan felt more comfortable trading with powers that had no common border with her, including Germany, Italy, Japan, and France. The United States was too far away and too little involved with South Asia to play a role in Afghanistan at that time.

As the clouds of World War II gathered over Europe, Afghanistan, which rarely enjoyed an international spotlight in the best of circumstances, faded still further from foreign attention. At least one country saw its potential, however. Nazi Germany, which had developed good relations with Kabul during the 1930s, once again tried to involve the nation in a diversionary probe into the Northwest Frontier Province. Hitler promised the Afghans restoration of their eighteenth-century Durrani Empire, which had stretched far into today's Pakistan and India, if they would tie up a few British divisions along the border. It must be recalled that at that time Soviet Russia was all but allied to the Nazis by the Molotov-Ribbentrop treaty, and that Britain, standing alone in Europe, seemed to be on the brink of defeat. With a pro-Axis colossus to the north and a weakened British India to the south and east, the temptation for Afghanistan to expand at the expense of the latter must have been considerable. But instead of accepting the offer, Kabul firmly declared its neutrality on August 17, 1940, again refusing to take up arms in another country's cause.

Soviet involvement in World War II and postwar preoccupation with Europe and East Asia left Afghanistan in relative peace in the 1950s. After Stalin's death in 1953, however, the ebullient new Soviet leader, Nikita Khrushchev, opened up a new chapter in Soviet foreign policy by actively wooing selected Third World clients, among them Afghanistan.

The new policy involved buying favor by extending foreign aid and low-interest, long-term, deferred-payment loans in what were then considered huge amounts—$100 million in the case of a package accepted by Afghanistan in 1955. The following year, an even more fateful decision found the Afghans agreeing to a Soviet offer to equip and train their armed forces.

These arrangements flew in the face of deeply ingrained Afghan suspicions. In 1901, the dying Abdur Rahman Khan, who had been educated and supported by the tsar's men in central Asia before taking the throne in 1880, and who remained grateful for their hospitality ever after, is supposed to have told his heir, Habibullah, "my final words to you, my son, are 'never trust the Russians,'" a warning the latter might have done well to heed. Aside from Amanullah's dabbling in the Soviets' Indian intrigues of the early 1920s, relations between the two countries had usually been characterized on the Afghan side by cool and wary correctness.

Why, then, this sudden opening to the north?

Regarding economic development, the Afghans would doubtless have preferred to look further afield for help, just as they had done between the wars. Then, their choice had been Germany or Japan, but in the early 1950s these countries were still too devastated by the war to play a role. The logical choice was the United States, and the Afghans were among the first Third World recipients of U.S. aid. Unfortunately, however, the first project undertaken (reclamation of desert land in the Helmand Valley for agricultural purposes) was plagued with all of the teething problems that accompanied early U.S. aid programs. Begun on a private basis, it soon outran available private funding and was turned over to the U.S. government. Beset by technological and sociological problems—the U.S. advisers were at first ill-prepared for work in a poor Moslem land—the Helmand Valley Authority became an ongoing embarrassment for many years before finally starting to yield positive results in the 1970s.

By contrast, the Russians had a number of advantages: their own central Asian republics provided them with experience in working with Moslem peoples; these same republics produced linguists and interpreters who could communicate with the Afghans in their own languages; and the Soviet advisers, unlike their pampered American counterparts, were accustomed to about the same living standard as the Afghans, including immunity to some of the more virulent local diseases.

In time, Americans and Afghans working together were able to overcome most of these disadvantages, and American aid projects, though never reaching the scope of the Soviet program, provided a sufficient balance to keep Moscow from buying its way into control of the country. The circumferential paved highway system, for example, with its feeder roads off to the Soviet, Iranian, and Pakistani borders, were half Soviet-, half American-built.

The military aid program, however, had a much greater strategic significance, and here the Afghans could not adopt the same evenhanded policy as with civilian aid. Even with one standardized set of spare parts and ammunition, the costs and logistics of maintaining a modern military machine are outrageous; two incompatible sets (such as American and Soviet) in the same army present unimaginable problems.*

Forced to choose between East and West, the Afghans reluctantly and with well-founded apprehension settled on the East. It was a fatefully wrong choice, dictated by a combination of earlier British injustices, contemporary Afghan ambitions, and external factors over which Kabul had no control.

In 1947, the British had pulled out of India, leaving behind the two states of India and Pakistan. London had turned a deaf ear to Afghan

---

*In the 1960s and 1970s another studiously neutral state, Burma, in fact took arms deliveries from both the Soviet bloc and the West and somehow escaped logistical collapse. On the other hand, the Burmese army did not need to contend with external enemies, was largely ineffective when dealing with internal insurgents, and has only made a name for itself since those days by shooting civilian demonstrators.

appeals to abolish the Durand line and move the border east so as to
include Pashtuns now living outside Afghanistan. To do so would have
meant cutting into the new state of Pakistan, so weakening it that it
could not have survived. The infuriated Afghans reacted to the refusal
by voting against Pakistan's admission into the United Nations, the
only negative vote cast on that issue.

Internally, the Afghans felt a need for a stronger central government, one that could impose its will on the chronically rebellious tribesmen
on the periphery. To this end—and to confront Pakistan on anything
like an equal basis—Afghanistan needed a modern, disciplined army
equipped with modern technology. The Afghans tried to get aid from
the United States, whose military aid to Pakistan was already making
the Afghans' position that much more precarious, but Washington was
committed to Pakistan as the linchpin in a series of overlapping mutual defense treaties set up to deter Soviet expansionism.

One U.S. option was to bring Afghanistan, too, into one of the defensive
pacts. But this would have entailed an impossible commitment to defend
a remote, landlocked country on the Soviet border, plus taking on some
measure of responsibility for solving the Pashtunistan issue. It also would
have required an Afghan willingness to jettison their traditional neutrality, a most unlikely step for them to take. By arming Afghanistan
without first achieving strong influence in Kabul, Washington might
have been faced with the outbreak of a hot war between an ally (Pakistan) and a client whose potential for waging it was thanks only to
American weapons.

Growing Soviet Influence

A side benefit to the Afghans for accepting both economic and military
aid from the Soviets was the diplomatic support Moscow was willing
to extend in the Pashtunistan dispute. This support was firm, consistent, and of immense help in improving the Soviet image.

Thus, the Soviet Union profited all around from the new relationship. The aid projects benefited it by providing good-quality Afghan
fruit, natural gas, and cement for Soviet consumers at below-world-
market prices. The Afghan economy was bound tighter and tighter to
the Soviet economy, adding a security buffer on the USSR's south-
ern periphery. Support for Afghanistan's Pashtunistan aspirations not
only discomfited a U.S. ally but made points for Moscow in India,

Pakistan's main enemy. (For its part, the United States refused to take sides in the Pashtunistan issue but limited itself to trying to patch up the quarrel, to no great effect.)

Most important of all, the opportunity to train Afghan army and air force officers in the USSR—a necessity if they were to use Soviet weapons—gave the Soviets untrammeled access to a key group of potential agents. "Power grows out of a gun barrel," said Mao Zedong, and nowhere on earth is the saying more apt than in Afghanistan. This is not to say that in 1956 there was any Soviet master plan or timetable for taking over in Afghanistan, but only that Moscow wanted to build up a coterie of legally armed sympathizers who in any political crisis could wield potent, perhaps decisive, influence.

From the Kabul end, the Afghan prime minister who engineered the aid program was Mohammed Daoud, a first cousin of the king and a wily politician. He became prime minister in 1953 but was ordered to resign in 1963, in part because the leading royal family patriarchs, who effectively ran the Afghan government as a family corporation, became uneasy over the country's worsening relations with Pakistan (Daoud was obsessed with Pashtunistan) and its growing dependence on the USSR. Daoud might have refused to step down—he already had a powerful following in the army, thanks to the abundant Soviet hardware he had procured—but he obeyed the order, paving the way for the king to try to reform Afghanistan into a constitutional monarchy. The constitution itself, adopted after considerable debate by a national *loya jirga* (grand assembly), was promulgated in 1964.

From the Soviet standpoint, these were not welcome developments. Daoud was no Communist, but as someone who had staked much of his career on acquiring Soviet aid, he was vulnerable to discreet pressure. He was also, due to a poor relationship with the American ambassador, Angus Ward, cold toward the United States. Moreover, he had been for the Soviets a single reference point in a unitary political setup that had no such distracting elements as opposition parties or a free press.

Afghanistan's transformation into a parliamentary system signaled the need for new Soviet tactics. No sooner had Daoud resigned than a small group of Afghan intellectuals, undoubtedly under Soviet tutelage, began working to form a Marxist-Leninist party. On January 1, 1965, after a year and a half of effort, some twenty-seven delegates, supposedly representing more than one hundred sympathizers, gathered clandestinely at the home of their senior member, Nur Mohammed Taraki, to hold the founding congress of the People's Democratic Party of Afghanistan (PDPA).

It was the dawn not only of a new year but of a new era. From that day onward, Soviet involvement in internal Afghan political affairs acquired an institutional arm.

NOTES

1. Arnold, *Afghanistan*, 5–10.
2. Gregorian, *Emergence*, 238.
3. Nollau and Wiehe, *Russia's South Flank*, 98, 101.
4. Polyakov and Chugunov, *Konets basmachestva*, 101.

CHAPTER 4

VANGUARD PARTIES AND WATERSHED YEARS

His thoughts are over the mountains;
the danger is over his shoulder.
Russian saying

The founding of the PDPA in 1965 came as the Soviet Union was turning away from the tentative internal reforms of the Khrushchev era but was continuing his policy of pushing for ever-greater influence abroad. The next fifteen years would register generally positive results for the Kremlin as it steamrollered and sabotaged the various internal and external oppositions that rose to challenge it. But these years would also see the accumulating costs of such aggressive policies, costs that ultimately would prove unsustainable.

Soviet Third World Policies

To put the formation of the PDPA in a larger frame, we must step back and look at the development of Soviet policy toward the Third World since the end of World War II. It is true that the optimism of the 1950s, which anticipated a wave of Marxist-Leninist revolutions in countries just freed from colonial rule, had proven premature. It is also true that the face-off with the United States over Cuba in 1962 had revealed the Soviet inability to project its military power intercontinentally, and that the USSR had been helpless to avoid or mitigate such setbacks as the ouster of Patrice Lumumba in the Congo in 1960. The massacre of Indonesian Communists later in 1965 merely confirmed the limits of Soviet power. But these events only served to underscore the need for discretion, not to induce the USSR to forsake its foreign ambitions.

It merely meant that in this increasingly complex world, the old simplistic Soviet ideological formulae had to be modified. Accordingly, a theory of "the noncapitalist path of development," first introduced at the 1960 Conference of Communist and Workers' Parties, embraced some heretical (by the standards of the time) concepts: (1) socialism can be achieved by peaceful means in new states where classes have not developed as they have under advanced capitalism; (2) it is beneficial for such states to stay in the world capitalist system while they develop; and (3) such states should encourage "controlled private initiative in the service of social progress."[1]

These concepts were then expanded to embrace the need for development of a "vanguard" (i.e., Marxist-Leninist) party to lead the way into the bright future, hand in hand with a united front of other "progressive forces," all of which should be dedicated to defending the state's political and economic independence and carrying on the "struggle against imperialism."[2]

It was anticipated that this would be a relatively painless process, lasting anywhere from a few months to a decade, during which a nationalist revolution would transform itself into a socialist one after conditions for the dictatorship of the proletariat had been established. In economic terms, it was a plan to exploit capitalism to destroy capitalism, a modern version of the old Leninist dictum that when the time came to hang the capitalists they would scramble for the opportunity to sell their executioners the rope. The unspoken expectation was that the USSR would have a greater and greater guiding influence as the new states underwent the expected transformation into socialism.

But these optimistic forecasts were seriously dimmed when first Ghana (1966) and then Egypt (following the abortive Six-Day War against Israel in 1967) departed from the paths foreseen by Moscow. By 1969, the official line had reverted to traditional Marxist thinking, including the need for successive nationalist, bourgeois, and socialist revolutions. Only after the third would a nation be officially transferred from the capitalist camp to the socialist side of the ledger. A modification in 1973 saw the Soviets postulating a third category (other than socialist and capitalist), which they termed "multistructured" (*mnogouklyadnyy*) and which they described as being an unstable, temporary transition form, destined soon to become either socialist or capitalist.

The Foundation and Masking of the PDPA

The formation of the PDPA in Afghanistan occurred in the middle of this developing ideological line, on January 1, 1965. In itself, the appearance of an Afghan Marxist-Leninist party was a remarkable phenomenon. Every other country then bordering on the USSR, including such politically backward nations as Korea, Mongolia, and Iran, had a domestic Communist party within six years of the Soviet October Revolution. The next-to-last was Norway, whose party dates from 1923, yet it would be more than forty years before the PDPA came into existence. Unlike Third World nations beyond the reach of Soviet power, Afghanistan bordered on the USSR and had no other regional protector; there was no need to mask the PDPA's essence.

Nevertheless, true to Soviet Third World policy of the day, there was no open admission of the party's true ideological colors. In fact, special care was taken to conceal its Marxist-Leninist nature: PDPA officials were never invited to international conferences of Communist and workers' parties, nor did they contribute to such journals as *Problems of Peace and Socialism*. They never followed such mandatory rituals as the dispatch of congratulatory telegrams to Soviet leaders on key Communist holy days (October Revolution Day, May Day, or Lenin's birthday). The PDPA was never included in Soviet listings of fraternal parties. Even after the party came to power in the coup of April 1978, its leaders initially continued to protest that it was merely "national democratic" in nature. So successful was the camouflage that even the authoritative annual *Hoover Institution Yearbook on International Communist Affairs* had no listing for an Afghan party until 1980.

The policy of masking newly installed Marxist regimes would persist for another fifteen years. In Grenada, most of the ploys used in Afghanistan would be repeated when the Marxist-Leninist New Jewel Movement (NJM) came to power in 1979; as revealed by secret party papers uncovered by the later U.S. invasion, the collaboration of non-Communists was considered an essential element of camouflage, without which the revolution stood in danger of immediate overthrow. The papers revealed that the Soviets themselves in private referred to the NJM as a "Communist party," that the NJM took its direction from the CPSU

Central Committee's International Department (ID), and that state-to-state relations took a backseat to the party link.[3]

Party Split—Parcham and Khalq

In Afghanistan, the preservation of secrecy was seriously complicated by the fact that the Afghan Communist movement was riven with factionalism even before it formally constituted itself as a party. Two factions, *Parcham* (Banner) and *Khalq* (Masses)—each named after its official journal—represented distinct groups of Afghan Communists: the bureaucrat- or officer-bred, city-raised, wealthier, "establishment" Parchamis, and the relatively poor, less-sophisticated offspring of rural Pashtun tribal figures, the Khalqis. Of the two, the Parchamis understood better the need for concealing the PDPA's orientation and ambitions under the cloak of a truly democratic, if leftist, political party. For their part, the Khalqis considered such subterfuge the worst kind of cowardice and opportunism, and they pushed for an openly and militantly Marxist-Leninist line, including the need for a revolutionary overthrow of the existing order.

The split between the two actually antedated the party's 1965 founding congress; according to one party history, the struggle for unity among proto-Communists had been going on since 1948, was resolved successfully in 1964, but was only "consummated in the First Congress of the PDPA." The agreement reached was reflected in the even division of power in the PDPA's top ranks between adherents of Parcham and Khalq. Much later, the Soviet press was to acknowledge that the split "appeared as long ago as the Constituent Congress."[4]

The very fact that two such disparate and mutually hostile groups of Afghans could sit down together and work out a solution is a strong indication that some outside power was refereeing the dispute. Afghans, once committed to a conflict, rarely stop short of total victory or defeat. The Soviets provided the only logical source of arbitration, even though, in accordance with the party line of the day, they clearly favored the Parchamis' guile over the Khalqis' fervor. Thus, although there is no documentary proof as yet that the Soviets actively promoted formation of the PDPA, there is good reason to believe they did so, and that they were instrumental in achieving the first temporary Parcham-Khalq reconciliation. Like several subsequent reconciliations, it would be of short duration.

In one respect, the factionalism may have been of positive benefit to the Soviets. The Parchami line was definitely more attractive to them, because the only practical way of building up mass support in Afghanistan was to conceal the party's real colors. Nevertheless, the militant Khalqis were useful in their own right, attracting as they did a more daring, activist element among the youth, even though they would never be more than a strident minority in an overwhelmingly religious and conservative population.

The outcome of the founding congress reflected a judicious mix of the two philosophies. The publicly issued party platform, a rambling essay of more than five thousand words, made only two passing references to socialism while focusing almost purely on "national, progressive, democratic" principles. But the outspokenly Marxist-Leninist party constitution (practically a carbon copy of the CPSU constitution), held secret and only revealed to new candidates when they were already fully trusted, left no doubt as to the PDPA's allegiance and subordination to Moscow.[5]

Whatever the Soviet role in papering over Parcham-Khalq differences at the founding congress, within two years they were unable to prevent the dispute from splitting the party in half. By 1967 there were two separate PDPAs, each with its own central committee and network of cells, identical only in name. The split would last until 1977, when the Soviets again were able to cobble together a shaky, temporary reconciliation.

The Soviets' failure to achieve any lasting success in solidifying and manipulating the PDPA was probably due mainly to a failure to understand Afghan society. In this, they cannot be faulted too heavily, for both factions of the PDPA were composed of people who themselves were largely out of step with their own national culture.

As the urban, upper-crust children of bureaucrats and officers, the Parchamis were unfamiliar with rural Afghanistan. The Khalqis, though originating in the country, were almost entirely recruited from young students who had been taken away from their native environment at an early age and sent to boarding school in Kabul. Both Parchamis and Khalqis reflected an instinctive obedience to traditional values but both probably wanted to impress the Soviets by appearing "modern" and thus downplayed these values. In particular, it was the Afghan dedication to principles of patronage and tribalism over any ideological consideration that seemed to baffle the Soviets.[6]

The PDPA and the Afghan Democratic Experiment

Whether under the Parcham or the Khalq banner, however, the PDPA as a credible force in a democratic structure made a poor showing in the parliamentary elections of 1965. Only four Parchamis and no Khalqis won their contests in a legislature of more than four hundred members. Possibly because of its failure in this election, the PDPA (which at that time was still formally unified) inspired a series of student riots which effectively brought the fledgling parliament to a standstill. A year later, more Communist disruptive tactics again halted parliamentary proceedings, this time degenerating into scuffling on the floor of the lower house. The Parchami chief, Babrak Karmal, was sent to the hospital with superficial abrasions but turned the event to his own advantage by grabbing spare bandages and wrapping them around his head, as if badly hurt, before appearing before followers who had gathered outside.[7] The government then took stern steps to prevent a recurrence of such disturbances, and these, plus popular disgust with the party's tactics and its own internal split, resulted in even less success in the 1969 elections, when only one Parchami and one Khalqi won seats.

Unfortunately for Afghanistan, the end of the experiment in constitutional monarchy was already looming. The king proved incapable of modernizing his country democratically, and in 1973 his first cousin, the former prime minister Mohammed Daoud, overthrew the monarchy in a nearly bloodless coup. His takeover had succeeded thanks primarily to the help he received from army and air force officers trained in the USSR, most of whom were sympathizers if not secret members of the Parcham branch of the PDPA. Those Parchamis who surrounded him in his new government had done so with the knowledge and blessing of the local KGB. (Writing in 1991 about efforts by the Khalqis in 1976 to discredit the Parchamis because of their association with Daoud, the KGB deputy chief in Kabul at that time testified, "Soviet intelligence was informed about the activity of the Parchamis in the Daoud government, which had been coordinated with and approved by the residency [KGB unit]. Almost all the Parchamis named by Amin as members of Daoud's Central Committee were delivering information to us.")[8]

The PDPA and Daoud

One may infer that the Parchamis (and the Soviets) had hoped that Daoud would become a pliant figurehead, or at least that he would eventually bequeath his power to those who had ushered him in. He was already an old man with severe health problems, including one collapsed lung, and their optimism would be understandable. But Daoud was also a wily politician and a fighter, whose understanding of PDPA ambitions was probably deeper than theirs of his. He immediately set up a "republic" in which he was president, prime minister, minister of defense, and foreign minister. He then proceeded to lop off or transfer to innocuous positions those PDPA officers who had helped him come to power, missing only one or two "sleepers" whose Soviet/PDPA connections he did not divine. He also let it be known that he would not tolerate Parchami recruiting in sensitive Afghan organizations, such as the military and police.

The process of distancing himself from the Parchamis took several years and was not immediately apparent to the victims. But Moscow was growing ever more uneasy as Daoud made up his differences with Pakistan over the Pashtunistan issue, began seeking significant military and economic aid from such non-Communist states as Egypt, India, Saudi Arabia, and Iran, and asked for a cutback in Soviet military advisers. By then, the Soviets must have realized they were on the verge of losing their economic and political investments in the country.

It was at about this time (1975) that the Khalqis, who had been almost completely shut out of the government from the beginning and were contemptuous of Daoud's decrees, began recruiting heavily in the Afghan military. When an illegal political group suddenly abandons its traditional recruiting among intellectuals, media personnel, and teachers, devoting itself instead to the armed forces, it is a signal that priorities have changed from long-range strategic growth to near-term armed conflict, and that radical action impends. That indeed was the Khalqi plan. The KGB deputy *rezident* in Kabul at that time has stated that Soviet intelligence was kept fully abreast of the PDPA's plans to seize power, though he stopped short of acknowledging KGB instigation of the coup plotting.[9]

Nevertheless, the mutual contempt between Parcham and Khalq was not one whit abated by the emergence of a common enemy (Daoud), their shared loyalty to Moscow-style Marxism-Leninism, or the peacemaking efforts of Soviet mediators. To the Parchamis, the Khalqis were still crude hicks, political bumpkins whose frank espousal of Marxism-Leninism would lead to catastrophe for the party in conservative Afghanistan. To the Khalqis, the Parchamis were city slickers whose close connections with the country's ruling circles had earned them the sobriquet of "the Royal Afghan Communist Party." Such urban-rural differences are commonplace in politics worldwide, but the essential Afghan ingredient of the Parcham/Khalq rivalry was its depth and ferocity, an implacable mutual hatred directly traceable to the Afghan blood-feud tradition. Only in such rare cases as that of the nominally Khalqi armored commander Mohammed Aslam Watanjar did loyalty to the Soviets seem to eclipse any local allegiance.*

The View from Moscow

From Moscow's standpoint, these differences must have seemed either frivolous or infuriating—or at least far less meaningful than the impending loss of all they had so diligently worked to achieve. Among other things, the increasingly acrimonious polemics between the factions had led to the first public revelations, by the Khalqis, of the party's dedication to Marxism-Leninism. A scathing Khalqi indictment of the Parchamis, in the form of a history of the party, was distributed to other parties in 1976 and published in Communist organs in Baghdad, Beirut, Delhi, and Belgrade. Moscow turned down a Parchami effort via the Soviet embassy in Kabul to have the CPSU ID distribute their rebuttal to thirty fraternal parties in Europe and Asia. It was time, Moscow is supposed to have noted drily, that the embassy realized that the ID was neither a postbox nor a forwarding address for anyone's correspondence.[10]

But Moscow's objection, if this report is true, should be interpreted less as a sign of lack of interest in the PDPA than as a desire to avoid taking sides and to keep the party's furious and self-destructive infighting from drawing unwanted attention to itself. Within a few months of each other, some of the same obscure Communist party journals that had published the Khalqi indictment (in Iraq and India, and in Aus-

*Starting in 1973, Watanjar compiled a remarkable success record in every Afghan government save one, supporting and, on demand, betraying consecutive Afghan leaders according to Moscow's approval ratings of the moment. His remarkable survival in spite of double crosses probably owes much to Soviet protection. As will be seen, his only fall from grace came in 1979 when the horse picked by both him and the Soviets to be a loser came home a winner—temporarily.

tralia as well) launched a low-key appeal for the Parcham and Khalq factions to patch up their differences and unite in a common struggle. The sudden, almost simultaneous concern of foreign pro-Soviet Communists for unity in a heretofore unknown party in an out-of-the-way country like Afghanistan was a sure sign of a Soviet guiding hand behind the scenes. Thereafter, however, all news about the PDPA in the foreign Communist press appears to have ceased. Moscow doubtless judged it better to press for unity quietly, while continuing to preserve the PDPA's non-Communist fig leaf, than to put public pressure for unity on the two factions from abroad. (And indeed, as noted above, virtually no Western scholar took note of the security lapse that revealed the PDPA's true colors.)

To reconcile the factions was no easy task, but if Daoud were to be toppled it had to be done. The Soviets failed to achieve intra-PDPA reconciliation in 1976, but a second try, in India, resulted in an agreement reached on July 4, 1977. This was the beginning of an unhappy ten-month Parcham-Khalq marriage, just long enough for the PDPA to carry off a coup d'état ("the Great Saur Revolution") against President Mohammed Daoud in April 1978, and to set up the Democratic Republic of Afghanistan (DRA). At that point, Afghanistan became the last in an impressive array of Third World countries where vanguard parties, established with Soviet encouragement and guidance if not under Soviet control, seized power in the mid-1970s. Preceding the PDPA on this course were the vanguard parties of Angola, Mozambique, Cambodia, Laos, Ethiopia, and Nicaragua.*

For Moscow, these "progressive" parties were an essential element in the inevitable, irresistible, irreversible tide of history that would sweep away old capitalist states and establish socialist ones in their place. Their investiture meant that in each country there would be an institutional structure more or less discreetly linked to the CPSU and capable of surviving the removal or death of any given leader. If in the later 1970s such parties were not always successful (e.g., the failed

---

*Some scholars have disputed Soviet involvement in or foreknowledge of Daoud's coup against the king or the PDPA's coup against Daoud. Morozov's revelations, though unaccountably leaving out key PDPA developments, show that the KGB's Afghan sources were deeply involved in both plots.

coup attempts in El Salvador, Guatemala, and South Africa), they could be viewed as having suffered only temporary reverses.[11]

In countries where the coups succeeded, the direct Soviet role in running the new ruling parties was consistently downplayed. Nevertheless, the Soviet Union tried to ensure via surrogates that success would elude anyone unwise enough to impede the proper course of history. For example, the Soviets often delegated to the East Germans the task of training and occasionally even administering the new regimes' security services.[12]

The Soviets saw the process of absorbing Third World countries under their ideological umbrella as taking place under a shifting "correlation of forces," with the socialist world achieving a steadily more marked ascendancy over its capitalist rivals. This ascendancy lay not only in an ever-improving Soviet military capability, with new and better missiles and warheads coming off the assembly lines in dizzying numbers, but in a ground swell of confidence. The United States, still suffering from its post-Vietnam syndrome, seemed indecisive and adrift in its international policies. NATO remained intact, but its future was cloudy as U.S. uncertainty proved contagious to the allies. The West appeared incapable of mounting effective opposition to the Soviets' self-assured, relentless march into the victorious future that Marxism had ordained.

In Europe, the psychological highpoint for the USSR came in 1977–78, when the United States and its NATO allies proved incapable of preventing the Soviet deployment in Eastern Europe of the highly accurate, triple-warheaded, intermediate-range SS-20 ballistic missile aimed at Western Europe. In March 1978, the United States suddenly backed off from an agreed-upon Western response to the SS-20—U.S. development and NATO deployment of the enhanced radiation weapon (ERW, also known as the neutron bomb)—thanks at least in part to a massive, worldwide Soviet overt and covert propaganda campaign.[13] Although other factors had entered into President Carter's last-moment decision to forego ERW deployment, the Soviets could be forgiven for believing that it was their own psychological warfare campaign that had resulted in his change of heart.

Little wonder, then, that whereas there might have been Kremlin debates about how far the Soviet Union should go in militarily defending its Third World clients, such discussions during the 1970s were "colored with optimism, almost euphoria, about the accelerating trend in the correlation of forces."[14]*

Nevertheless, there were problems in the Soviet Third World client states. The absence of direct Soviet control meant that such regimes were more or less free to take up policies that were counterproductive from the Soviet and even from their own standpoints. In Afghanistan, for example, the PDPA was only in power a month when the party's Khalqi faction was able to oust the Parchami faction (which was favored by the Soviets) and embark on orthodox socialist policies that dismayed not only the Afghan people but the PDPA's Soviet patrons.**

Afghan unhappiness with the new regime's revolutionary socialist policies led first to passive and then to ever more active resistance, culminating in open rebellion. In varying degrees, the same anti-Marxist popular reaction was also being felt in other Third World states where vanguard parties had seized power.[15]

The Watershed Decision to Invade

Such resistance required some kind of Soviet response, especially because it was tarnishing Marxism-Leninism and undercutting the image of the historical invincibility of socialism the Soviets had been at such pains to create. The dilemma was especially sharp in Afghanistan, the USSR's neighbor, where resistance forces by the end of 1979 appeared poised for victory. Having failed to convince the Khalqis to moder-

*In a fascinating reflection of Soviet doublethink, the most avid former defender of Soviet aggression in Afghanistan, Alexander Prokhanov, on conceding in 1988 that the invasion had been a mistake, had a unique explanation: in 1979 the West, he said, was confidently asserting that "socialism was receding, and Afghanistan provided an opportunity to show it was still advancing." (*Christian Science Monitor*, April 13, 1988, p. 1.) At that time if any reputable analyst in the West was feeling great confidence about the future of Western democracy, he was keeping discreetly silent about it.

**Intriguingly, developments in Grenada the following year also saw the triumph of the "Khalqi" Bernard Coard over the "Parchami" Maurice Bishop. Unlike the situation in Afghanistan, Bishop was firmly in power before he was overthrown by the more militantly Marxist-Leninist faction.

ate their policies, the Soviets finally resorted to the one means at which they were acknowledged experts—armed invasion.

With the experience of Hungary (1956) and Czechoslovakia (1968) to draw on, the Soviets felt they would have little problem in dealing with the "primitive" Afghans. In KGB chief Yury Andropov they had the principal architect of the vitally important preliminary deception ploys that had undercut Hungarian and Czechoslovak resistance before it could be mobilized. Once official opposition was taken care of, the USSR's leaders had no reason to doubt that the Soviet army, reputedly the best in the world, could make short work of the rebellious tribesmen.

Even so, the decision to invade, as later admitted by CPSU general secretary Leonid Brezhnev, had not been an easy one. It was one thing to assert that the victory of socialism was historically inevitable, but quite another to use Soviet troops to make sure history did not miss the path.

In fact, as revealed ten years after, the decision to invade was made by only four men: Brezhnev, Andropov, Defense Minister Dmitri Ustinov, and Foreign Minister Andrey Gromyko. Not even Eduard Shevardnadze, then an alternate Politburo member and later to be foreign minister, was consulted; he only learned of the invasion from the media after it was under way. According to a November 1989 article in the Soviet army's official organ, the decision was taken on December 12, 1979, though it seems probable that contingency plans for the invasion must have been laid well before that date.[16]*

By a remarkable historical coincidence, that same day was the one chosen by NATO to announce its intention to deploy Pershing II bal-

---

*Some analysts (e.g., Melvin A. Goodman, "Foreign Policy and Decision-Making in the USSR," in Hafeez Malik, ed., *Domestic Determinants of Soviet Foreign Policy towards South Asia and the Middle East* [London: Macmillan, 1990], pp. 98–99) have claimed that the Soviet decision to invade involved the Central Committee and even all "key party institutions," but this has been conclusively contradicted by numerous authoritative Soviet sources. There is some question whether the decision rested with just the four named here or whether ideological guru Mikhail Suslov and Prime Minister Aleksey Kosygin also were involved. In probably the most definitive description, a Soviet congressional investigative commission named only the four, as reported by TASS on December 24, 1989.

listic missiles and ground-launched cruise missiles in Western Europe as a response to the Soviet SS-20 threat.[17] Appropriately, the Soviet decision was secret, the NATO decision open. If ever a day must be picked to signal the beginning of the end for the Soviet Empire, December 12, 1979, deserves first consideration for the honor.

At the time, however, the turning point was anything but obvious. U.S. secretary of state Cyrus Vance and his European colleagues "instinctively understood that after ERW it was especially important to NATO that the theater nuclear force issue be dealt with firmly, but with a united alliance and under visible American leadership."[18] Brave words, but it would take nearly four years to prepare the missiles and their bases, four years of opportunity for the powerful, multifaceted Soviet psychological warfare apparatus to force another humiliating U.S. reversal by building a ground swell of popular opposition in Europe.

Such an effort indeed took place, but although the campaign was noisy and enjoyed some success, it failed in the end to accomplish its purpose. The NATO governments held firm, the missiles were deployed, and the balance of power in Europe shifted in a direction opposite to that intended by Moscow.

The contribution of Afghanistan to this development cannot be measured, but there is no question that it profoundly affected world opinion about the USSR by exploding three fundamental myths.

First, the Soviet invasion showed that the peace-loving image Moscow had been at such pains to create was a sham. The result was a public relations disaster of a magnitude not seen since Stalin signed the nonaggression pact with Hitler in 1939. Not only was the USSR itself blackened, but such Soviet-sponsored front groups as the World Peace Council (Moscow's favorite) were forced into uncomfortable silence or into outright support of the invasion.

Second, and even more significantly, the invasion exposed the highly touted Soviet army's feet of clay. Despite the best efforts of Soviet propagandists (and of some military spokesmen in the West, whose livelihood depended on the degree of their funders' belief in the Soviet menace), there was no way that the Soviet failure to annihilate the poorly armed, disorganized Afghan resistance could be interpreted as anything but proof of some basic Soviet military weaknesses. The initial attack, aided by clever deception, succeeded admirably and displayed a frighteningly efficient coordination of various branches of service.

But once the troops had landed and taken their primary objectives, they were bewildered by the unconventional means employed against them. Unprepared for partisan warfare, the Soviet military machine showed weaknesses not only for this kind of conflict but on a much more basic level: the enlisted men, junior officers, and even middle-grade officers were unwilling to make decisions without orders from superiors. (Those who overcame their dependence on commands from above would later prove a political and social irritant when they refused discipline at home.)

And finally, the invasion laid to rest the already moribund ideological myth that universal popular demand would lead to the inevitable global victory of communism. If communism had a future, it would be thanks only to force—and, at that, more effective force than what the Soviet Union was able to display in Afghanistan.

These truths fundamentally altered the world's view of the Soviet Union. Nowhere would they have a more revolutionary impact than inside the USSR itself.

NOTES

1. Pennar, *USSR and Arabs,* 3–4.
2. *Ibid.* 5–9.
3. Seabury and McDougall, eds., *Grenada Papers,* 69, 196.
4. *Kabul New Times,* November 5, 1984; *Pravda,* May 8, 1990 (FBIS-SOV-90-092, May 11, 1990, 13).
5. Arnold, *Two-Party Communism,* app. B.
6. See Roy, "Origins of the Afghan Communist Party."
7. Dupree, *Afghanistan,* 615.
8. Morozov, "Kabulskiy Rezident" (pt. 1), 38.
9. *Ibid.,* 38–39.
10. Arnold, *Two-Party Communism,* app. C; Morozov, "Kabulskiy Rezident" (pt. 1), 36.
11. Alexiev, "Soviet Stake in Angola," 140. See also Albright, "Vanguard Parties," 216–20.
12. MccGwire, *Military Objectives,* 229.
13. Vance, *Hard Choices,* 67–69, 92–96; Schulz and Godson, *Dezinformatsia,* 75, 133–34.
14. MccGwire, 229.
15. See Radu, ed., *New Insurgencies.*
16. *New York Times,* October 24, 1989, A-4; *Krasnaya Zvezda,* November 18, 1989, 3–4; Moscow TV, December 24, 1989 (FBIS-SOV-89–248, December 28, 1989, 72–74).
17. Vance, 96.
18. *Ibid.*

CHAPTER 5

THE THREE-PILLARS THEORY
AND ITS APPLICATIONS

When two dogs fight, let the third keep his distance.
Russian saying

With the invasion of Afghanistan, Moscow entered on a struggle for domination of the country that would continue until the Soviet Union itself ceased to be, even though the most noticeable element, the Soviet military occupation forces, was almost entirely withdrawn in 1989. There were three consecutive phases to the struggle, corresponding to the three pillars that traditionally upheld Soviet power from 1917 to 1991: the CPSU apparat (that is, CPSU members employed full-time by the party), the military, and the secret police. Before dealing with the role of each of these in Afghanistan, we must look at them against the backdrop of Russian and Soviet history.

And here we are immediately confronted with controversy.

Among students of Soviet politics, there was an ongoing argument for many years about the degree to which institutions other than the CPSU had any say in running the country or solving its problems, internal as well as external. At one extreme were those who maintained that the party controlled everything, and that other institutions did nothing but salute and carry out orders. At the other end were those who insisted that there was considerable hidden autonomy in certain state institutions, particularly the military establishment and the secret police, whose prime importance for Soviet national security gave them some flexibility in fulfilling their mission and a considerable measure of independent authority.*

For the purposes of this book, the argument might appear to be of only tangential importance. Our major thesis is that each of the three institutions—the CPSU apparat, the Soviet military, and the KGB—had a turn as the chief instrument for imposing Moscow's rule on Kabul during the years 1978–91. Whether or to what extent the latter two were acting independently or under CPSU control is relatively immaterial to the main conclusion that each in turn took (or was given) primary responsibility for bringing Afghanistan under Soviet control. Nevertheless, each deserves separate examination.

Common Pillar Characteristics

The privileged position of the party was always recognized, but the armed forces and police also shared certain characteristics that gave them advantages not enjoyed by other Soviet institutions. These included an esprit de corps, a sense of prestige and bonding that most other Soviet organizations lacked. It was reinforced by the fact that both the police and military were closed, specialized bureaucracies that customarily dealt with highly classified information and hence were even more secretive than run-of-the-mill Soviet institutions. Although hard to measure, the sense of superiority that members derived from being in an exclusive club and privy to secret information conveyed a subtle (and not always so subtle!) sense of immunity to the laws that governed their fellow citizens. The higher pay scales (KGB) and imposing uniforms and medals (military) were further marks of superior status.[1]

As important as the mind-set was the practical matter of privileged communications. Both the KGB and the military had their closed networks, even though the former doubtless occasionally listened in on the latter for security purposes. The ability to communicate directly with professional colleagues without involving the Ministry of Communi-

---

*Some analysts believed in yet other pillars, including the state apparatus in general, the military-industrial complex, the technocrats, and various other groups. None of these, however, had the same cohesiveness and internal control as the basic three. Even the Ministry of Interior, which under CPSU rule (as today) had its own troops and served an internal security function, lacked the independence of the regular army and secret police.

cations or other outside ears undoubtedly reinforced the sense of clubbiness and exclusivity.*

Finally, promotions within the police and military were perhaps more attuned to professional ability than one found in the outside Soviet world, where toadying to party apparatchiks could be more important for advancement than doing one's job properly. Granted that both the military and the KGB had their own party apparatuses that reached from the highest to the lowest levels of the respective organizations, and granted that a party representative always sat on promotion panels, these apparatuses were themselves privileged and, except at the highest levels, isolated from the parallel party apparat that governed civilian life. The party representative on an army divisional staff, for example, was completely independent of the party committee in the region where the division was based,[2] and the secret police had been free of local party control since 1926.**

In fact the shoe at various times was on the other foot, with KGB men occupying important local party positions where they could know and influence party affairs without the local party having similar privileges in the KGB. Until Stalin's death, "the chief Chekists at all levels were not only members of the party committees but members of their inner-circle bureaus, as actual watchdogs over them."[3]

An understanding of the significance of each of the pillars and how they operated at home and abroad is essential to an understanding of how the experience of the Afghan war undercut the whole Soviet system. It is particularly important because each of the three Soviet institutions is similar in name and proclaimed function to a parallel institution in Western democracies, yet each differs from its Western counterpart in vital ways. In this regard, a substantial part of Western

---

*One of the KGB responsibilities that was immediately shifted to other hands after the failed antidemocratic coup attempt of August 1991 was that of handling all especially important government communications.

**So-called military councils (*voyennye sovety*), composed of ranking military officers at the Army or Front level and corresponding party secretaries at the oblast, *kray,* or republic level were supposed to monitor and even direct military activities on behalf of the CPSU Central Committee. But there was some doubt whether these shadowy councils actually fulfilled their watchdog role.

misapprehensions about the Soviet Union derived from the different definitions put on key words in the respective Soviet and Western contexts.

The Party Pillar

The party is our first case in point. The very word *party* is derived from the base word *part,* and it implies the existence of one or more other parts. In the West one thinks of a party as being a division of a political whole, with the existence of one or more rival parties assumed. But the CPSU was less a "party" than a "totality," an organization that had the self-assigned mission of completely dominating all facets of Soviet life, not only political but social, economic, cultural, and even technological. Only in early 1990 was the constitutional provision guaranteeing CPSU political primacy revoked, and even this step was probably designed as merely a necessary deception maneuver. It would take the failure of the reactionary August 1991 Kremlin coup attempt to destroy the real behind-the-scenes power the party continued to enjoy despite the constitutional change. Paradoxically, it was only at that point, after losing its control, that the CPSU had a chance to become a true party, but by then it was so discredited that the chances for revival were minimal.

The precipitous decline of the party's authority is a recent phenomenon, but already there is a tendency to forget how truly totalitarian it was, even until the 1980s decade. To justify and rationalize its position in society it had to claim both invincibility and complete infallibility, virtues it had so enthusiastically asserted for itself in earlier years that it appeared far less a party than a compulsory religion. Truth became a party monopoly, regardless of how baldly contradictory or improbable its Kremlin versions, and any incontrovertible opposing evidence was written off disdainfully as "bourgeois objectivism." Party rites and catechisms, complete with prophets, heretics, saints, and devils became standard fare in schools and the workplace. A flourishing, if astonishingly variable, historical mythology sprang up, with heroes and villains often switching places in response to new leadership changes. ("It takes a wise man to predict the past," once mused a gloomy Soviet observer.) Although there had been a significant mellowing of party authority by the 1980s, its basic prerogatives for unrestricted rule were unchallenged.

To enforce its truth monopoly the party relied on the concept of "democratic centralism," an outwardly acceptable if somewhat authoritarian doctrine (debate on any issue would be tolerated in the predecision stage, after which all argument would cease and all members would carry out the decision unquestioningly) that cloaked outright dictation from above. During the Stalin era, the debate phase usually proved fatally risky for those who used it to voice opposition, thus limiting still further their surviving colleagues' incentives for independent expression.

Election was another political term that had a radically different meaning in the Soviet Union. Whether within the party or to decide state positions, Soviet elections would have been better termed involuntary affirmations, rubber-stamp exercises whose outcomes were preordained by higher levels in every instance. They did, however, serve a political function by coercing virtually every citizen into performing a periodic proregime political act and thus committing himself, to whatever small degree and however unwillingly, to the policies of his government.

In theory and practice, the party was the ubiquitous controller of virtually all aspects of every citizen's life.

The Military Pillar

Understanding the role of the military in Russian and later in Soviet society is difficult for anyone brought up in a more civilian-oriented environment. Even under the tsars the army was an inordinately important part of the social structure, and, as chapter 2 showed, when Russian arms failed in the field, upheaval and reform at home followed. Late in World War I, "military defeats and incipient revolutionary anarchy smashed the *strongest link* in the hierarchical chain, the army," thus paving the way for the October Revolution.[4]

This is not to say that old Russia or even the Soviet Union was militaristic in the Prussian sense of the word. The army, while remaining an army, has always been more integrated with civilian life than in most countries. Under both tsarist and Communist rule, troops have regularly helped in such activities as construction projects, road building, harvesting, and snow removal, as well as serving as an emergency force during natural or man-made disasters. The society was not militaristic, but with all of these public-service roles and with universal military service, the army was almost always in view, a ubiquitous and respected part of Soviet life. "The soldiers are our brothers, our sons," said an otherwise dissident citizen to the author in 1990, though he hastened to exclude the generals and admirals from his wide-ranging family.

From the 1920s onward, the military also featured heavily in Soviet culture, but always in alliance with the party, a union that was sometimes carried to extremes. For example, a 1927 film, *The Forty-first,* dealt with a Bolshevik woman soldier cast away on a desert island with an ex-tsarist officer. The two fall in love, but when a capitalist rescue ship comes over the horizon, the girl does the Right Thing—and notches her forty-first kill—by liquidating her lover; the almighty Communist collective, though not physically present, has the last word.[5]*

Military themes in a country that had just undergone war, revolution, and then civil war were of course to be expected. What was innovative about Soviet propaganda was its continued and accelerating decades-long use of military terms for nonmilitary concerns. Teachers, for example, were exhorted to "storm the bastions of illiteracy"; virtually every government program was a "front"; there was a "battle for the potato harvest"; successful workers were "soldiers of the Revolution" if not "heroes of labor"; and, of course, the "conquest of capitalism" was the ultimate goal. This type of language only began to fade from the Soviet scene in the late 1980s. Even when couched in civilian terms, the slogans that were still in use in 1990 carried the tone of military commands.**

As in most societies, top military officers in the Soviet Union have been traditionally wary of sociopolitical innovation. They tended to

---

*Usually Soviet movies were more explicit in their glorification of the collective, dwelling on the cavalry charge, the artillery barrage, the running and stumbling infantrymen on the attack in their thousands. The theme of the collective comes through indirectly even in films that focus on individuals. *The Storks Are Flying*, a post–World War II production dealing with a wartime love story, was one of the first Soviet films without a blatant propaganda message. But it ends with the heroine—who has gone to the train station to greet her returning lover—suddenly realizing he has been killed at the front, and she runs through the masses of other soldiers, giving individual flowers from her bouquet to each. The individual has perished, but the collective survives.

**In October 1990, the following slogan was supposed to inspire the cultural elite of Samarkand: "Literary and artistic figures! Enrich the spiritual world, actively mold the civic attitude of man, actively and clearly reflect the course of *perestroyka!*" The world at large was the target of an Uncle-Sam-Needs-You–type poster whose main figure was a serious worker whose pointed finger demanded, "YOU! Have You Learned to Work in the New Fashion?"

be one of the most fundamentally conservative forces in society, "perhaps irrevocably conservative" in the words of one observer. This was particularly true when, under Leonid Brezhnev, they got virtually everything they asked for. Unlike the situation in some other politically primitive societies, however, the military rarely played any obviously active political role. On the contrary, its main concern was not with ideology or political processes; it demanded only resources, respect, and sufficient access to the top leaders to ensure both.[6]

Until Afghanistan, the Soviet people had an almost mystical faith in their army, revered for its victory over the Nazis in World War II and regarded as one of the few Soviet institutions deserving of honest respect. Its fall from grace began in the early years of the Afghan war and by 1991 had become precipitous.

The KGB Pillar

The KGB and its predecessor Soviet secret police organizations were unique from many standpoints, and for a Westerner their role in Soviet life is even harder to appreciate than the CPSU's or the Soviet army's. It has often been said, for example, that the KGB combined the functions of the FBI, CIA, Coast Guard, and border patrol. It was all of these and more, for in its dispensation and administration of punishments it was a Justice Department, in its collection of all information for the leaders it was a *New York Times*, in its assessment of popular moods it was a Gallup poll, and in its enforcement of the parroting of party slogans it was a sort of (fortunately imaginary) Madison Avenue Enforcement Agency.

The former USSR is doubtless the only country whose secret police was founded before the state itself. The "All-Russian Extraordinary Commission for Fighting Counterrevolution, Speculation, and Sabotage," abbreviated in common parlance to the "extraordinary commission," initials CheKa, was founded on December 20, 1917, five years almost to the day before the USSR itself. The terms *Cheka* for the organization and *Chekist* for one of its operatives remained in vogue from then until at least the end of 1991, regardless of the parent organization's subsequent name changes.

Although it later went through many reorganizations under different names and associated acronyms (GPU, OGPU, GUGB, NKVD, NKGB, MGB, KI, and finally KGB), the secret police retained the essence of its role in Soviet life almost until the very end of the Soviet Union itself. Only as 1992 dawned did the hydra-headed KGB (which henceforth is how we will refer to the Soviet secret police in all its various incarnations) at last appear moribund, a victim of the demise of the Soviet Union itself, but even then its end was not entirely self-evident; after all, if the USSR could have a prenatal secret police, might it not also have a posthumous one?*

Although the KGB carved out for itself a unique niche in history, it was heir to a long tradition of official conspiracy. The tsarist secret service, the *okhrana,* was also known to carry conspiracy to absurd and self-defeating ends. One *okhrana* agent, on orders, assassinated a Russian grand duke to establish himself as a true revolutionary. Another, Roman Malinovsky, was a confidant of Lenin who at any time could have killed or arranged the arrest of the Bolshevik leader, yet whose position of trust was considered so important to his police handlers that they would never consider jeopardizing his security for any such ephemeral goal. In the end he would outlive them, their organization, and the very government for which they all worked. Only after the revolution, when the *okhrana* files were opened, did the Bolsheviks discover his real role and put him before a firing squad.

A somewhat similar operation at the end of World War II saw Soviet intelligence officers deliberately feed genuine Soviet agents disguised as refugees to an agent they had placed as a security expert in an émigré organization in Germany. Aware of their recruitment, the agent would soon force genuine confessions from these unfortunates (who would then meet instant death) and thus facilitate his own rise to the position of security chief.

These examples of conspiracy are important reminders of the KGB's willingness to make significant tactical sacrifices in the interests of long-range strategic goals. We will encounter indications of less vio-

*In November 1991, the KGB's foreign espionage arm was broken off and christened the Central Intelligence Service, and a domestic federal counterespionage and police force, the Interrepublican Council for Security, was set up. At year's end, it was still unclear whether either or both of these might survive into the commonwealth phase of the former Soviet Union.

lent but more sophisticated operations in our discussion of the organization's activities in Afghanistan.

Under Lenin and Stalin, the KGB became the main organ of terror and enforcer of rigid ideological orthodoxy. The midnight knock on the door, the torture-filled interrogations, the forced confessions of utterly improbable crimes, the banishment to labor camps, the pistol-bullet executions were all carried out by the secret police. Later, the KGB would become the innovator of random terror, where oppositionists might be murdered anonymously, receive prison or labor camp sentences, be locked up and given painful treatment for "psychiatric illnesses," be forced into involuntary emigration—or be left mysteriously untouched, to become the target of suspicion among other dissidents.

But the KGB's most peculiar facet (and here it had nothing in common with the *okhrana*) was its responsibility for knowing the objective truth about any given situation while at the same time ensuring that only the party-approved line—almost invariably a lie—was voiced. As aptly noted by the late Soviet émigré Andrey Amalrik, the KGB spent billions domestically to suppress all dissent and then billions more to find out what the Soviet people really thought. As the unique repository of objective truth in a government that operated in a sea of self-generated exaggerations or outright lies, the KGB was critically important to the leadership and herein lay one little-recognized source of its immense power.

The responsibility for knowing the truth required it to run a huge army of domestic informants and foreign agents whose reports funneled into Moscow from all corners of the globe. Nevertheless, the almost unconscious assumption by Western observers that past Soviet leaders were at the end of a limpid stream of complete, objective information on the basis of which they laid elaborate, infallible schemes was badly flawed. In the absence of free media and untrammeled investigative reporting, there was nothing to prevent the KGB from maintaining its monopoly of truth, but that very exclusivity was a vulnerability, for it prevented the voicing of conflicting opinion. The absence of alternative viewpoints was probably responsible for complacency that often led to disastrous miscalculations, from failing to guard against the Nazi surprise attack in 1941 to belief that Soviet arms could conquer Afghanistan.

The reverse side of knowing objective truth lay in denying objective truth to any but the KGB's Kremlin masters. This duty entailed not only carrying secrecy to absurd extremes, suppressing all information unfavorable to the Soviet Union and most of that favorable to the West, but actively promoting false information, *dezinformatsiya* in the KGB's own lexicon. Moreover, the KGB, no less than any other Soviet organization, found it impolitic to tell the leaders what they did not want to hear, or it suppressed information that ran counter to a policy that it thought worth carrying out.*

Relations Among the Pillars

Although the three pillars jockeyed with each other for advantage, this is not to say that a state of extreme tension and competition usually prevailed among them. On the contrary, throughout most of Soviet history they preserved a generally cooperative if uneasy coexistence. At the expense of other branches of the population—the peasantry and workers in whose name the October Revolution had been waged, the vast state bureaucracy, and even the party's own apparat (our third pillar)—the military and police usually prospered to the limits the economy would tolerate. The CPSU leadership, whose hold on power in the end rested on the bayonets of the one and card files of the other, always had a strong stake in catering to the needs of these organizations, which in turn preserved a wary but not openly hostile relationship with each other.

There were exceptions to this uneasy concord. During the purges of the 1930s, the secret police reigned supreme, cutting vast swathes through the party, the military, and even their own ranks. The military in particular suffered grievous losses in the purges, with virtually 100 percent casualties all the way down to the brigade commander level. Almost fatally weakened by the carnage, the Red Army performed disgracefully in the Winter War with Finland (1939–40) and in the early

---

*The old official Soviet attitude toward the sanctity of information is perhaps best illustrated by the tale of the American journalist who, in trying to track down a story about a mass murderer on the loose in Moscow, finally succeeds in getting through to the Central Committee Information Department, only to be told, "This is the *information* department. We collect information—we do not give it out." (Andrew Nagorski, *Reluctant Farewell* [New York: Holt, Rinehart & Winston, 1985], p. 50.)

months of World War II. Only by restoring the army's prestige, relaxing ideological straitjackets, and appealing to patriotism was Stalin able eventually to rally his country for a successful defense against the Germans. As the war progressed, the Soviet army became the most important pillar of all. But even before the war's end in 1945, Stalin was already whittling away at the military and showing renewed favor to the secret police, which for the first eight years of the postwar era again played the most important role.

Effects of Stalin's Death on the Secret Police

The importance of the secret police as a state institution and its relative independence of the party was illustrated at the time of Stalin's death. In April 1943, Stalin had split off state security functions from the People's Commissariat (later Ministry) of Internal Affairs, where they had rested since 1934, and set them up as a separate Commissariat/Ministry of State Security. Lavrenty Beria, who previously had been responsible for both functions in the *state* apparatus, was only allowed to remain commissar/minister of internal affairs. Nevertheless, he retained responsibility for both functions along *party* lines by virtue of his position in the Politburo. If the party had been as dominant as some think, the party position would have given him adequate control over state security. This, apparently, was not his perception of the situation, for less than forty-eight hours after Stalin's death in March 1953, he had seized the state lines of control by abolishing the Ministry of State Security and sweeping it back into the Ministry of Internal Affairs (MVD) as merely one of the latter's chief directorates.

The party and military chiefs undoubtedly condoned and probably promoted Beria's power grab, although with considerable misgivings. They had little choice, for Stalin had been readying a new purge, one that would have counted among its victims not only Beria himself but all the rest of the old guard of Stalin's closest party and military advisers. To the extent that the secret police were doubtless responsible for planning and executing the purge, they had to be brought immediately to heel by the man who knew them best, Beria. At the same time, police control over the population could not be relaxed in this time of crisis. As the announcement of Stalin's death spelled out, "the most important task of the party and government is to ensure . . . the greatest unity of leadership and the prevention of any kind of disorder or panic."[7]

Beria, like his eventual successor Yury Andropov, had consistently projected the public image of a liberal while secretly introducing the most vicious methods against all real and imagined state enemies. In the first weeks after Stalin's death, whether as part of the liberal disguise or under pressure from other members of the Presidium (then the name of the Politburo), he and they oversaw a series of measures that had the effect of denigrating the police image: an amnesty for old people, mothers with children under ten, all children under eighteen, and pregnant women (none of whose incarceration in labor camps had been admitted previously); a public admission that the "doctors' plot" (an alleged conspiracy to poison Stalin and the intended keystone of the purge that was to have followed) had been fabricated; the arrest of the secret policeman responsible for the "Georgian plot," another fabricated conspiracy; and the first rehabilitation of a Politburo member purged by Stalin, the seventy-five-year-old G. I. Petrovskiy.[8]* Even as Beria's personal power was enhanced, that of the KGB pillar was being cut back.

As police power appeared to wane, the perception of liberalization extended to the minority Soviet republics and beyond, to the East European satellites. Great Russian** chauvinism was attacked and Russians were removed from leadership positions in the Ukraine and Latvia. In East Germany, the government admitted to having committed "serious mistakes" by overly rigid enforcement of socialist principles.

This confession produced a swift and violent reaction. On June 17, 1953, less than a week after the first guarded admissions, there were demonstrations throughout the German Democratic Republic (GDR), with students and workers hurling rocks at the Soviet army tanks deployed to intimidate them. It was the first open anti-Soviet mass activity in Eastern Europe since the end of the war, and although it was quickly

---

*Significantly, however, the amnesty did not extend to most political prisoners. As reported by Solzhenitsyn, only three out of three thousand "politicals" at No. 2 Camp Division in Kengir were released. Instead, large numbers of common criminals were unleashed on the Soviet public "like a plague of rats."(Alexander Solzhenitsyn, *The Gulag Archipelago*, vol. 3, *Katorga Exile* [New York: Harper and Row, 1973, 1974, 1976], p. 280.)

**See glossary under Russian, Great.

suppressed, it set a precedent that would be followed by other satellites in turn.

With the whole Soviet edifice tottering, it might have been assumed that the new Soviet leaders would again fall back on the police and its chief, Beria. Instead, on June 25 or 26, at a secret session of the Presidium, the other members arrested Beria at gunpoint and sometime later liquidated him. The success of this maneuver was thanks only to a successful conspiracy between the rest of the party leadership and the military high command, including the redoubtable World War II hero Marshal Giorgi Zhukov, who deployed his tanks around the Kremlin to prevent a Beria countercoup. The two "junior pillars" had joined forces to overthrow the previously dominant third pillar.[9] The feelings of the party toward the secret police at this time were later inadvertently revealed by Khrushchev when, in referring to one of his closest colleagues, Ivan A. Serov (who would soon take over the secret police), he made cryptic reference to "a few dubious things about him, as there are about all Chekists."[10]

Although Beria's downfall resulted in no known civil disobedience in the Soviet public at large, it caused a psychological revolution in the forced labor camps. Prisoners reviled and ridiculed camp guards, who appeared uncertain and frightened:

Beria had fallen, and he had bequeathed the "blot" on his name to his faithful Organs. Until then, no prisoner and no *free man*, if he valued his life, had dared even to think of doubting the crystalline purity of each and every MVD officer, but now it was enough to call one of those reptiles a "Beria-ite," and he was defenseless![11]

The epaulets with the blue borders . . . hitherto the most respected, the least questionable in the armed forces at large, had suddenly become a stigma, not just in the eyes of prisoners . . . but even perhaps in the eyes of the government.[12]

On July 22, less than two weeks after Beria was publicly denounced, five industrial projects at the Vorkuta forced labor camp went on strike. Although by August 11 the strike had been broken by regular army troops (with heavy prisoner casualties), the camp guards never regained their authority, despite attempts to do so by arbitrary violence. More unrest followed, culminating in May 1954 in a forty-day uprising by the prisoners of the Kengir labor camp, a rebellion that was finally crushed only through the use of aircraft, armor, and massed troops.[13]

Formation of the KGB

A year after Stalin's death, on March 13, 1954, the state security functions were again divorced from a discredited MVD and set up under a new Committee for State Security (KGB), "attached to the Council of Ministers of the USSR," a phrase that indicated a radical downgrading of secret police authority. Beria's replacement, Serov, was not a member or even alternate member of the CPSU Presidium, and the secret police lost most of their privileged party positions throughout the country. The apparent initial intent was to place a firm governmental hand on their activities so as to prevent repetition of the Stalin-era abuses.

But the remaining two pillars were inherently unstable without their third leg. The MVD never did regain its old prestige, but the more secretive KGB, over time, was slowly rebuilt. In 1978 it became the "KGB of the USSR," thus increasing its prestige, and by 1990, it had again become the sturdiest leg of the triad. This was a slow process that involved no purges or serious reorganizations; unlike the first generation of Soviet power, which saw the secret police change names eight times, the KGB remained the KGB from 1954 until its fragmentation in late 1991.

In his famous "secret speech" at the twentieth CPSU congress in February 1956, Khrushchev reasserted the primacy of the party. In cataloguing Stalin's crimes of the 1930s, he concentrated almost entirely on the sufferings of the party and of "good Communists," giving only passing mention to the ordeals of the military. The tribulations of the non-Communist public were barely mentioned, and he made no reference at all to the 1938–39 purge of the secret police themselves.

Nevertheless, the Khrushchev speech avoided criticizing the secret police as an institution. He put the blame on "provocateurs, who had infiltrated state security organs, together with conscienceless careerists [who] began to protect with the party name the mass terror against party cadres . . ." He named a few of the individual villains but was careful not to blast the concept of a secret police. On the contrary, in his public statements at the time and later, he praised the Chekists and advocated strengthening state security organs.[14]

Moreover, the strength of the military pillar could not be ignored. In January 1956, before the twentieth congress, Marshal Zhukov had thrown down the gauntlet to party officials who wanted to retain local CPSU control over the military. He demanded an end to district party criticism of commanders' activities and called for a strengthening of such commanders' authority. Later, during the congress, he gave warning that the generals "would not stand for a Stalinist treatment of the army."[15]

1956 Eastern European Revolts

And in fact Khrushchev was soon to need the support of both other pillars to maintain control over Eastern Europe. The secret speech, like the GDR's admissions of Communist errors in 1953, gave legitimacy to the unrest that was spreading across the whole empire. In September-October 1956, first Poland and then Hungary defied Soviet hegemony, and the CPSU was powerless to reassert its total control. Poland, because it remained Communist and because of its large population and legendary willingness to do battle with invaders no matter what the odds, was allowed to pursue its own course. But little Hungary, under Imre Nagy, wanted to leave the Warsaw Pact, to declare itself neutral, and to become a democracy. This was intolerable to Moscow, which used the ruse of negotiations to buy time while it readied several armored divisions for an invasion.

On October 30, 1956, Radio Moscow broadcast that all Soviet troops would be withdrawn from Budapest as soon as the Nagy government desired, and that the Soviets were ready to start discussions on the general position of Soviet troops in Hungary. The Soviet ambassador, Yury Andropov, confirmed this declaration, earnestly assuring the Hungarians that reported Soviet troop movements into Hungary at that time were merely to facilitate transportation of the departing garrisons. In fact, the ambassador was continuing the discussions even as Soviet armored divisions were pouring across the border to crush the revolution. As the outnumbered, outgunned Hungarians fought their last, hopeless battles, Radio Kossuth and the Hungarian News Agency teletype sent out their final, desperate appeals to the world, but to no avail. Andropov, later

to be chief of the KGB and then CPSU general secretary, performed
the last act of Soviet betrayal by promising Imre Nagy safe conduct
from his asylum in the Yugoslav embassy, only then to have him arrested
and later executed.[16]*

If the CPSU pillar had demonstrated its ineffectiveness in Poland
by failing to prevent the demise of a firmly pro-Moscow party, the
military pillar had gained strength from its bloody victory over the
Hungarians. At the same time, the fate of Hungarian secret police officers
unfortunate enough to be identified by their countrymen was an especially chilling object lesson to the KGB. Alone among Hungarian
institutions, the Ministry of Interior's State Security Division or State
Security Forces (*Allam Vedelmi Osztaly* [AVO], or *Allam Vedelmi Hatosag*
[AVH]) remained loyal to Moscow—and suffered accordingly. The
revolutionaries systematically hunted down and lynched AVO/AVH
officers wherever they could be found. Often identified by their un-
official "uniforms" of leather jackets and good-quality brown shoes,
the victims were most often hanged from lampposts, but in some cases
were quite literally torn to pieces by enraged mobs. By contrast, the
military, which in any case mostly sided with the revolution, met no
such retribution. Even most Communist party officials were merely
disarmed and dismissed with contempt, rarely suffering any physical
harm.[17]**

Soviet Military in 1957 Power Struggles

The prestige of the military took another jump the following year,
when it intervened in an internal struggle. In June 1957, faced with
an intraparty revolt in which a majority of the Presidium voted to demote
him, Khrushchev convened an emergency meeting of the Central
Committee and called on Marshal Zhukov, the minister of defense, to

---

*Andropov was reportedly far more than a simple executor of the Kremlin's will;
according to Arkady Shevchenko, he was the engineer of the Hungarian operation
and the only one with a clear vision of what should be done.
**It is not impossible that the spontaneous vigilante justice meted out to the AVO/
AVH provided a strong incentive for the KGB in later years, as the Soviet edifice
itself began to totter, to project a "progressive" image, as if they were in the vanguard of the reform movement rather than hoping to hold it back.

have military aircraft airlift Khrushchev's supporters to Moscow from the outlying districts. The maneuver was successful. Khrushchev received majority support from the Central Committee, and Marshal Zhukov was rewarded with a full membership in the Presidium, the first military man to hold such an exalted party rank.

In October, however, while on a trip to Albania, he was summarily recalled and dismissed for having plotted an overthrow of the regime ("Bonapartism"), for disagreeing with the party leadership on policy matters, for sponsoring his own personality cult, for administering the army "in a nonparty manner," and for attacking military-party organs. One may dismiss the most serious of these charges (plotting a coup) as typical Khrushchevian verbal extravagance, especially because Zhukov was neither shot nor even stripped of his decorations but merely removed from the Presidium and retired in disgrace. Nevertheless, his record of opposing party control over the military is well documented, and his dismissal dealt a severe blow to the military pillar. Significantly, his replacement, Marshal Malinovskiy, did not get a seat on the Presidium, nor would any other minister of defense receive an equivalent honor until Marshal A. A. Grechko became a full Politburo member in 1973.

By downgrading first the secret police and then the military, Khrushchev increased the relative strength of the party pillar at their expense, but he also paved the way for his own eventual downfall. It is true that as CPSU first secretary he wielded immense personal power, enough to preserve his authority for seven years, but in the end he had no maneuvering room when his subordinates finally revolted. Perhaps his single most fateful error was to infuriate the apparat that supported him by dissipating its powers in two ways: decreeing the separation of agricultural from industrial party apparatuses, and limiting the terms in party office all the way up to the Presidium level. (City and regional party bureau officials could only remain for six years before being replaced; Presidium members could stay a total of fifteen years, in three five-year terms.)[18]

Khrushchev's Downfall

No longer supported by the military or police and precariously balanced atop the last pillar, which he himself was undercutting, Khrushchev in effect committed political suicide.

The consequences of this elementary political error were illustrated when Khrushchev learned of the plot to unseat him. Bursting in on the October 1964 Presidium meeting where the other members were discussing his removal, he demanded to know what was going on. On being informed that they were discussing his dismissal, he shouted, "You're crazy!" and, in his capacity as commander-in-chief of the army, instantly telephoned Minister of Defense Malinovskiy, ordering him to arrest the conspirators. The latter refused, noting that as a good Communist he would follow only the instructions of the Central Committee. (One can picture the marshal's complacent malevolence in citing the party's supreme authority to the man who earlier had used that same authority to humiliate the military.) Khrushchev then rang KGB chief Semichastnyy with the same order, but was again rebuffed. With no other guns to call on, Khrushchev resigned.[19]

In fact, as was later revealed, both the previous and then-acting chief of the KGB (Shelepin and Semichastnyy, respectively) had taken a leading part in preparing Khrushchev's downfall by keeping him and his family under personal and telephone surveillance and readying troops for the coup. Shelepin's reward was membership on the Presidium (soon to be again named the Politburo), and Semichastnyy's a membership on the Central Committee. (The military, which simply stood aside, reaped no immediate benefit.) But the real winner was Leonid Brezhnev, who though only informed of the coup plot at the last minute, was chosen as a compromise party leader by the other logical aspirants for the position—Kosygin, Shelepin, and Suslov.[20]

Rise of Brezhnev

Even to the few who recognized Brezhnev's name at that time, he was a largely unknown figure whose promises to continue and accelerate Khrushchev's reforms sounded believable, even though most analysts thought that he would serve only as a temporary stand-in leader. Sooner or later, they predicted, one of the better-known Kremlin figures, such as Suslov or Shelepin, would assume the reins of power. But gray, unremarkable Brezhnev, the consummate bureaucrat, survived by balancing between the various power groups that sustained him, playing one off against another and rewarding each in turn. The appeasement of these blocs entailed turning back the clock, perhaps not all the way to Stalinism, but far enough to cause increasing apprehension at home and abroad.

The maneuvering sustained Brezhnev in power but did not gain him respect:

> Other world class leaders are original personalities who mold government power and their programs. But the biggest bureaucrat will remain what he always was—the tool of someone else's will. The first three Soviet leaders were original politicians: Lenin, Stalin, and Khrushchev. But at the head of the present, fourth administration of the Soviet superpower, for the first time we have a superbureaucrat. He is an imitator of his predecessors, a fulfiller who realizes the will of the trinity of real power in the country: the party apparatus, the political police, and the army. This is his strength and what has preserved him from internal revolt; and this is also his impotence, that makes his power as chief of state and leader of the party ephemeral.[21]*

But Brezhnev, as Avtorkhanov acknowledges, was more than just an arranger of consensus among the elites. As his power grew, he discarded the title of first secretary—there were lots of other first secretaries at all levels of the CPSU apparat—and revived Stalin's unique title of general secretary, which he established for himself at the twenty-third CPSU congress in 1966.

Realizing the threat from Shelepin, whose keen ambitions, new position on the Presidium, and still-powerful connections in the KGB made him a potential rival, Brezhnev sent him on a foredoomed diplomatic mission to England and Germany. Both countries had powerful Ukrainian émigré communities that were enraged by recent revelations that the KGB had murdered their leaders, Bandera and Rebet, and Shelepin was greeted with stormy demonstrations. Later, Brezhnev disposed of other potential rivals, including Semichastnyy (whom he dismissed from the KGB and Central Committee in 1967), by other stratagems.[22]

---

*The same view was also current in Moscow in the early 1970s, when a saying denied the existence of a personality cult on the basis that "there can be no personality cult without a personality."

Thus, in the very early part of Brezhnev's rule, the KGB appears to have done no better than stay even, or perhaps even to have lost some ground in the ongoing struggle for influence. The military, by contrast, appears to have gained immediate favor and been granted virtually all its wishes from the outset of Brezhnev's administration.[23] Except for a brief expansion in 1960–61, the strength of Soviet forces had held steady or even contracted from 1955 to 1965, the main span of Khrushchev's administration. Starting in 1965, however, they embarked on a steady expansion that lasted until 1976. In 1973 Minister of Defense Marshal Grechko regained for the military the Politburo seat lost with Zhukov's ouster sixteen years before. By 1976 the military held thirty seats in the CPSU Central Committee, by far the largest representation from any bureaucratic group.[24]

The Soviet military budget also expanded steadily, and it was during the 1970s that Moscow for the first time deployed a blue-water navy that could project Soviet power to all corners of the globe. Nevertheless, despite the favor shown the military, Brezhnev, like Khrushchev, understood that he could not offend the KGB as an institution, and he was not slow to promote its interests once he had a coterie of loyal supporters in its ranks.

The 1968 Invasion of Czechoslovakia

Before the invasion of Afghanistan, Brezhnev was faced with only one other serious external challenge: the 1968 "Prague Spring" in Czechoslovakia. Although he ultimately had to rely on a military invasion to crush the democratization process, he mobilized the resources of his CPSU and KGB pillars first in an attempt to avoid the invasion, next to facilitate it, and finally to minimize its consequences. It is noteworthy, however, that only the military enjoyed an unqualified success in fulfilling its mission.

The CPSU was a complete failure, as shown by its inability to emasculate the democratic movement in Czechoslovakia during the early months of 1968. Although in February Brezhnev successfully forced Prague's party leader, Alexander Dubcek, to rewrite a "revisionist and liquidationist speech" on the twentieth anniversary of the Communist coup d'état in Prague, thereafter the CPSU's ability to influence events in Prague dwindled steadily.[25]

Between March and August, Moscow tried to accomplish a "silent invasion" by having Czechoslovakia request the stationing of Soviet troops in the country, but this was refused. Pressure to permit the holding of Warsaw Pact maneuvers in the country did succeed, but after arriving early and overstaying their welcome, the Soviet troops finally acceded to the government's demand that they leave.[26]

While the CPSU was floundering, the KGB was fulfilling its informational and disinformational duties in preparation for reestablishing Soviet control. These involved not only the collection of accurate information on the real situation (to be disseminated only to a restricted circle of Soviet leaders), but also the deliberate spreading of false information to the rest of the world.

A cache of Western small arms, in crates conveniently marked with English-language stencils, was "discovered" and widely trumpeted. Eight American tanks were reportedly rendezvousing with three West German tanks in Czechoslovakia, and American Special Forces were allegedly preparing to invade in the guise of West German tourists. Virulently anti-Semitic pamphlets directed against leading liberals were disseminated, as were propaganda brochures calling on workers to reject the intellectual liberals and support "healthy party cadres." But the Czechoslovak government denounced the arms cache as a provocation and noted that the "American and German" tanks were actually Soviet-built armor on loan from the Czechoslovak army to an American movie crew for filming *The Bridge at Remagen*. The "American troops disguised as German tourists" were clearly real German tourists, and the blue-collar appeal attracted few supporters. All in all, it was not the KGB's most shining hour.[27]*

Once the invasion was under way, however, the KGB did better. Two highly placed Soviet agents, Czechoslovak News Agency chief

---

*Thus, the former acting chief of the KGB station in Washington, General Kalugin, found that his reports refuting the Soviet propaganda line in 1968 that the United States was busily subverting Czechoslovakia had been shortstopped and destroyed on receipt in Moscow. Such information, if available to the top leaders of that day, might have had a deterrent effect on the decision to reimpose orthodox communism in Czechoslovakia with Warsaw Pact troops as was done in August that year.

Miroslav Sulek and Central Communications Administration boss Karel
Hoffman also played a part. Sulek, who had been "vacationing" in the
Soviet Union, returned hastily on the eve of the invasion and ordered
his employees to clear all broadcasts with him personally. As the invasion
got under way he handed them the text of an invitation to the Soviets
by unnamed leading party and state functionaries, but the employees
refused to broadcast it.

Although Sulek failed in this attempt, Hoffman was able to cut
communications within Czechoslovakia and to the outside world by
shutting down Prague's transmitter just as Dubcek was about to read
a Presidium statement denouncing the invasion as a violation of international law and of the principles of socialist-bloc relations.[28] The
Dubcek statement eventually became available, but the Soviets were
spared the embarrassment of having the last appeals from the drown-
ing government broadcast live to the world, as had happened in Hungary twelve years before.

This success was almost certainly due to the foresight of Yury Andropov
who, as recently appointed KGB chief, undoubtedly still remembered
the damage done to the USSR in general and himself personally by
the free flow of information out of Budapest in 1956. He and the CPSU
propagandists, both during the Czechoslovakian operation and after
it, bent every effort to minimize the international embarrassment that
it would inevitably cause. As a damage-control operation, these efforts enjoyed only spotty success. They did best in the Third World,
which was encouraged to view the Warsaw Pact invasion as at worst
merely a no-fault argument between fat-cat European states and thus
of no relevance to them, or at worst the result of evil American imperialist machinations. At home in the USSR, the small, courageous
demonstrations against the invasion were instantly and ruthlessly suppressed, the demonstrators carted off to jail and held incommunicado.
In Western Europe, however, the effect of the invasion was to shatter
anew the partially and painfully reconstructed transnational Communist movement, left in tatters after the Hungarian Revolution.

Andropov and Dissidence

Andropov's contributions dealing with the 1968 Czechoslovak problem
undoubtedly helped the upswing in KGB fortunes that followed. At
least as important in promoting official support for the "organs," however,

was the Kremlin's perceived need to stamp out domestic dissidence. Inspired by Khrushchev's revelations of Stalin's misdeeds, released by the decline of mass terror as the regime's standard disciplinary tool, spiced by the personal contacts of Soviet citizens abroad and free-world visitors to the USSR, and increased exponentially by the availability of mass-distribution technologies (radios, tape recorders, typewriters, copying machines, photography, etc.), dissidence was threatening the regime's most cherished advantage, its monopoly over truth.

It was, in short, again an informational problem, and in Andropov and the KGB the regime found its most effective weapons. Through a long and mixed campaign of harrassment, selective terror, forced psychiatric treatment, occasional torture, permitted emigration (sometimes banishment) abroad, sentences to prison or labor camps, and complicated intrigue, the KGB finally managed to quell most of the overt dissent in the country, though it would take a full fifteen years from the first trials in 1965 to the trailing off of the most obvious dissident manifestations. Throughout the process, the KGB gained in official authority and prestige. In 1966 there were only four KGB representatives on republic party bureaus, in 1971 seven, in 1976 twelve, and in 1981 fourteen. Andropov became a full Politburo member in 1973 and was given the rank of army general (unheard of since Beria's days) in 1976; in 1978, three deputy KGB chiefs also became army generals.[29]

From the late 1960s, the public rehabilitation of the KGB in the USSR proceeded apace. The regime published thousands of documentary and fictional works aimed at glorifying the service and extolling its activities in thwarting the evil designs of internal and external enemies. Andropov's secret police predecessors may have done as good or better a job of domestic and foreign spying, but none was his equal in informational manipulation: stifling, distorting, and often inventing, depending on the needs of the country, the service, and himself—in reverse order of priority.

The fortunes of the military also continued to improve through the early and middle range of Brezhnev's years in power, though they appear to have leveled off and possibly even to have started a slight decline after 1976. The defense budget grew at a rate of 4 to 5 percent annually from the mid-1960s to 1976, and at about 2 percent per year thereafter, about the same rate as the economy as a whole. Some Western ana-

lysts began to see a breakdown of the close military-CPSU relationship as early as 1976, whereas the KGB-CPSU honeymoon would last
until the succession struggle that broke out on Brezhnev's death in 1982.[30]
In any case, the period leading up to 1976 was, according to one set
of analysts, the "golden age" of party-military and party-KGB relations.[31] But the seeds of institutional clashes were already rooted and
were beginning to be fertilized by the rot and corruption of the privileged party structure that Brezhnev had nurtured. Their germination
and flowering would follow the invasion of Afghanistan.

NOTES

1. Knight, "KGB and Civil-Military Relations," 101.
2. Colton, *Soldiers*, 30–31.
3. Avtorkhanov, "Andropov i ego pravleniye," 26. Avtorkhanov was one of the first to spell out the three-pillars theory.
4. Sinyavskiy, *Soviet Civilization*, 14.
5. Kenez, *Birth of the Propaganda State*, 211, 215.
6. Colton, *Commissars*, 288.
7. *Ibid.*, 131.
8. *Ibid.*, 137–38.
9. Khrushchev, *Khrushchev Remembers*, 336.
10. *Ibid.*, 338.
11. Solzhenitsyn, *Gulag* 3:281.
12. *Ibid.*, 285.
13. *Ibid.*, 298–331.
14. Knight, *KGB: Police and Politics*, 52–53.
15. Paloczi-Horvath, *Khrushchev*, 190, 203.
16. Shevchenko, *Breaking with Moscow*, 80. For a detailed, comprehensive, and moving description of the revolution, see Lasky, ed., *The Hungarian Revolution*.
17. Lasky, 64, 72, 165, 189, 193.
18. Shevchenko, 125.
19. Sakharov, *Memoirs*, 237.
20. Knight, "KGB and Civil-Military Relations," 100; Shevchenko, 126, 128.
21. Avtorkhanov, *Sila i bessiliye Brezhneva*, 5.
22. *Ibid.*, 22–26.
23. Colton, "Perspectives," 26.
24. Colton, *Commissars*, 201, 245, 271.
25. Bittman, *Deception Game*, 180.
26. *Ibid.*, 181, 191, 193–95.
27. *Ibid.*, 188–89.
28. *Ibid.*, 194–95.
29. Carrott, "Political Change," 77, and Knight, "KGB and Civil-Military Relations," 103–4.
30. Knight, *KGB: Police and Politics*, 104.
31. Colton, "Perspectives," 25–29. The term appears to have been coined in this context in Azreal, *Soviet Civilian Leadership*, 2.

CHAPTER 6

CPSU RULE IN AFGHANISTAN: 1978–82 AND BEYOND

The Afghan adventure [embodies] all of the danger
and irrationality of a closed totalitarian society.
Andrei Sakharov

The Road to the 1978 Coup

In the 1950s, the Soviet Union had invested in Afghanistan economically with a massive aid program; in the 1960s and early 1970s, it had made a political investment via the PDPA. Neither of these had been successful in securing a dominant role for the USSR in the country, but neither had been very costly, and it would have been relatively painless to abandon both had circumstances dictated. The coming to power of the PDPA in 1978, however, involved more than another speculative experiment that could be written off with a shrug. A new, ideological dimension was present, meaning that Moscow's involvement in Afghan affairs was now less an investment than a commitment.

It is not likely that this prospect caused the Kremlin undue nervousness at the time. It was the spring of 1978, and ideology had again become a dominating feature of Soviet foreign policy. The triumph of a pro-Soviet vanguard party in Afghanistan was probably seen as just one more victory in the Communist-capitalist world competition, one more plus for the Soviet side in what Moscow called the "changing correlation of forces."

For the Soviets, Afghanistan offered advantages over such other new client states as far-off Angola or Laos. Unlike these, it was a next-

door neighbor, with a long history of close relations with Moscow.
Via the military training program that had been going on in the USSR
for more than twenty years, Soviet civilian and military intelligence
officers had had long-term contact with Afghan officers of all ranks.
These contacts could then be developed further via the Soviet military advisers sent to Afghanistan to help maintain old weapons or introduce
new ones.

A similar situation had developed on the civilian side, with an active
Soviet embassy social program to keep up contacts with progressive
Afghans. Especially within the newly established PDPA (only thirteen
years old in 1978), Soviet influence was dominant in both the Parchami
and Khalqi factions.

With these advantages, the Soviets had developed a wide network
of more-or-less clandestine and more-or-less controlled Afghan sources.
The basic problem for those in charge of these assets, then as for the
next decade, lay in perceiving the degree to which the Afghan agents
really were under control, and in exploiting the relationships to Moscow's
best advantage. In neither respect did Soviet officials shine.

Even under the best of circumstances, when agents were dependent
on their handlers for money, hard-to-get consumer goods, prestige, or
other benefits such as medical care, *control* was at best a relative term.
To persuade a proud, individualistic Afghan to follow a course that
he did not devise for himself required a large measure of tact, not always
a Soviet strong suit. It was difficult enough when the agents were out-
of-power PDPA functionaries or young military officers still subordinate to old-guard conservative generals; it became much harder when
these same agents took over the country. They remained just as committed to Marxism-Leninism, but especially the Khalqis now thought
they were entitled to achieve socialism in their own Afghan way, rather
than following someone else's model. They were obedient to Soviet
instruction only when it suited their purposes.

"The Great Saur Revolution"

On the night of April 17, two men (later identified by Parchamis
as the Khalqi-faction Alemyar brothers) shot dead a leading Parchami
theoretician, Mir Akbar Khyber, on the street in front of his Kabul home.
PDPA agitators then succeeded in turning his funeral on April 19 into
a huge street demonstration, where rumors flew that the murder was

the work of Daoud's secret police, the CIA, or other dark forces. Six days later, in a midnight police raid, Daoud rounded up and jailed all the leading PDPA cadres, both Parchami and Khalqi, with one key exception. This was Hafizullah Amin (the second-ranking Khalqi behind Nur Mohammed Taraki), who was held under loose house arrest for more than ten hours before finally being taken to jail late on the morning of April 26. Coincidentally, Amin was also the designated point man for activating secret PDPA sympathizers among the Afghan officer corps in a coup originally planned for August 1978, and he used his temporary freedom to issue the prearranged coup instructions. He was already in periodic contact with the KGB at this time, but once he decided to act, he had to move too fast to clear his moves with the Soviets even if he had wanted to—which he did not.*

One can only conjecture how the Soviets might have handled the Parcham-Khalq controversy if the coup (later dignified as the "Great Saur Revolution," named for the Islamic month that spans April and May) had proceeded as originally scheduled. As it was, Amin's control during the initial stage ensured that any possible secret Soviet plan to ease the Parchamis into a dominant position in the new Afghan power structure was doomed to failure from the outset. Key second-echelon Parchami officials with planned coup roles, such as Nur Ahmad Nur, were left in the dark by Amin as the coup proceeded, and only Khalqis were active.[1]

Soviet Involvement in the Saur Coup

As the coup developed, the Soviets put on a noisy and obviously false act of not knowing what was going on. For example, Soviet diplomats busily pumped their Western counterparts for biographic data on the new Afghan leaders, as if they had never heard of the very Parchamis and Khalqis they so often—and with such fine impartiality—had hosted at the Soviet embassy. As we have noted, the KGB had close connec-

---

*An Afghan émigré told the author that the delay in jailing Amin was thanks to the intercession of Lt. Col. Pacha Sarbaz, the third in command of military intelligence, who was also a secret Khalqi, if not a KGB agent. Interestingly, Alexander Morozov, the KGB deputy chief in Kabul at that time, in a 1991 memoir makes no mention of the Khyber murder as the prelude to Daoud's crackdown, and merely notes that it was "strange" that Daoud did not jail Amin along with Taraki.

tions and regular meetings with leading members of both factions, including Amin. According to an authoritative 1991 account in *Novoye Vremya* (New Times) by the former KGB deputy chief in Kabul, Amin feared that the KGB might be too timid to allow him to proceed (in 1976 they had advised him that a coup would be premature), and he is supposed to have given orders "not to breathe a word to the Russians" as he set the coup in motion. The KGB, however, was fully aware of all his moves, but whether through lack of will or through lack of time made no effort to stay his hand.[2]

In chapter 8 we will touch further on KGB disinformation, but it is worth mentioning here that efforts to prove the Soviets were completely unwitting and uninvolved with the coup continued both outside and inside the USSR until the middle of 1991. A good example, whether or not directly KGB inspired, can be found in one book, where the author raises the question but, instead of refuting the evidence, shifts the ground from Soviet involvement by misquoting this author and accusing him of anti-Afghan racial prejudice.[3] Another example appeared in the Soviet Union shortly after the August 1991 Moscow coup attempt that destroyed the old government structure, though it obviously was written beforehand. In "Shtorm-333" of *Nash Sovremennik* (a hard-line Communist journal), a dramatization of purportedly documentary material has Brezhnev convening a Kremlin meeting of the Politburo "Afghanistan Commission" (Brezhnev, Gromyko, Andropov, Ustinov, Ponomarev, Arkhipov, and assorted deputies) on April 29, 1978, to learn who Taraki is, and to judge whether Moscow should recognize the new regime.[4]

The previously cited *Novoye Vremya* article of about the same time confirms the judgment of many that the Soviets (particularly the CPSU International Department and the KGB) were quite close to Taraki and were aware of the coup plans, even though Amin tried to keep the plans secret. The Parchamis were caught by surprise by the timing, but not the Soviets, whose sources kept them abreast of developments at all times, though they made no move to warn President Daoud. Such a warning "never even occurred to those [in the know] in Kabul or Moscow."[5]

Moreover, from the outset of the coup the Soviets were in the thick of things, in some cases taking part (helping launch air sorties from Bagram air base, for example), and accompanying the ground forces that secured Kabul airport. Given the tight political discipline required of Soviet army officers, it is most improbable that any advisers on duty in Afghanistan would have taken such action without express permission from the highest levels in Moscow. An intriguing indication that such permission preceded the coup is found in a request that Soviet servicemen be given medals for participation in "military actions" in Afghanistan from April 22, 1978, onward—four days *before* the coup got under way.[6]

The fighting lasted for only a little more than a day, starting at 9:00 in the morning of the 27th of April. At 4:00 the next morning, Daoud and his family, including infants, were confronted by rebel forces in the presidential palace and ordered to surrender. In a last act of defiance, Daoud reportedly drew his pistol and fired at one of the soldiers, wounding him slightly. The entire family was then mowed down in a hail of gunfire. Shortly thereafter, all resistance by Afghan army units loyal to Daoud ceased.

Role of the CPSU International Department

The emplacement of the PDPA as the ruling party meant that responsibility for Afghan affairs became concentrated in the CPSU apparat, specifically in the International Department of the Central Committee. It is true that both the Soviet military (in its training of Afghan officers) and the KGB (in its handling of Afghan agents inside and outside the PDPA) were vitally important for Moscow throughout this era. But it was the CPSU that, having prepared for the Parcham-Khalq armistice, played the dominant role. Its first representative in Kabul after the late-April 1978 coup was Nikolay Simonenko, chief of the Afghanistan section of the ID, who arrived in Kabul by mid-May as head of a whole group of ID advisers.[7]

From the outset the ID's handling of Afghan problems was marked by ineptitude. Some of the problems can be laid to sheer bad luck. For example, the original PDPA coup plans foresaw overthrowing Daoud in the Afghan month of Assad (August-September). The decision to move in April appears to have been taken by the Khalqis in response to fast-moving events.

But the main difficulty lay in the whole institution of the ID and its aging, rigid, Stalin-trained staff, typified by its chief, Boris Ponomarev. Ponomarev was a functionary of the old Comintern until it was disbanded in 1943. He then became a member of the newly formed ID, which took over the Comintern function of enunciating and enforcing the CPSU line among foreign Communist parties. After Stalin's death in 1953, the ID's authority was less ruthlessly applied, but the basic attitude remained.

Ponomarev worked his way up to become chief of the ID, a position he held for more than thirty years until his retirement in February 1986. In later years, the ID's responsibility was for nonruling Communist parties, "fraternal" ruling and nonruling parties (such as Afghanistan's PDPA), and such major fronts as the World Peace Council, World Federation of Trade Unions, and the Afro-Asian Peoples' Solidarity Organization.

The peculiar nature of the ID's function as an ideological watchdog gave it far more authority over its foreign affiliates than other Soviet institutions had over theirs. Where the foreign party was in charge, as the PDPA was in Afghanistan after 1978, the ID eclipsed such foreign-oriented state organs as the Ministry of Foreign Affairs and Ministry of Foreign Trade. Dealing with foreign countries on a day-to-day basis, the ID provided the most authoritative channel for passing information from Afghanistan and instructions from Moscow.[8] In Simonenko, however, the ID did not have one of its leading lights. On arrival in Kabul, he promptly allowed himself to be recruited by Amin as a partisan of the Khalqi cause, only later backtracking on advice from the KGB.[9]

Parcham-Khalq Fight Renews

On taking power, the PDPA renamed the government the Democratic Republic of Afghanistan (DRA). In the first DRA cabinet, whose members were announced a few days later, all portfolios went to PDPA officers. Moreover, there was an obvious and careful effort to alternate between Parcham and Khalq in the pecking order. Although this represented an obviously prenegotiated balance between the two factions, in fact the Khalqis held the upper hand because they controlled most of the state's weapons.

This was not what the Soviets and Parchamis had planned. The Khalqis were given the Ministry of Interior and its attendant police forces, but the minister of defense was a Parchami, Gen. Abdul Qader. The Soviets probably assumed that the two forces would each remain loyal to its chief's faction, thus striking a balance, but in fact the Khalqis were as dominant in the army as in the police, especially after Amin's exclusive use of Khalqi officers for the coup. With virtually all of the guns under their command, the Khalqis made short political work of the Parchamis, sending them off into diplomatic exile in June and July 1978. Those remaining in Afghanistan, if of sufficient stature to enjoy a measure of Soviet protection, at first were merely neutered politically. Gen. Abdul Qader, for example, though nominally minister of defense, was isolated and closely watched by Khalqi agents.

The CPSU failure to control or at least to manipulate the Parcham-Khalq controversy at this critical stage represented the first of several serious errors. The basic Soviet weakness was an inability to understand Afghan culture and the way Afghan loyalties—like other Afghan values—are personal, individual, and usually rooted in tribalism and patronage.

The Soviets, brought up in a society where a person's primary loyalty was supposed to be only to an impersonal collective, did not understand that for Afghans party institutional loyalty was an alien concept, the least important of social imperatives. To an Afghan Communist, it was far less the *party* that was deserving of loyalty than it was the individual party *member* who had recruited him—and that recruiter in turn was more than likely linked to him by prior family or tribal relations.[10]

If there was one positive accomplishment for the Soviets at this stage of the Parcham-Khalq dispute (and this can only be deduced indirectly), it was their successful insistence that the Khalqis spare the lives of at least the six leading Parchamis, who had held important posts in the first DRA government. These were sent abroad as ambassadors. Most of those remaining also enjoyed some protection, at least at first; as the result of Soviet "advice" to Taraki, Parchamis continued to hold "at least 30 percent of Party and government posts" inside the country.[11]

First Parcham Coup Attempt

Before the new ambassadors had unpacked their bags, they were preparing to regain power in Kabul. According to later Khalqi literature, a coup plot had been devised by Parchami chief Babrak Karmal on the eve of his departure for Prague to take up his duties as ambassador there. It involved having all of the Parchami ambassadors return "secretly" to Kabul in time for the Eid holidays at the end of the holy Islamic month of Ramadan, which in 1978 fell on September 4. On that day of celebration—which may have been the date originally set for the PDPA coup against Daoud—they would use their Parchami followers still in the armed forces to disarm Khalqi comrades and take power.

Allegedly, the plot was uncovered before it could unfold when the conspirators mistakenly informed the Afghan ambassador to India, Pacha Gul Wafadar, who, as a loyal but closet Khalqi, promptly advised Amin and Taraki. Those intended participants unfortunate enough to be still in Afghanistan were imprisoned, tortured, and in many cases executed. The guilty ambassadors, ignoring a Kabul recall order, promptly vanished, in at least three cases emptying the embassy tills of all official funds as they decamped. They would reappear as high government officials on the coattails of the invading Soviet forces in 1979.

There can be little doubt that this plot represents yet another Soviet blunder. It is scarcely credible that Karmal could have worked out the details of so complex a conspiracy in the hectic days before his posting abroad (he had lost the political fight with the Khalqis only the week before) and then coordinated it among Afghan ambassadors dispersed in capitals throughout Eastern and Western Europe, the Soviet Union, South Asia, and North America. Just the logistics and security problems attendant on infiltrating six well-known figures across the border simultaneously would have been unmanageable without the assistance of some well-greased organization, in this case presumably the KGB.*

At the very least, the conspirators must have had the use of the sophisticated Soviet communications network for their purposes. More probably, the Soviets themselves were coordinating the entire operation. The report that the plot was blown by the Afghan ambassador to India could well represent yet another Soviet error, inasmuch as mistakenly confiding in a member of the wrong faction is a far more understandable mistake for a Soviet to make than for an Afghan.

---

*Again Morozov leaves a gaping hole in his account, never mentioning the plot or even the fact that the various ambassadors had been stripped of their party and state ranks, and had dropped from sight as refugees in Eastern Europe.

Why would the Soviets want to encourage a new coup? The Khalqis were just as dedicated Marxist-Leninists and just as loyal to Moscow as were the Parchamis. Soviet advisers were rapidly spreading throughout the new government to guide its first steps. But the Khalqis were determined to push Afghanistan into socialism in the shortest length of time, and to do it in their own way, politely ignoring guidance from the Soviets, let alone accepting help from the loathed Parchamis. This independent attitude must have held echoes for the Soviets of Marshal Tito's removal of Yugoslavia from Moscow's control in 1948; in the ideologically oriented Soviet foreign policy of the late 1970s, Khalqi assertiveness probably seemed a dangerous and impermissible deviation.

But perhaps more to the point, the Khalqi program was politically harebrained. The combined Parcham-Khalq PDPA had been a tiny minority in an overwhelmingly conservative Afghan population. By cutting that minority in half and eliminating most of its technically competent members (the Parchamis were stronger in the civilian bureaucracy than the Khalqis), the Khalqis were undermining their own fragile grasp on power. Moreover, by insisting on an immediate doctrinaire Marxist-Leninist approach, they were much more likely to inflame a potentially lethal public reaction against themselves than were the more devious, go-slow Parchamis.

The detailed program of the Parchami conspirators, as published by the Khalqis some weeks later, reflected an understanding of these realities. After seizing power, the Parchamis intended to enlist the support not only of the defeated Khalqis but of as many non-PDPA elements as they possibly could to make the new government work. Included in the plan was formation of a United National Front to act as a nongovernmental support mechanism. (If further circumstantial evidence of Soviet involvement in the 1978 coup is needed, these were precisely the measures the Soviet-controlled puppet government introduced after the 1979 invasion, including plans for a United National Front.)

This sort of right-wing opportunism was anathema to the Khalqis, who proceeded with their suicidal program of forced-draft Sovietization of Afghan society. The Afghan national flag became a blood-red clone of the Soviet Union's, the clergy were relentlessly persecuted, land was expropriated and redistributed (but in such a fashion that it was unprofitable for everybody), age-old customs of arranged marriages were outlawed, and rural debts were canceled. Khalqi agitators and teachers, backed by squads of police or the military, went into the countryside, arrested (and sometimes executed) mullahs and other village dignitaries, and proclaimed the new order.

The result was as predictable as it was violent. Street demonstrations might do for expressing dissident political opinion in Kabul and a few other big towns, but grass-roots Afghanistan has never had time for such half measures. Left on their own as their protective cordons were redeployed to take care of other villages, Kabul's representatives were regularly shot. Troops would be sent in to restore order, but would then have to be withdrawn to take care of other trouble spots. Soon, spontaneous assassinations gave way to more organized resistance, first on a local level and then by province until it became nationwide. The jihad was born.

CPSU Accommodation to the Khalqis

The CPSU, having failed to prevent this development, was faced with the option of going along with the Khalqis or again trying to unseat them. Its first choice was accommodation.

Immediately after the first news of the Parchami coup plot and its failure, congratulatory messages were exchanged between Moscow and Kabul. In December, just after Kabul published its detailed description of the conspiracy, virtually the entire PDPA leadership went to Moscow to sign a far-reaching Afghan-Soviet friendship agreement. Had Moscow still been bent on unseating the Khalqis, it could scarcely have arranged a better opportunity than the simultaneous presence in Moscow of all leading members of the faction.

Naturally, a coup would have sparked an international and domestic Afghan outcry, especially after the Khalqis had taken the prudent predeparture step of exposing the conspiracy (but without implicating the Soviets directly) and thus establishing Soviet responsibility for any similar development that might occur while they were absent from Kabul. But compared to the furor a year later, after the Soviet military invasion, the public relations loss to the USSR would have been inconsequential.

Soviet accommodation went beyond simple acceptance of the Khalqis' hold on power; it now included a significant ideological concession. As we have noted, the PDPA on taking power in April had been careful to avoid calling itself socialist, probably at the insistence of the Parchamis and Soviets. With the temporary elimination of the Parchamis from the political equation, the Khalqis had become outspoken about their socialist ambitions. Until early 1979, the Soviets had avoided taking a stand on the issue, but at that point they suddenly became more and more explicit about the DRA's "socialist orientation."[12]

It was the wrong time to back the Khalqis, but it took Moscow several months to understand the gravity of its error. In January, resistance mobilization had reached the stage of threatening provincial capitals; in February the American ambassador to Kabul, Adolph ("Spike") Dubs, was kidnapped and killed under murky circumstances that if nothing else illustrated the impotence of the Kabul government and its KGB advisers; and in March Soviet advisers and their dependents in Herat were massacred and their bodies mutilated in an uprising that temporarily took over the country's third-largest city. During the spring, the death toll among Soviet advisers reportedly rose to about one hundred per month.

There are indications that the Soviets may have contemplated another Parchami coup attempt as early as the spring of 1979, possibly coordinated with Soviet military intervention. If so, it was frustrated, and the remaining unhappy Parchamis in the DRA government, again the victims of a new purge and repression, suffered accordingly. Whatever the Soviet behind-the-scenes machinations, before the middle of June a decision must have been taken to distance Moscow from the Kabul regime ideologically. As of that time, references in Soviet media to the socialist nature of the PDPA had ceased.[13]

September 1979 Coup Plot

But what to do about Amin, whose headlong rush to socialism, contrary to all Soviet advice about the need for moderation, was driving the country inexorably to massive counterrevolution? The best that the Soviets could devise was another coup.

It must not have seemed a difficult operation to mount. Granted that Amin had his own group of dedicated followers among the Khalqis, especially in the army, but he had antagonized not only all the Parchamis (thousands of whom he had had expelled from the party, imprisoned, tortured, and/or executed, depending on his mood of the moment) but a great many Khalqis as well. First among these was Nur Mohammed Taraki, nominal chief of the party, a somewhat weak-willed intellectual whom Amin had shouldered aside in his drive to power. Taraki's followers, though tending also to be relatively mild-mannered intellectuals, permeated the Afghan bureaucracy. In addition, the Soviets could call on the services of those Khalqis with whom they had established their own private connections, including at least some of the military officers whom Amin considered to be his own, and especially the secret police. And finally, they still kept closely in touch with Babrak Karmal and the other Parchami ambassadors who had fled so precipitously after the failure of the 1978 coup plot.

With these assets in hand, the Soviets must have felt fairly confident of success. Taraki's trip to Havana in September for a Non-Aligned Movement meeting offered them a chance to sidetrack him briefly in Moscow on his way home, and to effect a reconciliation meeting with Karmal. At the same time, key Soviet agents in Kabul, including the ministers of interior (Watanjar), frontier affairs (Mazdooryar), and communications (Gulabzoy), and the chief of the secret police (Sarwari), were probably alerted to help Taraki overcome any resistance by Amin. The plan was doubtless to blame all DRA/PDPA's multiple failures on Amin and then, after executing him, hold a happy reconciliation with the Parchamis and give Karmal a place of honor in a newly recombined Parcham-Khalq government that would moderate the Khalqi policy of trying to impose instant socialism. As a first step, the new regime would invoke Article 51 of the United Nations charter and invite Soviet troops to come in and clean out the resistance.

Soviet preparations to fulfill their side of such an arrangement were illustrated by a special levy of conscripts called up in June 1979, two months after the normal draft had taken place. These troops were then assigned to the Kushka Regiment, which suddenly expanded from a skeletal staff of 120 to its full strength of 1,800–2,000, including officers flown in from East Germany and Czechoslovakia.[14]

Unbeknownst to the Soviets, however, Amin had his own faithful people reporting to him, including the head of Taraki's security detail while on his trip to Havana, Major Taroon. In Moscow, Taroon and other members of the Afghan delegation were waiting in an anteroom while Taraki visited Brezhnev in the latter's office when then– foreign minister Andrey Gromyko breezed through the outer office, innocently inquiring of those waiting outside whether they had yet seen Babrak Karmal. Thus warned, Taroon quickly elicited details of the impending coup and sent them off to Kabul in a telegram in Pushtu, apparently succeeding in avoiding any prompt Soviet intercept by the use of this obscure language.

Those involved in the conspiracy in Kabul were supposed to arrest Amin just before Taraki arrived home, using Ministry of Interior troops ostensibly deployed to protect Taraki's motorcade from the airport. But Amin countermanded the orders and substituted his own army troops for the guard. A shocked Taraki found himself greeted and embraced by the leader who was supposed to be already under arrest.

There followed a somewhat embarrassed standoff that lasted for several days as both sides jockeyed for position. Eventually, Soviet ambassador Puzanov took a hand in the proceedings by giving his personal guarantee to Amin over the telephone that no harm would come to him if he joined Puzanov and Taraki for a reconciliation meeting. Over the objections of his closest advisers, Amin agreed—and drove into a waiting ambush in which his loyal aide Taroon was mortally wounded.

Amin, however, escaped, and from then on Taraki's days were numbered. Although Watanjar, Mazdooryar, Gulabzoy, and Sarwari escaped with their lives and took refuge in the Soviet embassy, Taraki was seized before he could follow suit. At first uncertain how to proceed with his embarrassingly high-profile prisoner, Amin waited about three weeks and then, perceiving no Soviet intention to rescue or defend Taraki, had him suffocated. After another month, Puzanov was withdrawn at Amin's insistence, but only after Amin's foreign minister, Shah Wali, publicly exposed the ambassador's duplicity.*

Again there was a mutually embarrassing face-off, now between Amin and the Soviets, with neither quite sure how to proceed. There was one last reported coup attempt in October, this one involving a coor-

---

*There are curious contradictions about the circumstances and consequences of Taraki's death. One Soviet version was given corroborative detail as late as 1989 by Gromyko, who said Brezhnev had "burst into tears" on hearing of how his good friend Taraki had been "brutally murdered in his study," finding the crime "too much to bear." Gromyko implied that Brezhnev's emotionalism over Taraki then became a major factor in triggering the invasion. (*Observer* [London], April 2, 1989, p. 23.) But the Soviets (and specifically Gromyko) sent numerous signals implying they had no objection to Amin's victory or intention of interfering in Afghan affairs. (Arnold, *Two-Party Communism*, 92–93.) The subsequent Gromyko version has a strong odor of disinformation.

dinated effort by troops loyal to Watanjar and a Nazi-style nationalist organization under Soviet influence, but it was a feeble, last-ditch
effort that came to nothing.

Not long after, the Soviets must have decided that the time had come
to do away with abortive coups and deception, and to handle Afghanistan
by the one invariably successful method they had employed elsewhere:
outright military invasion. As in their other efforts along these lines
(Hungary in 1956 and Czechoslovakia in 1968), they foresaw the difficulty
of putting a legal face on their actions, particularly in the graceful disposal
of the former leadership. At the time, they may well have considered
this the main problem confronting them.

Disposing of Amin

The authoritative report on how the Soviets planned to proceed—
and even on how they did proceed—with the removal of Amin remains
buried in secret Soviet archives. The following rendition is an attempt
to reconcile several different, conflicting stories from persons claiming firsthand or at worst reliable secondhand information, among them
a KGB defector, a claimed KGB participant, and a leftist Pakistani writer
who later talked to surviving members of Amin's family.*

The original Soviet plan was to have First Deputy Minister of Internal Affairs Viktor Semenovich Paputin persuade Amin to issue an
invitation for Soviet troops to come in and, acting independently, put
down the resistance. Paputin arrived on November 28, but he failed
in his mission and departed on December 13. (Assuming that he cabled
his report and awaited a reply before leaving, this timing suggests that
it was his report that triggered the December 12 Kremlin decision to
proceed with the invasion. See chapter 4.)

Paputin, presumably after making a personal report in the Kremlin,
appears to have returned again to Kabul without publicity to oversee
personally the stronger measures that were then in motion. On the morning
of December 26, a jubilant Amin, believing he was getting more Soviet
assistance but that it would be under Afghan command (or at worst
joint Afghan/Soviet command), informed an Arab journalist that the

---

*It must be emphasized that this rendition is merely the author's own interpretation
of what probably happened, based in part on his discounting of perceived biases among
some of the primary sources, which are listed in endnote 18.

Soviets respected the independence and integrity of Afghanistan, and that they had decided not to press for permanent bases. "Soviet forces," he said, "are coming to help put down the rebellion."[15] What he did not realize was that it was he whom Moscow considered the primary rebel.

The intention at this stage seems to have been to disable but not kill Amin at midday of December 27 by drugging him and putting him under Soviet "medical" supervision. At 6:00 P.M., Soviet forces, which had been arriving in Kabul by air since December 24, would swing into action, taking over key government installations. Meanwhile, the Afghan army—immobilized, disarmed, and left leaderless by a series of Soviet ruses that included removal of vehicle batteries for "winterizing," recall of old ammunition pending issuance of new supplies, and a large party thrown by a visiting Soviet delegation on December 27—would be taken out of the picture.

Just as envisaged in the September coup plot, Babrak Karmal and other Parchamis would be returned to power, and Amin, when he awoke, would be left with the choice of stepping down gracefully or being indicted for the murder of Taraki. Presumably, in either case he would be induced by whatever means necessary to confirm that the Soviet invasion was in response to his specific invitation (or perhaps, alternatively, to confess that he had been a CIA spy for many years—both equally false allegations).

But just as before, the plans came unstuck. Amin's Soviet cook, responsible for administering a disabling drug at lunch on December 27, found that his employer had little appetite and ate so sparingly that, after a brief loss of consciousness, he was back in action, if shakily, by 2:00 P.M. This meant that the Soviets had to resort to a second fallback plan of taking Amin's redoubt by force. The KGB troops responsible for this action were informed of their mission at the last moment. They wore Afghan army uniforms, and, mistaken for mutineers, at first were greeted with a spirited defense. After the front line of Afghan defenders heard Russian yells among the attackers, however, they realized their mistake and ceased resisting but were cut down anyway. This led the surviving Afghans to fight on desperately, but by then they had already lost vital ground.

In the preliminary skirmish, the commander of the attacking force, KGB Colonel Boyarinov, who had been head of the KGB terrorist training unit, was killed by heavy machine-gun fire, some say by his own troops. (Having given the order that no one be permitted to leave the palace alive, the colonel allegedly forgot and stepped out a door to call for reinforcements.) His death allegedly blinded his enraged troops to the order to take Amin alive, and they proceeded to sweep through the palace, exterminating all life by giving each room a grenade or two and a burst of machine-gun fire. Amin's body was later found in a basement room, his head partly blown away by a grenade, but no one knew his specific killer. A more gaudy but less credible account of his death has him standing at the bar with his arm around a mistress when cut down by the invading assault team.

Other Soviet Covering Actions

The same case of mistaken identity greeted the Soviet forces targeted on Radio Kabul, which was supposed to be silenced so that a prerecorded message by Babrak Karmal could be read over a transmitter with Radio Kabul's frequency but located in the Soviet Union. The desperate defenders, expecting they would be killed by those they mistook for their countrymen, succeeded in delaying the takeover long enough that both radio programs were broadcast simultaneously, to the confusion of all. The following day, plumbers had a job clearing the sewer lines of employees' party cards that had been flushed in panic during the attack.[16]

The assault on Radio Kabul failed to meet its timetable, but the concentration on communications elsewhere was a success. Here, it was the Soviet minister of communications himself, Nikolay Vladimirovich Talyzin, who played the principal role. He was shown in the December 25, 1979, edition of the *Kabul Times* arriving at Kabul airport accompanied by a large retinue of beefy, unsmiling aides. The swift Soviet success in blowing up at least two out of three main Kabul telephone exchanges on December 27 doubtless owes something to these sturdy fellows. By evening of that day, Amin could communicate with his army commanders only by radio.[17]*

---

*In 1980 Talyzin was rewarded by being made a deputy chairman of the USSR Council of Ministers, and in 1985 he became an alternate Politburo member and chief of the State Planning Committee (GOSPLAN), but in 1989 Mikhail Gorbachev fired him from all his party and state posts. His dangerous mission to Kabul may have been in atonement for his failure to intercept Taroon's warning telegram to Amin in Pushtu the previous September.

Ironically, virtually all sources reporting on this confused time imply that the Soviets could have taken most of their targets almost without bloodshed simply by declaring who they were. Such was the respect that the Khalqis, especially the elite guards units responsible for Amin's security, had for the Soviets that they would have been trusted until the last moment. In the attack on Amin's redoubt, for example, the defenders who mistakenly laid down their arms had been trained in the USSR and wanted to greet their attackers as old friends. The Soviet penchant for elaborate camouflage probably cost the attackers a good many unnecessary casualties.

Although the invasion was a military success it was a political disaster. Somewhere, under unknown but apparently violent circumstances, Paputin paid for his failure with his life. His death reportedly occurred on December 28, but there is still no resolution of the two conflicting rumors about how it happened: either from wounds suffered in the palace battle or by his own hand in the Moscow airport on his return. His obituary in the Soviet press was conspicuous by the absence of condolences by high-ranking officials, normal in such situations, indicating that his passing was not mourned by those in power.[18]

The military component of Soviet policy at this stage was what grabbed the world's attention, but it was only partly an end in its own right. Certainly the Kremlin saw military advantages in pushing its frontiers outward, but it viewed the invasion more as merely a drastic means to establish a *political* end: consolidation of a stable, pro-Moscow Afghan government that would avoid self-destruction via Khalqi-style extremism. The initial invading force numbered about seventy thousand, most of it deployed to defend fixed installations and lines of communication. After three months, with resistance solidifying in the countryside, it had built to eighty thousand, but from the Kremlin's standpoint the main mission then and for about two more years was still only to intimidate the resistance and provide a high-tech backup for the Afghan armed forces that were supposed to do most of the real fighting.

Parcham-Khalq Conflict under the Soviets

Following the invasion, Soviet coaching was intensive in both the civilian and military fields. Some five thousand "advisers" kept tabs on the military, but at least as many were eventually assigned to the civilian sector. Although many of the Soviet civilians were appointed for their technical know-how, the most important group was that assigned to party and ideological work. For example, the PDPA Central Committee alone hosted thirty-five Soviet advisers, plus two or three more for each of its departments. No party document, from a slogan to a plenum resolution, could be issued until it had been forwarded to the Soviet embassy via the advisory staff and received back through the same channel with the necessary corrections.[19]

One of the goals of tight CPSU control over the PDPA was doubtless to suppress the Parcham-Khalq controversy and enforce some degree of cooperation between the warring factions. As in May 1978, there was a new balance between Parcham and Khalq at the highest PDPA levels, but with a subtle difference: almost all the Khalqis were either persons who for one or another reason had avoided the earlier factional struggles, or persons who owed their careers—and in some cases their lives—to their Soviet contacts. (At least three top-level Khalqis, for example, were among those who had participated in the failed 1979 coup and received asylum in the Soviet embassy afterward.) The Parchamis, by contrast, were those who had been in the forefront of the factional struggle, and were dedicated to it. They too, of course, owed their present prestige to the Soviets, on whose coattails they had returned to Afghanistan.

Thus, the Soviets had a firm grip over both the leading Parchamis and most of the leading Khalqis. Interestingly, however, although the advisers seemed to have absolute power over their Afghan colleagues, they themselves soon fell victim to "clientism." Ten years later, a Soviet paper was to observe that Soviet advisers, "having no idea of the objective causes for the appearance and growth of differences in the PDPA . . . fell under the influence of their own 'advisers,' becoming even more ardent Khalqists or Parchamists than the Afghans themselves."[20] The Parchami patrons were the CPSU and KGB, whereas the Khalqis, whose main strength lay in the military and uniformed police, depended on the Soviet military.

Creation of a Non-Communist Façade
A secondary task was to alter the PDPA's image for both the Afghan and international audiences. To soften the appearance of bayonet-imposed communism, a great effort was put forth to portray Karmal and his cohorts as believers in Islam. (The image of piety suffered greatly when Karmal was photographed wearing shoes while at prayer in a

mosque, however.) *Socialism* suddenly vanished from the party lexicon. The Saur coup of 1978 was redefined as a "national democratic revolution," and such ill-advised Khalqi steps as turning the national flag red were revoked. In his inaugural speech, Babrak Karmal called for support from his countrymen in an oddly un-Marxist order: religious believers, religious leaders, the military, traders, capitalists, landowners, artisans, shepherds, nomads, government officials, intellectuals, youth, and—oh yes—"working men and women, peasant men and women."[21]

All during 1980 and early 1981 there were unceasing efforts to launch the National Fatherland Front that the 1978 Parchami conspirators had been accused of planning. When its founding congress was finally held on June 15, 1981, most of the constituent organizations were patterned on typical Soviet fronts of the era, representing youth, women, trade unions, poets and writers, journalists, artists, and peace-solidarity-and-friendship activists. In addition, there were a few peculiarly Afghan groups, including a High Jirga of Tribal Representatives and a Council of Clergymen and Scholars.

Just as in Grenada the year before, another part of the program to obfuscate the Communist origins and dedication of the PDPA was to "broaden the base" of the government by including prominent individuals with no overt links to the USSR or the PDPA. Some of these were in fact genuine non-Communists, whereas others were figures whose Soviet sympathies had been obvious for years. Eight real non-Communists, appointed as "advisers" to the government and its individual ministries, were featured in the Afghan media, as were statistics on the number of non-Communists allegedly appointed to middle-level positions, but none were given any independent executive power.[22] Gradually, the propaganda campaign about them wound down, dying away completely by the middle of 1981. In June the Revolutionary Council was expanded by fifteen members, but if any were nonparty the fact was no longer considered worthy of mention.

For the truly non-Communist Afghan collaborators, the lure for involvement had been a mixture of patriotism, PDPA assurances that it was indeed evolving away from Soviet-style Marxism-Leninism, and above all a Soviet promise to withdraw the occupation army in the near future. When these promises were not met, the collaborators drifted away: two received ambassadorial posts, one went to his grave, two vanished in an unknown limbo, and three defected to the West. By mid-1982 the innocent were gone; the remaining ostensibly nonparty figures were without exception those with previously suspected PDPA/Soviet links. The government had lost its last feeble claim to legitimacy.

Growing Resistance and the Degradation of the PDPA

Meanwhile, the surge of Afghan resentment against the invaders was massive. It was not nationalism as we know it; the resistance was not fighting for a flag or a government system but out of outrage against an alien, infidel invader. The PDPA, which under the Khalqis had been despised for its atheism and socialist sloganeering, gained nothing by demonstratively turning its back on these outward signs of Marxism-Leninism; the maneuver was correctly perceived as nothing but a feint, and the quisling regime nothing more than a puppet, even less acceptable than the Khalqis, who though more openly Marxist were at least in control as native Afghans. Under the Soviets, with their demeaning demands for full control over all government decisions, the proud Afghans were reduced to the status of nineteenth-century colonial peoples under the heel of Western European empires.

At the start of the occupation, the majority of PDPA members—perhaps 85 percent—were Khalqis, and their strongholds were in the army and the regular police. The Soviets provided the minority Parchamis with an equalizer in the form of a new secret police, whose chief was Najib (he has used only the single name, and its more religious variant, Najibullah, though he has also been called Mohammed Najibullah and Mohammed Najibullah Ahmadzai), a burly, street-scrapping medical student during the PDPA's formative years, and one of those ambassadors (he was assigned to Tehran) who had absconded with his embassy's funds when he decamped in 1978.

Over time, the Parchamis would gain on the Khalqis numerically, to the point that in the late 1980s the two were probably roughly equal in numbers, but from the outset basic government decision making was in Parchami hands. Meanwhile, the intellectual quality of party membership declined, even as its claimed membership increased. In 1978, Taraki had claimed, with only slight exaggeration, that the PDPA was a party of schoolteachers; by 1982, when a party conference revealed the makeup of the middle and upper levels of its membership, the educational level had fallen considerably.[23] The proportion of party members in the armed services (including police and secret police) rose steadily through the early 1980s, stabilizing at about 65 percent from 1985 to the end of the decade.

Impact of the Invasion on the First World

As anticipated by the Kremlin, the invasion caused a worldwide uproar. Unlike earlier Soviet invasions of its European satellites, however, this uproar could not be stilled by Soviet diversions and propaganda ploys, the sealing off of Afghanistan from objective journalism, or simply the healing passage of time.

In the United States, a heretofore somewhat indecisive President Carter, declaring that the invasion had made "a more dramatic change in my own opinion of what the Soviets' ultimate goals are" than anything else they had done while he was in office, undertook a broad spectrum of responses, some expected, some unanticipated by the Soviets. The postponement of ratifying the Strategic Arms Limitations Treaty (SALT) II was one expected penalty (though it probably would not have passed the U.S. Senate anyway), as was, perhaps, the abandoning of a plan to open reciprocal consulates in Kiev and New York City. Most economic and cultural exchanges were suspended, trade was severely restricted, and Soviet fishing privileges in American waters were curtailed. The Soviets may have considered these as possible short-term penalties that would have to be suffered only temporarily before the benefits were quietly restored.

Much more serious and unexpected was the denial of seventeen million tons of U.S. wheat that the Soviets badly needed to tide them over their third bad harvest year in a row. Moreover, a military dimension was apparent when the president announced formation of a rapid deployment force in the Middle East and declared that the oil supplies of that region were a vital security interest of the United States (the Carter Doctrine). And probably least expected and psychologically most devastating, the United States boycotted the Moscow-hosted 1980 Olympics, convincing many of its allies to follow suit. It is hard to overestimate the pain that this blow inflicted or the damage it did to Soviet prestige in the USSR's own citizens' eyes.

But the worst First World consequence of the invasion from the Soviet standpoint was the steeling of Western resolve, and the militancy of free-world determination to prevent further Soviet expansion. In the last months of his administration, Jimmy Carter belatedly began an arms buildup, but in the 1980 elections he was swept from office by an even more militant Ronald Reagan. The Soviet invasion of Afghanistan—and the Afghans' heroic response to it—focused the attention of the world on Moscow's ambitions even more sharply than its last previous resort to arms, the 1968 invasion of Czechoslovakia.

The reaction of other First World governments was somewhat more tepid than that of the United States. West Germany, caught in a mild depression, actually increased its exports to the USSR by 30 percent in the first half of 1980, and other grain producers hastened to take advantage of the U.S. decision to close off its own shipments. But they could not make up the shortfall entirely, and many who profited economically salved their consciences (and perhaps bowed to public opinion) by joining the U.S. Olympics boycott.

Non-Soviet Communist Reactions

Moscow also lost considerable support among First World Communist parties. The Belgian, English, Italian, Spanish, and Swedish parties criticized the invasion openly, with the Partito Comunista Italiano (PCI) calling it an "inadmissible violation of . . . the principles of independence, sovereignty, and non-interference."[24] The Communist parties of France, Finland, Denmark, Portugal, and Luxembourg all supported the invasion, but these later were to suffer drastic losses in popularity at the polls, losses from which they never recovered.

Within the Warsaw Pact, there was firm approval only from the German Democratic Republic, Bulgaria, and Czechoslovakia. Romania was the only Pact member to criticize the invasion openly, but both Poland and Hungary gave their support to it in noticeably tepid form, the Hungarians delaying their official approval until January 20, 1980. Yugoslavia and Albania condemned the invasion. In Asia, the main critical voice was that of China, whereas the parties of Laos, Cambodia, Mongolia, and Vietnam dutifully followed the Soviet line. Interestingly, North Korea did not subscribe to a document of solidarity with the new regime signed by other parties in February 1980.[25]

The Polish Tinderbox

But more than official reaction was at stake in Eastern Europe. On July 1, 1980, the restive Polish citizenry, which had been bought off by a series of weak Communist leaders who had given them food subsidies beyond the capability of the state to pay, suddenly faced food price rises of 30 to 90 percent. A wave of strikes followed. On August 31, forced to its knees by the strikes, the Polish government startled the world by signing an agreement with Polish labor leader Lech Walesa to legalize free trade unions. No such worker revolt had ever before succeeded in a Communist state. On October 24, the Solidarity trade union movement was officially registered as a legal entity. The flight from the Polish Workers Party (Communist), which in the next two years would cut membership by about 30 percent, had already begun.

These developments were watched from Moscow with increasing unease. Nothing less than the party's monopoly of power was being threatened, not only in Poland but by extension in the Soviet Union itself. On August 20, 1980, the Soviets resumed jamming of Western radio broadcasts, which were of course following the Polish developments with great interest and reporting on them in detail. In September *Pravda* presented the Poles with its third authoritative warning in three weeks about the consequences of too much permissiveness. There followed a slight relaxation of the propaganda offensive, but as fall turned to winter and unrest in Poland spread, the authorities proved incapable of handling the crisis, and tension became extreme. President Carter talked of the "unprecedented [Soviet] military buildup" on Poland's borders, and members of his administration said that the Soviets had "completed military preparations for a possible intervention," which might be "only one day away." In early 1981, the gloomy estimate varied from "odds favor a Soviet invasion" to the flat prediction that it was "inevitable." TASS, meantime, lent weight to these views on December 9, 1980, by declaring that the Polish unions were engaging in a "counterrevolutionary struggle."[26]

And indeed Soviet troops were on high alert in the western parts of the USSR during this period, ready to move within hours if necessary. The 1981 Soviet spring maneuvers on Polish territory, code-named "*Soyuz* (Union) 81," began in March and lasted until April 7, a Warsaw Pact–record twenty-two days that recalled similar maneuvers on the eve of the 1968 attack on Czechoslovakia. It was reported in April that Warsaw Pact commander-in-chief Marshal Viktor G. Kulikov had been urging Brezhnev to use military force to bring the Poles back to heel. Later it was revealed that in both 1980 and 1981 there had been "strong and continuous pressure on the Soviet Politburo and on Brezhnev personally" to invade.[27] Most analysts of Soviet-Polish relations during this tense period have ignored the Afghan factor, especially as it bears on the Soviet decision not to use force. Certainly there were many other deterrents involved, including the legendary fighting spirit of thirty-six million hell-for-leather Poles, an aroused and remilitarizing United States that specifically warned the Soviets against any such move, and the USSR's own economic and social problems.

Nevertheless, if it had not been for Afghanistan the West (and especially the United States) would not have been so aroused; the Soviet economic problems and sense of aimlessness, though serious, could have been eclipsed by a politico-military triumph; and even the willingness of the Poles to fight the Soviet army juggernaut might have been less if the Afghans had not been showing that it could be done. (The Poles were aware of Afghan events through Radio Free Europe and a largely unrestricted flow of literature from Western Europe, especially France, where interest in Afghanistan was intense in the Polish exile community.[28]) These are all imponderable factors, but there can be little question that the old men in the Kremlin would have been far more willing to risk an invasion of Poland if the Afghan albatross had not already been weighing them down.

Third World Reactions

Soviet fortunes were scarcely better in the Third World. Newborn nations that had watched the Soviet conquests of Hungary and Czechoslovakia with relative equanimity became suddenly very sensitive. To them, the sight of one rich, mostly Caucasian country beating up on smaller rich Caucasian countries had not been a matter of great concern. But when that same rich bully went after one of their own, it became quite another matter. From the time the first United Nations General Assembly resolution calling for the withdrawal of foreign forces passed by an overwhelming vote in January 1980 (104 for, 18 against, 18 abstentions), until the ninth and last such vote in November 1987

(123 for, 19 against, 11 abstentions), the majority pressing for a Soviet withdrawal swelled steadily.

Not only did the Third World look askance at the Soviet Union, but the latter itself began to have second thoughts about propping up some of the allies it had collected in developing countries. The PDPA's failure to get control of Afghanistan was surely one of the main influences leading to the conclusion that "by the early 1980s, there was a general recognition in Soviet theoretical literature that earlier hopes for strong clients and lasting influence resulting from the promotion of Marxist-Leninist vanguard party-states were not being realized."[29]

Crisis Role of Polish Military

By the end of 1981, the CPSU's claims to infallibility and ideological perfection were sounding increasingly hollow, both inside and outside the USSR. Its failure to enforce conformity on the Poles via Konstantin Rusakov's Ruling Communist Parties Department of the CPSU Central Committee was a serious embarrassment. On December 13, 1981, the Polish army and other security forces (including the secret police) under Gen. Wojciech Jaruzelski swung into action, declaring martial law, rounding up Solidarity leaders and other dissidents, and imposing a three-day total blackout on all but fully state-controlled communications. Poland's evolution away from Marxism-Leninism was stopped in its tracks. It was a forced move; in 1992 Gen. Viktor Dubynin declared that Soviet troops had been poised to take over Poland in December 1981 if Jaruzelski had failed to impose martial law.[30]

Over the next year, Jaruzelski himself took over more and more party and state posts, by the end of 1982 being first secretary of the party, prime minister, minister of defense, and chairman of the military council. These moves were accompanied by a "creeping militarization of public life; first the countryside and later towns and cities as well were put under the direct administration of military task forces."[31]

In seizing power, Jaruzelski did not downgrade the party; he merely arrogated its functions to the army, himself, and those civilian members of the apparat he felt were worth retaining. The coup gave an excuse for purging the party of deadwood and too obviously corrupt officials, but Jaruzelski and those around him operated in the name of the party, not the army. There is little precise information on the Soviet military and KGB roles in the imposition of martial law in December 1981, but there can be little doubt that both institutions were immediately and intimately involved, probably more so than the CPSU itself. They, after all, were in direct touch with the Polish action units responsible for running the country.

The CPSU supported Jaruzelski happily, especially because of his nominal deference to the Polish party, but the resort to martial law widened the gulf between the CPSU and the West European Communist parties. In Italy, PCI chief Enrico Berlinguer ostentatiously ruled out any further special ties with the CPSU, thus enraging CPSU ideologues to the point that, forgetting their militant atheism, they branded the PCI's leaders heretics as well as traitors.[32]

CPSU's Decline

In the Soviet Union, an increasingly enfeebled Brezhnev had entered the last year of his life. Surrounded by corrupt party cronies, each with his own Mafia-like fiefdom, Brezhnev could still play a role as a symbol of continuity and unity, but he was no longer an active participant. Both he and the party were visibly losing prestige at home and abroad. Domestically, there was a growing overall pessimism about where the Soviet Union was heading. Ahead of his time, the perceptive American George Pfeiffer in 1980 had already detected a mass loss of "confidence and belief in socialism's moral superiority" among his Moscow friends, which they ascribed to a lack of "powerful leadership."[33]

December 1981, like December 1979, was a fateful turning point. If the rise of the military was typified by the Polish "internal invasion," the decline of the party was symbolized in the USSR by the onset of ideology chief Mikhail Suslov's final illness. Felled by a stroke in December, the Gray Cardinal would die in January 1982. Brezhnev's own death the following November would be only a footnote; by then he was just a figurehead. The CPSU then entered a decline from which it would never recover.

Brezhnev's successor, Yury Andropov, tried to turn things around by imposing harsher penalties for infractions of party discipline. From Brezhnev's death until 1986 there were approximately 430,000 expulsions from the party, even as the overall membership swelled from about 17.5 million to slightly more than 19 million. The educational level of members also improved somewhat. But such statistics reflect neither the quality of membership (careerism had essentially eclipsed idealism as a motive for joining) nor the level of morale nor the reputation of the party, all of which were falling not only at home but abroad. Through its heavy-handed methods, "by 1985 the USSR had achieved the remarkable feat of alienating almost every country in the world, Communist and non-Communist alike,"[34] perhaps first and foremost its own citizenry.

Gorbachev and the CPSU

When Mikhail Gorbachev came to power in early 1985, it was with the firm intention of improving the CPSU's control over Soviet society. He would cling to belief in the leading role of the party until at least 1989, despite his calls for decentralization of decision making and less party interference in management at the local level. For the first few years, his speeches called for enhancing, not diminishing, the party's role; he wanted to make Marxism-Leninism work.[35] At least through 1989, he rejected the idea of multiparty democracy.

Although the party continued to grow marginally, it was during the mid-1980s that its youth branch, the Komsomol, showed its first decline. Between 1984 and 1989, the organization dropped from forty-one million to thirty-one million members, with four million of those in the last year alone. In 1988, Pravda decried the loss of party authority, correctly ascribing it to the people's disdain for party bureaucrats. A year later a public opinion poll on the prestige of the CPSU showed that 73 percent of its own members believed the membership was made up of "mediocrities or [persons] of low professional qualifications."[36] A year later 90 percent of the population believed that party errors had arrested the USSR's development, and the percentage of those who had no faith whatsoever in the party had grown in one year from 23 percent to 35 percent.[37]

The tide of party prestige continued to run out during the early months of 1990. Contrary to Gorbachev's wishes, hard-line statements, and frantic political maneuvering in December 1989, the CPSU in February demonstratively forsook its monopoly of political power. According to CPSU ideology chief Vadim Medvedev, there was no choice, as mass demonstrations shook Moscow; the decision was necessary, he said, to avert a "cataclysmic explosion." [38] Shortly after, Article 6 of the Soviet constitution, guaranteeing the party's monopoly, was formally stricken from the document.

For a few heady months there was talk of pluralism and discussion about how this might be brought about. In a wry commentary, the previously orthodox but now liberal *Moscow News* noted that "in bag races victory goes not to the one who runs better, but to the one who runs better in a bag. We were better than the others to run in the bag of a one-party system, but now victory will go to him who can run best not in a bag but unhindered." [39] Between January 1990 and July 1991, four million out of nineteen million party members demonstrated their wish to be unhindered by turning in their party cards, while many more simply stopped paying their dues. [40]

But the forces of reaction were gathering, and in late spring one began to see references to "democratic centralism," "democratic humanism," and other such old, self-canceling Soviet expressions. These did not sit well with the public, and in June 1990, to preserve his power, Gorbachev divorced party and state at the highest levels of both, preserving only his own dual roles of party general secretary and president.

By early autumn 1990, the conservatives had swung Gorbachev to their side, and at the end of the year it appeared that the party might be staging a comeback. The resignation in December of Foreign Minister Eduard Shevardnadze, accompanied by his warning of a coming antidemocratic coup, dramatized but did not improve the situation.

Nevertheless, even if reaction had won, it probably would not have been able to restore the party to anything but a figurehead role. In 1978, the KGB was not permitted to give any kind of advice to CPSU Central Committee members, or meddle in their affairs in general, [41] but by 1990 that had changed completely. An expert analyst of the Soviet Union, Alexander Rahr, after a visit to the country in the fall of 1990, determined to his own satisfaction that the party truly had relinquished its control over the army and KGB, leaving administration of the state to these two entities plus Gorbachev. [42] As it was, reaction again began to recede as Gorbachev, in the late spring of 1991, began to swing again toward the liberals, eventually provoking the August coup attempt.

But by then, signs of the debasement of Communism as a theory and the CPSU as its instrument ranged from the wryly humorous to the shockingly bitter, and there was no turning back. People grinned when the atheistic party's main organ, *Pravda,* found it necessary to save itself from bankruptcy by publishing the Bible, but there were also sharper edges. In May, a radio announcer concluded a program ridiculing the official version of how a Soviet soldier had died abroad ("from putrefaction") as follows: "I wonder how many more of our boys will die as a result of putrefaction in the corpse of Soviet Communist totalitarianism?"[43]

In 1991 Soviet communism died under an avalanche of popular revulsion. Beside that stupendous collapse, the CPSU's failure to win in Afghanistan ten years earlier might appear inconsequential; the party had had, after all, many more fundamental weaknesses and stresses to contend with at home in the USSR than in far-off Afghanistan, a much greater challenge to its claimed leadership of a monolithic international movement from the Chinese than from the bickering PDPA factions, and a far more insidious threat to ideological conformity from the global communications revolution than from the *mujahidin*'s militant Islam.

Nevertheless, just as an avalanche must start with some small concrete movement that triggers the awesome release of pent-up energy, so the collapse of Soviet communism required some clearly definable proof that the system was not working. Afghanistan was one such proof, perhaps the most important one.

NOTES

1. Anwar, *Tragedy of Afghanistan*, 102.
2. Morozov, "Kabulskiy Rezident" (pt. 2), 36–39.
3. Anwar, 103.
4. Ivanov, " 'Shtorm-333'," 149.
5. Arnold, *Two-Party Communism*, 15–19, 52–60; Morozov (pt. 2), 38.
6. Bradsher, *Afghanistan*, 83; Saikal and Maley, *Regime Change*, 34; *Krasnaya Zvezda*, October 12, 1989, 2.
7. Morozov (pt. 2), 38.
8. See Fukuyama, "Patterns of Soviet . . . Diplomacy," and Adams, "Incremental Activism."
9. Morozov (pt. 2), 38.
10. Roy, "Origins," 43.
11. Anwar, 118.
12. Bradsher, 96–97.
13. Arnold, *Two-Party Communism*, 84–86.
14. Alexiev, "Inside the Soviet Army," 6.
15. Rees, "Afghanistan's Role," 3.
16. "A Fatal Thirty-Minute Error: The Soviet Invasion of Afghanistan as Seen from the Precincts of Kabul Radio," *Afghan Realities*, no. 6 (July 1982), 10–11.
17. Arnold, *Two-Party Communism*, 224; Anwar, 189.
18. Anwar, 187–193; Girardet, *Afghanistan*, 14; U.S. Department of State, *Tales*; Arnold, *Afghanistan*, 92–93; Malyshev, "Kak my brali dvorets Amina," 58–59; *Le Monde diplomatique*, September 1983, 13.
19. Dorronsoro and Lobato, "The Militia in Afghanistan," 106.
20. *New Times* 12 (March 20–26, 1990): 8.
21. *Kabul Times*, January 2, 1980.
22. Arnold, *Two-Party Communism*, 103–4.
23. *Ibid.*, 124–25.
24. *Background Brief* ("Afghanistan"), March 1980, 7.
25. *Ibid.*, 6–7.
26. *New York Times*, September 28, 1980, 6; December 4, 1980, 1; December 8, 1980, 1; December 9, 1980, 1, 8; January 2, 1981, 3; February 19, 1981, 31.

27. Staar, *USSR Foreign Policies*, 157–58, 173; Bialer, *Soviet Paradox*, 223.
28. See Smolar, "Afghanistan et Pologne," 91–95.
29. Fukuyama, "Patterns," 5.
30. *San Francisco Examiner*, March 15, 1992, A-4.
31. Wesson, ed., *1983 Yearbook*, 293.
32. Kennan Institute, *Meeting Report* (Dr. Joan Barth Urban), April 30, 1986.
33. See Pfeiffer, "Russian Disorders."
34. Sakwa, *Soviet Politics*, 127–28, 285.
35. *Slavic Review* 48, no. 2 (Summer 1989): 313–14.
36. *Sobesednik* no. 45 (298) (November 1989): 2; *Pravda*, May 2, 1988, 1 and October 16, 1989, 1.
37. Teague, "Is the Party Over?" 4.
38. *Independent*, February 9, 1990, 10.
39. *Moscow News*, April 15, 1990, 3.
40. See Teague and Tolz, "CPSU R.I.P."
41. Morozov (pt. 2), 39.
42. Kennan Institute, *Meeting Report* (Alexander Rahr), January 14, 1991.
43. Radio Rossii, May 29, 1991 (FBIS-SOV-91-104, May 30, 1991, 20).

CHAPTER 7

THE MILITARY STEPS IN (1982–85)

The state expands, the people grow sickly.
Vassily Klyuchevskiy

The Ascendancy of the Military

The start of the Afghan war coincided with the Soviet Union's modern "time of troubles," the beginning of a protracted interregnum that in the first half of the 1980s would see the incapacitation and deaths of three national leaders in rapid succession. Weakened by the rampant corruption under Brezhnev and unable to claim significant prestige either at home or abroad, the party was already the feeblest of the three pillars by the end of the 1970s. It continued to lose strength as one after another sick or senile general secretary—Brezhnev, then Andropov, then Chernenko—was seen shakily mounting the reviewing stand at Lenin's tomb to take the May 1 and November 7 holiday salutes from their vigorous, superbly equipped troops. The contrast between the leaders and the led was stark.

The absence of vigorous leadership compounded a typical Soviet administrative ailment, the inability to innovate. In an environment where information was constantly being warped and impeded, and where there was virtually absolute job security for those in power, there was always a longer-than-normal gap between cause and effect, between a growing problem and a policy reaction. Thus, well into the 1980s the party would continue to pursue its dedication to Third World Marxist-Leninist vanguard parties such as the PDPA, long after many such junior partners—and especially the PDPA—had proven themselves incapable of effective rule. Soviet disenchantment with these parties was a slow and agonizing process that went on for a number of years.[1] Soviet support for unpopular vanguard ruling parties was perceived in the West as nothing but thinly disguised imperialism, and in the end it would carry huge delayed-action economic and political costs for Moscow.

During this time of uncertainty, the Soviet defense establishment dug in to preserve its perquisities against ever more insistent civilian demands for a greater share of the national economic pie. The military's erstwhile most generous provider, Leonid Brezhnev, had begun losing enthusiasm for the military's insatiable appetite as early as 1976, and in any case he had ceased to be an effective leader for several years before he died in November 1982. The faltering Soviet economy after 1976 could not sustain the 4–5 percent annual growth rate in the defense sector as before, but the sheer bulk of the defense establishment and the impetus imparted to it in earlier times gave it a virtually irresistible momentum.*

Moreover, Brezhnev's continuation as nominal leader during the late 1970s and early 1980s while suffering from growing weakness was symbolic of the party's own nominal but increasingly uncertain control over all state institutions, particularly the military. The army, though bowing in ritual fashion to the CPSU and its leading role, doubtless felt comfortably secure in its position of privilege and disdainful of the fussy, ineffective civilian party bureaucrats.

This is not to say that the army's top brass disapproved of the party as an institution within the military. On the contrary, until the end they viewed it as a kind of binding political cement, an essential ingredient in keeping their own multiethnic forces unified, and thus, indirectly, a means of holding the disintegrating empire together. But this did not necessarily imply great respect for the civilians in charge or for their world views.

---

*Outside estimates of the military's share of the Soviet gross national product varied wildly from about 6 percent to 40 percent during this period. In 1991, thanks to *glasnost*, much more data became available, and though the controversy was not stilled, the figure for Soviet government spending on defense was revealed as between 26 percent (1990) and 36 percent (1991) of all government spending. (Stephen Foye, "Soviet High Command," p. 13.) The U.S. percentage of government spending devoted to defense is roughly comparable, but only because a much smaller portion of the U.S. economy is in government rather than private hands.

The military's disdain for the civilian bosses was rarely made explicit, but beginning in 1979 one spokesman, Chief of Staff Marshal Nikolay V. Ogarkov, more than made up for his colleagues' discreet silence. In numerous writings and speeches, Ogarkov disputed the official party line that a nuclear war was unwinnable, lobbied unceasingly for more investment in defense, and did his best to whip up fears of an impending invasion from the West. He all but identified Brezhnev by name in voicing his contempt for détente and "almost certainly crossed the line between permissible—or at least tolerable—lobbying and rank insubordination." So outspoken did he become that a "senior Soviet diplomat" accused him privately of "unparty-like behavior," the same charge laid against Marshal Zhukov on his ouster in 1957.[2]

In normal circumstances, such insubordination would have been rewarded with instant demotion or retirement. Instead, however, despite CPSU leaders' growing anxiety over his hawkish statements, Ogarkov continued to survive as chief of staff not only through the balance of Brezhnev's administration, but through that of Andropov and half of Chernenko's. His ability to keep his post and continue to give independent statements was indicative of mounting military influence.

In September 1983, ten months after Brezhnev's death, Ogarkov showed both his own and the military's political importance when he led a press conference, televised to the world, concerning the Soviet air force's downing of a Korean Airlines 747 that had strayed into Soviet airspace off Sakhalin Island with the loss of all 269 aboard. Normally, any public handling of such an extremely sensitive international incident would have been run by the CPSU general secretary or a ranking party figure appointed by him. Granted that Andropov had just become incommunicado because of terminal kidney failure, the duty still should have devolved on one of the other Politburo members rather than merely the chief of the general staff. A few months later, with Andropov's officially admitted "bad cold" clearly something more serious, a prescient scholar observed that "behind the scene, the threads of intrigue are being woven, and warring groups of party boyars are being formed in the fight for Andropov's legacy. [Only] he who has the army's blessing will inherit it."[3]

When the civilian hierarchy finally decided Ogarkov had to go, it was only because he seemed poised to use the military's clout to take over as minister of defense when the terminally ill Dmitri Ustinov was approaching death. It was a sign of the military's continued influence that even then the civilians felt the need to ease him out in a most gingerly fashion and to give him an important post as commander-in-chief of the western theater of military activity.[4]

But the army's immense political weight and immunity from outside discipline were just as destructive to its effectiveness as the CPSU's were for the civilian administration. Like the party, the military suffered from an armor-plated disregard of its own failings and of the need for fresh approaches. Simply by being unable to win on the Afghan battlefield, for example, it had already demonstrated its incompetence, but had not yet been made to pay any significant penalty.

True, the army seemed to realize that it had a morale problem—the punishments for infractions of military laws were made more severe in 1983, for example—but the full impact of its disgrace still lay some years in the future. Like the CPSU before it and the KGB after, this stage's principal tool of Soviet hegemony in Afghanistan would suffer wounds whose real pain would only be felt much later.

The Afghan Military after the Invasion

In Afghanistan, Kabul's army since the 1950s had also enjoyed relatively generous funding, but there was no corresponding popular reverence for it, nor was it perceived as a collective. Some individual divisions had good or bad reputations, at least among foreigners curious enough to find out, but it is doubtful most Afghans cared about such matters. Soldiers, like everyone else in the society, tended to be individualistic, as anyone who has ever witnessed Afghan troops attempting close-order drill can attest.

The original Soviet intention had been to capture the Afghan army intact and use it, under Soviet control, as the main force to overcome the resistance. But the various deceptions used at the time of the invasion to disarm the Afghan forces had failed, oddly, to arouse admiration and obedience in the breasts of the deceived. Sporadic resistance to the invaders by Afghan army units soon ceased, but the massive desertions that ensued left the Soviet forces with Afghan troops that were too few in number and too dispirited in morale to handle the intended mission.

What the Soviet general staff expected the impact of the invasion on the DRA army to be can only be conjectured, but it was clearly far more devastating than anticipated. From about one hundred thousand in late 1979, the army had shrunk to between twenty and twenty-five thousand by the end of 1980, and it never would regain its former strength. Desertion and draft evasion, though never quite keeping level with conscription, in spite of the draconian enrollment methods that soon came into vogue, posed a never-ending problem.

To an outsider—and even to Soviet citizens themselves in later years—the Soviet failure to anticipate the Afghan reaction to the invasion is incredible. The miscalculation was probably based on the twin beliefs that enough Afghan army officers had been recruited to carry the day, and that such agents would continue to enjoy the support of their troops after the invasion. Both assumptions were far off the mark. The presumption of troop obedience to their officers might have held up in the days when a unit consisted of officers and men from the same village or region. Ironically, it may have been early Soviet advice to the Afghans to get away from the concept of home guard units and build a homogeneous conscript army that dissolved the strongest loyalty link between officers and men.

(In 1882, the Englishman Edward Hensman—apparently in reference to similar errors by British military/colonial planners—praised the individual Afghan fighting man, but noted that "once he is asked to sink his identity and become merely a unit in a battalion he loses all self-confidence and is likely to think more of getting away than of stubbornly holding his ground as he would have done with his own friends led by his own chief."[5])

Afghan draft resistance resulted in a decline in both the quantity and quality of troops: mainly it was the slow, the stupid, and the overaged or underaged who failed to evade conscription. When more capable youths volunteered or were drafted, they often donned the uniform only for the purpose of acquiring a free weapon before taking the first opportunity to desert and join a resistance group.

For years, the Soviet training programs for Afghan officers had covered all branches of service, but the longest courses—and hence those offering the best opportunities for recruitment—were in such high-technology fields as armor and the air force. It was here that the Soviets enjoyed their most significant penetrations of the armed forces.[6] But officers alone do not make an army, and gaps opened between Communist officers and non-Communist enlisted men; moreover, the loyalty of even many nominally Communist officers to their Soviet mentors evaporated with the invasion.

Thus, to compensate for the meltdown of the DRA army, the Soviets had to increase their own force commitment. The initial invading contingent had numbered seventy thousand, probably considered adequate for the purpose at the time, but this had to be boosted to eighty-five thousand before the summer of 1980. Also, although Moscow's main aim in 1980–81 was almost certainly political, the methods used by the Soviet forces from the outset reflected either another instance of incredible political blindness or the Soviet military acting independently of the Kremlin.

Initial Soviet Strategies and Tactics

Some observers have claimed that it was only at the end of 1980, after Soviet advisers were killed while trying to set up civil action programs to help win over the population, that the policy changed from "winning [the Afghans'] hearts and minds to getting their attention by other ways."[7] Others dispute the reported delay in the Soviet resort to "other ways." According to one U.S. military analyst, the invaders had given up on reaching a peaceful solution by June 1980. The follow-on military strategy was to secure communications centers and the land links between them, hold casualties to a minimum, exploit the Soviet advantage in high technology, firepower, and mobility, limit by terror tactics the infiltration of resistance groups, and adopt a scorched-earth policy wherever resistance appeared.[8]

From the first days of the war there were reports of the Soviet use of lethal chemical warfare (CW) agents, reports that grew in frequency and credibility in the months that followed. They included films by a Western journalist of a chemical attack, testimony by Soviet POWs responsible for decontamination operations, and chemical evidence taken from the bodies of dead Soviet soldiers, as well as eyewitness accounts from hundreds of Afghan refugees. The accumulated evidence led one expert to conclude unequivocally that "the [Soviet] use of lethal chemicals—blood and nerve agents—in Afghanistan has been proven beyond question," though "the use of mycotoxins, artificially manufactured biological weapons, is still the subject of some controversy."[9]

The Soviet motive behind the use of CW was probably less a hope that the weapon would prove decisive than an interest in testing it out in combat conditions. The targets chosen were invariably in remote areas, beyond the view of most foreign observers. By 1983 or 1984, when the international outcry over the use of CW grew too stormy, such operations "greatly diminished or stopped," not only in Afghanistan but in Indochina, where they also had been reported. The discovery there of mycotoxins, which can develop naturally only in cold climates, was considered a particularly damning indication of Soviet-sponsored CW operations.[10]

A French doctor in charge of a volunteer medical corps, *Médecins sans Frontières,* asserted in 1983 that Soviet military units had used terror as a deliberate weapon to intimidate the Afghan population from at latest mid-1980. Arriving in their armored personnel carriers (APCs) at villages that had already been forewarned through the Afghan bush telegraph and evacuated, the Soviets would set fire to crops and buildings, loot the few poor belongings left behind, and then retreat after leaving booby traps in place. Villagers who had not fled, mostly those too ancient to escape, would be taken off for interrogation or summarily shot. "The effect sought was terror, not strictly military victory." These operations were mostly shut down at the end of 1980, giving way to a campaign of terror from the air (bombing, strafing, sowing of anti-personnel mines) in 1981.[11]

Both this source and others reported the deliberate destruction of hospitals, both old civilian buildings and the field hospitals with large red crosses on their roofs set up by French organizations. These attacks, mostly from the air, would continue as long as the Soviet air force was involved in the war.[12]

It was impossible for the Soviets to rely on the understrength Afghan army to pacify the countryside, yet it was not part of the Soviet plan to take heavy casualties in their own forces. In some areas, where unprotected troops were likely to come under sniper fire, they would stay out of sight and relatively safe within their steel-walled vehicles. After driving into a town, they would remain buttoned up, sometimes for several hours, and then depart, leaving any Afghan witnesses bemused and somewhat contemptuous.

For their part, *mujahidin* in the early days of the war often dressed in martyrs' white robes and would sometimes charge an armored force, counting on their belief in Allah to achieve victory against the infidels. A cruel Darwinian process of natural selection swiftly put an end to such tactics. Though largely uneducated, the Afghans quickly adapted to the conditions that the Soviets' superior technology forced on them.

The Soviet strategists and tacticians were much slower to adapt. The original armored sweep evolved into a hammer-and-anvil type of operation, intended to crush resistance forces between the advancing armor and a blocking force deployed ahead of it; but so slow, cumbersome, and unimaginative were these attacks that the resistance could either avoid contact or exploit the situation operationally. The sweeps stuck to the open roads, and though supported by helicopters were vulnerable to ambushes from the high ground that overlooked bridges and defiles. There was no effort to use light infantry as a flanking force to clear the ground on either side of the line of advance. Losses of Soviet armor in the first year was estimated by one amateur observer who traveled over much of the country with the *mujahidin* at perhaps one thousand.[13] (Later Soviet admissions that they lost fewer than fifteen hundred killed during that first year of the war seem low for this if no other reason.)

The Afghan Army in 1981

By the end of 1980, there was apparently a decision to stand down on Soviet actions and let the Afghan army, now somewhat improved in numbers and capability, handle ground operations. To make service more attractive for officers, the Kabul regime in January 1981 doubled military salaries and bestowed promotions and medals with a lavish hand, especially on the higher ranks. For enlisted men, the approach was more stick than carrot: the draft age was lowered, the tour of duty was extended, and press gangs roamed the streets hunting down possible draft evaders. Although there were also a few positive incentives such as rewards for voluntary enlisting or reenlisting, the main reliance was on force. In September the reservist age limit was raised to thirty-five.

These moves were accompanied by a renewed emphasis on ideology and discipline. Fading noticeably from the media was advocacy for "broadening the base" of government by employing non-PDPA executives; that tactic had only infuriated the doctrinaire Khalqis without materially improving the DRA's domestic popularity ratings, and the pendulum now swung back to more authoritarian rule. In line with the new policy, in June 1981 the PDPA Politburo took on three hard-line figures with military/security backgrounds and functions: Minister of Communications Aslam Watanjar (a former tank commander and almost certainly an agent of Soviet civilian or military intelligence), Minister of Defense Maj. Gen. Mohammed Rafii (also a Soviet-trained tank specialist and probable agent), and State Security chief Najib (trained and advised by the KGB).

Soviet participation in combat operations during 1981 was confined largely to air attacks, artillery support, some use of armor, and moral encouragement to their unhappy Afghan allies. It was not a successful mix, as some six ground offensives during 1981 resulted in defeats or, at best, only partial and temporary victories for the combined Soviet/Afghan forces.[14]

With both the DRA and Soviet forces showing some reluctance for combat, and the resistance just getting organized, casualties were relatively low on both sides in 1981. A West European volunteer doctor described the Soviet strategy as one of trying to strangle the resistance by interdicting food and medical supplies being smuggled in from Pakistan. The level of combat, he said, was "very, very low," as witness the fact that his surgical field hospital, intended to care for *mujahidin* wounded, had had almost no business.[15]

In this second year of the war, resistance forces controlled the countryside only a few kilometers out of Kabul, and they had no hesitation in moving about by daylight. Although Soviet air supremacy was not challenged in these early stages, and although the armored Mi-24 helicopter gunships were terrifyingly immune to small-arms fire from below, it was hard for air crews to spot individual guerrillas in their naturally camouflaged robes, almost invisible against the mountain backgrounds, at more than a hundred yards' range. Moreover, the poor quality of air-ground communications sometimes led them to attack DRA troops—and accompanying Soviet advisers—with misplaced friendly fire.[16]

The resistance could scarcely be said to have had a strategy in this initial phase, but it quickly adopted innovative tactics. One was to lay ambushes in defiles where helicopters called in for support would have to fly below the level of surrounding ridges. This exposed their unarmored upper parts to the 12.7mm (.50 caliber) machine guns that were the resistance's heaviest weapon in those days.

Another tactic was to focus sniper fire on Afghan officers at every opportunity. The soldiers under their command, usually undertrained teenage conscripts, would often flee or desert to the *mujahidin* as soon as the officer fell.

The most radical resistance group, Gulbuddin Hekmatyar's Hezb-e-Islami, also experimented with taking a Soviet hostage, an elderly geologist named Okrimyuk, in 1981. After extended unsuccessful negotiations with the Soviets, however, he was executed.

Soviet Political Developments and the 1982 Change in Policy

As the CPSU lost credibility at home, both the military and KGB pillars gained strength at its expense, but of the two the military at first did better than the KGB. Even before Brezhnev died, the main responsibility for solving the Afghanistan problem already lay in the military's hands, but it was initially hamstrung by the party's insistence on having the DRA try to gain popularity by broadening the base of the Afghan government and limiting the military's freedom of action. The change in the Kremlin's priorities, illustrated by the election of one intelligence and two military officers to the PDPA Politburo (Najib, Watanjar, and Rafii) was also probably associated with early signs of the Kremlin's diminishing faith in Third World vanguard parties in general and the PDPA in particular.

Late in 1981 or in early 1982, probably to the satisfaction of the Soviet high command and professional officer corps, the main responsibility for settling the Afghan problem was handed to them. The troop level, which had stayed at 85,000 for two years, jumped to 105,000, and Soviet direct participation in combat against the resistance climbed sharply. Although about 80 percent of the occupation forces were conscript units responsible mainly for defending installations and communications, the other 20 percent were highly trained, physically fit professional soldiers from airborne and other elite divisions. The demoralized regime forces were still part of the combat picture but—just as with the American experience in Vietnam in the 1960s—the role of the indigenous troops atrophied as the superpower mentor took over more responsibility for the fighting.

New Soviet Military Initiatives

The Soviet army reverted to large-scale ground sweeps, now augmented with heliborne operations, to surround and destroy resistance concentrations. Although initially successful in some cases, the largest such offensives in 1982, against the Panjshir Valley in April and May and again in September, failed to inflict more than slight casualties on the resistance, while exposing the Soviets to higher-than-normal losses. Ahmad Shah Massoud, the famous resistance leader who was headquartered in the Panjshir, evacuated civilians from the valley floor, laid ambushes up the side valleys, and pressed home attacks as the Soviets withdrew.

So successful was Massoud that the Soviets concluded a six-month truce with him in January 1983, an interlude that he used to build up and organize his forces. At the end of six months, both sides continued to honor the truce in the Panjshir until the spring of 1984. The terms of the agreement did, however, give Massoud a free hand to operate elsewhere, and during this time he launched frequent attacks against Soviet convoys and outposts in the north. His operations benefited from Western aid to the resistance, which, though slow to materialize and often usurped by resistance groups more favored by the Pakistanis, began making itself felt in 1983, resulting in successful ambushes and other small-scale guerrilla attacks.

The Soviets, too, were improving their capabilities and committing more sophisticated weapons to the war. On the ground, the Soviets seemed to be in an experimental stage, launching probing attacks here and there to test the efficiency of various combinations of ground, air, and airborne forces. In the air, they increased the volume of retribution sorties against villages suspected of harboring resistance fighters.

Turning Point in the Panjshir

The decisive turning point in the Afghan war came in April 1984, with the failure of the seventh Soviet assault on the Panjshir Valley. In many ways, that failed attack reflected in an Afghan microcosm the political, military, and intelligence failures that eventually would bring down the Soviet Union itself.

By the beginning of 1984, Massoud must have known that the Soviets were preparing some kind of action against him. It was clear that the occupiers could not accept with equanimity his increasing military capabilities and continued implacable hostility. Massoud's main base in the Panjshir Valley was a dagger poised over the heart of the Soviet air force in eastern Afghanistan, the Bagram air base. That dagger also threatened the Salang Pass road, the main land artery of supply to the Kabul regime from the Soviet Union. The annihilation of Massoud and his forces was thus of critical importance.

To accomplish their mission, the Soviets sought to combine the capabilities of the PDPA, a large Soviet/Afghan military strike force, Soviet air and ground units located in central Asia, and a special KGB/KHAD assassination team whose mission was to liquidate Massoud personally. It was a massive operation that required careful coordination among all three pillars.

Details of the operation were not long in reaching Massoud's ears, thus illustrating one of its basic vulnerabilities, the lack of security. Massoud himself would later express astonishment over his comprehensive knowledge of Soviet capabilities and intentions compared to their ignorance of his own. If he had any doubts about what was coming, they were probably laid to rest when in February the Soviets proposed that their old truce be renewed; deception may be a Soviet specialty, but whether by instinct or foreknowledge, Massoud immediately recognized the ploy as a means of making him lower his guard.[17]

If the Soviets' plans were clear to Massoud, his were obviously a surprise to them. In March, his men launched unusually large, devastating ambushes of convoys from the Soviet Union. Many of these contained the gasoline and diesel supplies intended to fuel the forthcoming offensive, and their destruction forced the occupiers to requisition all available supplies in Kabul to make up for the shortfall.[18]

Impact of Panjshir Battle inside Afghanistan

This initial military setback undoubtedly had a psychological impact on the Soviets' Afghan allies. The PDPA, in its effort to strengthen the armed forces, had been appealing to party members (who enjoyed immunity from conscription) to volunteer for the army. In the face of Massoud's resoundingly successful ambushes, however, party members showed even less than normal enthusiasm for heeding this call, so the PDPA—presumably under Soviet pressure—selected a large number of "volunteers" from its ranks to partake in the offensive. Inasmuch as the Parcham branch of the party dominated its administration, it was not surprising that those chosen to risk death as "hero-volunteers" were selected from the ranks of the rival Khalq branch. The bitter hostility between the two was exacerbated, and of the two thousand to six thousand Afghan troops participating in the assault, some four hundred reportedly deserted on their way to the front.[19]

If the CPSU's surrogate in Afghanistan received a blow, so did the KGB's. Not only did Massoud's intelligence net warn of the coming military offensive against him, but it easily disposed of the threat against him personally. A key role in the Communist operation had been assigned to a twenty-three-man assassination team, led by a Massoud confidant who had been recruited by KHAD. But this man in fact remained Massoud's real agent all along, and he betrayed the entire operation to Massoud at his first opportunity, resulting in annihilation of the team. (To protect this man's family, held hostage by the regime, Massoud at first reported that the would-be assassin had been killed in the attempt; only later did his survival and true role as Massoud's agent emerge).[20]

But it was probably the Soviet military whose prestige and spirit took the worst pounding. The assault reportedly involved twenty thousand Soviet soldiers, four hundred tanks, and large numbers of aircraft. Spare troops garrisoned in central Asia were brought in, some to take part directly, others to assume the duties of locally stationed forces committed to the battle. The attack began on April 20, 1984, with saturation bombing by up to two hundred Tu-16 strategic medium bombers that had been deployed from western parts of the USSR and launched from bases just north of the Afghan-Soviet border. On April 21, a rolling artillery barrage was followed by infantry, armor, and leapfrogging special-forces heliborne units, supported by Su-25 ground assault aircraft and Mi-24 helicopter gunships. New weapons included napalmlike liquid fire bombs. A month later the attack had ground to a halt with most of its territorial objectives secured but at a cost of some five hundred Soviet casualties, termed by one reporter a "costly success."[21]

But the "success" was neither complete nor permanent. Ahmad Shah Massoud and most of his forces escaped unscathed while inflicting punishing blows on the attackers. The Communist occupation, never complete, only lasted for the summer. A renewed Soviet offensive in September to clear the valley of areas reoccupied by the resistance was a halfhearted affair, and by winter the valley was again in Massoud's hands.

There would be other large battles won and lost by both sides in the ensuing four years before the Soviets began their withdrawal. But not even the introduction in 1986 of Stinger missiles—which destroyed Soviet air supremacy and forced the infantry into costly, unprotected ground action—was as fateful psychologically as the failure of this largest, most comprehensive assault since the invasion itself. Moreover, it was especially galling to the Soviet troops that their sacrifices went unnoted in their own media, which portrayed the entire operation as a glorious victory for their Afghan surrogates.

(Writing much later, after the Soviet troop withdrawal, the journalist Artem Borovik related how a colleague, on submitting a story for a book about combat in Afghanistan, had been told by an editor to change all the Russian, Ukrainian, and Georgian names to Afghan ones; he did so, and in so doing mortally offended those who had taken part in the battles he described.)[22]

First Soviet Reaction to Military Failure

Back at the Kremlin, the defeat at Panjshir came too late to have an immediate effect on the critical battle for succession after the death in January 1984 of Yury Andropov. As predicted by Avtorkhanov just before Andropov's death, the struggle of party boyars appears to have been decided in good part by the military. Andropov's choice as heir to the party throne had been Mikhail Gorbachev, a young, somewhat radical and unconventional fellow from the Stavropol region. But just as Andropov himself had thwarted Brezhnev's choice of Konstantin Chernenko as his successor, so Andropov's nominee was now shunted aside. Ironically, it was that same Chernenko, now semisenile and in obviously failing health, who was propelled into the general secretary's chair as a compromise stand-in, while the various other party and state factions battled it out in the background.

For the military, Chernenko was an excellent—if not the best possible—choice, for it meant that established state policies, including the military's fat share of the budget, would continue undisturbed as long as no dynamic new leader was on the scene. The military's prestige at the top level and its disdain for international opinion was illustrated a few days before the Panjshir operation when the pilot who shot down the Korean Airlines 747 the previous September was nominated for the USSR's highest military decoration, Hero of the Soviet Union. But the zenith of the growing military influence in the Kremlin was about to pass.

During the first eight months of 1984, there was a gradual increase in the Soviet press in human-interest stories about the Afghan war. The first cautious admission of Soviet casualties had begun only in 1983, but 1984 saw an effort to "Kiplingize" the war by portraying it as painful, dramatic, heroic, and selfless. Only then did individual deaths in combat begin to be glorified, although on a very selective basis and without indicating that any soldiers but those publicized had died. To outsiders, the admission, however limited, of soldiers killed "doing their internationalist duty" (the stock propaganda phrase) seemed to reflect both an overweening confidence in the correctness of Soviet behavior and a consequent greater willingness to be frank about at least some of the war's distressing aspects.

This was very likely the view of the hard-bitten Marshal Ogarkov, whose belief in the glory aspects of military service was never in question. In fact he probably was instrumental in pushing the propaganda campaign, for the heroic treatment of the war in Soviet media came to an abrupt halt with his transfer from the chief of staff position in October 1984.

The reverse side of that coin may have been the leaders' perception of public apathy and disaffection and a belief that glorifying the war would help to sell it. As early as 1983, one perceptive Western journalist was already reporting disillusionment among Soviet officers returning from battle.[23] Another sign of disaffection in the ranks came in a Soviet military journal's plaintive call in 1984 for "more materials on internationalism, heroic-patriotic indoctrination, and combat traditions of the CPSU, the Soviet people, and the armed forces."[24]

This interpretation is borne out by a curious aspect of Soviet propaganda. All Soviet operations in Afghanistan were portrayed as *defensive* in nature, as if this somehow would justify the USSR's participation. In human-interest stories during 1984, for example, there were twelve stories of helicopters rescuing troops under fire, twelve about mine clearing, seven about guard duty at lonely outposts, six about convoy duty, and ten about miscellaneous other defensive activities. When it became necessary to describe *offensive* operations, these were always described as training exercises, even though some of the participants were hailed for medals they received for calling down artillery fire or air strikes on their own positions when assaulting an enemy stronghold.[25]

Internationally, the Panjshir defeat may have had a bearing on Moscow's willingness to engage Washington in regular discussions about regional (i.e., Third World) conflicts. Starting in 1984 and continuing into the following years, these would evolve into annual or more frequent meetings at the assistant secretary of state level.[26]

As will be seen in chapter 9, there was also growing resentment about the war in the public at large. The Panjshir defeat must have influenced not only Soviet public opinion (despite regime efforts to black out news about it) but the politicking in the Kremlin, where a military failure of that magnitude could be neither concealed nor ignored. The resulting loss of support for the military appears to have been exploited politically by those maneuvering for power in the Kremlin, including those trying to break Ogarkov's iron grip on the chief of staff position and block his path to the top defense job.

The civilians were assisted by the enfeeblement of the military bloc as age took its toll. Ustinov had been not only minister of defense since 1976, but a Politburo and Secretariat member for many years before that. His replacement by an aging, gray nonentity, Marshal Sergey Sokolov, who never achieved more than candidate Politburo status, signaled a change in the political tide.*

The official most blessed by this change was Mikhail Gorbachev, who all through 1984 and up until his final confirmation as general secretary in March 1985 had been locked in a life-and-death political struggle with the last remaining top-level advocate of military interests, party secretary and Politburo member Grigoriy Romanov. The failure of the Soviet army in the Panjshir, followed by the removal of Ogarkov, the death of Ustinov, and the promotion of the feeble Sokolov

---

*Ustinov's appointment as minister of defense in 1976 is taken by some (e.g., Azrael, "Civil-Military Relations") to mean that, because Ustinov was a civilian, the military was already being downgraded at that time. But Ustinov had been in charge of defense industries since World War II, and though not a uniformed soldier was certainly a stout defender of the defense establishment. Marshal Sokolov was not nearly as forceful a champion of defense interests.

were all influential in determining the outcome of the succession struggle eventually won by Gorbachev. Even with these advantages, the fight was a close one, and without the Panjshir debacle, the balance might have swung to Romanov, whose close ties to the high command and the defense industries would have ensured their continued dominance of Soviet policy.

Initial Gorbachev Afghan Policies

Gorbachev had been Andropov's protégé. His inauguration was thus a victory not only for him personally but for the strongest remaining pillar, the KGB. Nevertheless, there was at first no diminution in Soviet military activity in Afghanistan. By December 1984, the troop level had risen from 105,000 to 115,000. A further rise to about 118,000 in 1985 probably represented the maximum number that could be supported logistically inside Afghanistan, given the country's primitive transportation network.[27] They were augmented by 30,000 other combat troops stationed just across the border in Soviet central Asia, ready for short-term use in specific operations, but there were finite limits on how many soldiers the general staff could deploy in the field— and for how long.[28]

Although Gorbachev is credited (deservedly) with having engineered the Soviet withdrawal in 1988–89, this was not necessarily his initial impulse: not only did Soviet force levels reach their maximum in 1985, *after* he became CPSU general secretary, but the level of fighting in the summer of 1985 was reported to have "escalated markedly."[29] In mid-1985 he himself threatened to raise the stakes by increasing his force commitment to a half-million soldiers, though this was clearly beyond the support capabilities available in Afghanistan.

This evidence contradicts what seems to have been a later effort to portray Gorbachev as always having sought a peaceful solution to the conflict. It seems probable, given other, more accessible examples of his administrative style, that he bluntly warned his marshals and generals in April 1985 that they had a free hand but a fixed time limit to solve the Afghan problem by arms, after which, regardless of the outcome, he intended to start withdrawing his forces. This speculation is buttressed by an otherwise undocumented assertion that at one point, presumably in 1985, he gave General Zaytsev (then commander in charge of the Afghan campaign) "1–2 years to turn the situation in Afghanistan around."[30] Before the end of the year, he had probably lost faith in any military victory.

Military operations in 1985 reflected an increase in volume and a somewhat more focused effort to destroy *mujahidin* forces rather than visit indiscriminate destruction on the civilian infrastructure. A large part of the effort seemed aimed at interdicting *mujahidin* supply lines. In part the switch in strategy may have been because of the deadline we have imputed to Gorbachev: it would have seemed suddenly more important to the high command to win the war quickly and expensively rather than by relatively cheap but slow attrition.

Another significant factor was the vast depopulation of the countryside that had already taken place—by 1987 more than 50 percent of the Afghan population had been killed or driven from their homes—thus reducing the number of targets and educating the remaining Afghans in better survival skills. Afghan civilian and military war deaths peaked in 1984, with 1,712 Soviet military operations yielding an estimated rate of sixteen Afghan dead per thousand population; in 1985, 2,013 operations resulted in a thirteen per thousand rate, the second highest of the war. Thereafter, engagements rose to 3,907 in 1986 and 4,450 in 1987, but Afghan war deaths dropped to eleven and then to nine per thousand, respectively. Much of the responsibility for the lower death rate in the later years was thanks to the introduction of Stinger missiles, which drastically cut the efficiency of air attacks, previously the main cause of Afghan casualties.[31]

Significance of the Stingers

In the Middle Ages, chivalry got its name not from good manners but from the horse that carried the rich, armor-plated, invulnerable warrior of that era into battle against others of his kind or a largely defenseless infantry. (With that kind of advantage, the horseman could occasionally afford good manners.) With the advent of the longbow, the age of chivalry came to an abrupt halt; the freeholding yeoman needed only to double-taper a piece of yew of his own height, string a proper thong, iron-tip an arrow made of aspen, and he had an equalizer. The cavalry was not dead, but it was no longer invincible.

What the longbow did for the English yeoman, the hand-held Stinger surface-to-air missile (SAM) did for the Afghan resistance against the

Soviet army's most effective weapon, the Mi-24 helicopter gunship. In the early 1980s a few Soviet-designed hand-held SA-7 missiles (roughly equivalent to the earlier American Redeye) found their way into *mujahidin* hands, but they were notoriously unreliable, easy to mislead with countermeasures, and cursed with a telltale trail of white smoke that led straight back to their launcher.

The Stingers were different. After a preliminary abortive appearance in mid-1986 (the climatic extremes were too much for their electronics components), a modified version made its dramatic debut at summer's end that year. On September 26, a flight of four gunships flying in formation in Nangarhar Province came under Stinger attack, and only one returned to base. From then on, Soviet aircraft losses soared; at the peak of their use the Stingers reportedly enjoyed a 68 percent kill rate.[32]

Suddenly vulnerable, gunships that used to range at will and visit destruction from the altitude of their choosing on both military and civilian targets were reduced to flying either so high as to be ineffective for much more than artillery spotting, or at minimum altitude and maximum speed. Although these tactics enabled them to avoid most Stingers, it reduced their combat efficiency markedly. Moreover, the low-level flights resulted in more accidental crashes and exposed them to machine-gun fire and even attack by RPG-7 hand-held antitank missiles, which were also in the *mujahidin* arsenal.

Soviet ground troops, accustomed to riding into battle in armored personnel carrier convoys under an air umbrella, found themselves on foot carrying out long flanking patrols to protect those same convoys, while exposing themselves to hostile fire. Casualties mounted and the level of morale, already low, dropped still further. Back at the Kremlin, the inability of the occupation forces to find an effective counter to the Stinger undoubtedly constituted yet another blow to the prestige of the military.

Domestic Decline of the Soviet Military

Shortly after taking power, Gorbachev informed his generals that they would no longer have first call on the nation's resources. At his first meeting with ranking field commanders in Minsk in July 1985, he made it abundantly clear that the military had to clean up its management, get rid of cost overruns, and become more efficient. Starting in 1986, unprecedented criticisms of the military in the Soviet press became more and more common, from examples of misbehavior among Soviet forces in Germany to open complaints about casualties in Afghanistan to objections about conscription deferments for the sons of party officials. Despite these indicators, however, the military's sheer bulk, huge budget, and traditional importance in society continued to make it a formidable opponent for the new, reform-minded CPSU general secretary.

In May 1987, however, the military's prestige in the Soviet Union suffered a grievously embarrassing blow when a nineteen-year-old German pilot, Matthias Rust, flew a single-engine Cessna four hundred miles from Finland to Moscow through the heart of Soviet air defenses and landed on Red Square without being intercepted. The unauthorized flight, he said, was merely to promote world peace, although he was unclear on how it would do so.

For the Soviet high command, however, peace was not the result. Defense Minister Sergey Sokolov was promptly retired, his place taken by the relatively young Dmitriy Yazov, who leapfrogged several senior officers to take the supreme defense post. Air defense chief Alexander Koldunov and several other senior officers were fired in disgrace, while at least four other officers were expelled from the party. For Gorbachev, the flight was a political godsend, enabling him to clean out the entrenched military old guard and thus strengthen his hand enough to carry out the drastic cuts in the military budget envisaged under his defense doctrine of "reasonable sufficiency."*

In fact, the flight was an almost suspiciously happy melding of a political need and an event that served it. There were many odd aspects of the Rust case: just prior to the incident there was a rash of articles in the Western press about Gorbachev's efforts to downgrade the military; the circumstances that permitted Rust, a minor, to rent a plane in Finland were never explained; during the flight, one MiG

---

*It would take until October 1988, however, to retire Marshal Nikolay Ogarkov, the most intense proponent of an expensive, offensively oriented military establishment. The following May, Ogarkov and eight other marshals and generals were dropped from the Central Committee, whereas only one new military member was added to the fourteen soldiers who survived the cut.

interceptor flew alongside him but made no effort to force down the obviously foreign plane; and Rust received a severe sentence that isolated him for several years in a Soviet labor camp, effectively removing him from the prying questions of Western authorities and journalists until interest in the case had largely subsided. Either Gorbachev was the beneficiary of a piece of extraordinary good luck, or someone had run an extremely clever operation to pull the rug from under his military opponents.*

The price of Gorbachev's local victory over the army was, however, probably far higher than he envisaged. By mid-1988, he was starting to withdraw his troops from Afghanistan, and popular disenchantment with the military was growing. At the end of the year, complaints about *dedovshchina*, the brutal hazing of new recruits by older hands that sometimes involved homosexual rape and had even led to murders, was getting more and more publicity. By 1989 media criticism included allegations of officer cowardice, drunkenness, and uncaring or even brutal behavior toward enlisted men in Afghanistan. More and more ugly incidents of racism began to be reported in both the foreign and Soviet press. The whole patriotic/military theme in Soviet propaganda was beginning to shred under growing public contempt.[33]

The government itself reflected this changing mood. The invasion of Afghanistan began to be associated publicly with "the excessive use of force in Soviet foreign policy" as early as 1988. In March 1989, students received automatic deferment from conscription. By November, all persons accused of—and the two thousand serving time for—everything from theft to murder in Afghanistan, including deserters, were cleared and/or released. In a cost-cutting and tension-reducing move, Gorbachev promised to cut his army by half a million men, a move unanimously approved by the Supreme Soviet and Congress of

---

*Gen. Oleg Kalugin, late of the KGB, while agreeing that the Rust incident had been remarkably fortuitous for Gorbachev, told the author in January 1992 that it had *not* been a KGB operation. Kalugin would not, however, necessarily have been privy to such a sensitive operation. Of the branches of Soviet military service, air defense—sometimes called the "agricultural sector of the defense effort" by other officers for its notorious inefficiency—would be perhaps the easiest to embarrass with a deception operation.

Peoples Deputies, which in March 1989 had seen at least three senior generals and two admirals defeated in the USSR's first truly free elections.[34]

Reeling under these blows, the army suffered a widening split between the top and middle ranks of officers. An overweight corps of generals (one general to every seven hundred other ranks, or six times as many proportionately as are found in the American army) was a bastion of conservatism that clung to the traditional concept of a conscript army under rigid army/party command. Younger officers, personified by a Maj. Vladimir Lopatin, demanded basic reform, including reliance on a relatively small volunteer military establishment along American lines, the removal of party controls over it, the appointment of a civilian minister of defense, abolition of nepotism, a cleanup of corruption, and the outlawing of *dedovshchina*.* According to one 1990 study, between 60 and 80 percent of middle-grade officers agreed that the services should be depoliticized, that is, no longer under CPSU control.[35]

By the end of 1989, about five hundred active and reserve officers had banded together in an informal union called *Shchit* (Shield), ostensibly to look after the welfare of the military and its dependents, but also to prevent misuse of the military as an arm of political repression. The Ministry of Defense was horrified but apparently incapable of disbanding the union. In May 1991, the union still carried enough weight that Yazov found it necessary to decry it as a group of "arrant time servers and renegades."[36]

The military became even more defensive after Soviet arms proved ineffective in defending Iraq against the onslaught of modern Ameri-

---

*Lopatin, a young (born 1961) maverick political officer with the naval air arm until 1988 when he won election to the Congress of Peoples Deputies, was so outspoken an advocate of military reform that he was expelled from the CPSU in the spring of 1990, only to be reinstated a few months later, perhaps in the vain hope he could be swayed by party discipline. As head of a temporary congressional subcommittee on military reform, he at first enjoyed Gorbachev's patronage but later was criticized by Gorbachev when the latter moved far to the right in late 1990. Lopatin then allied himself with Yeltsin in September 1990 and was made deputy head of a Russian committee on security.

can weapons in early 1991. But the most telling sign of sensitivity came when the military high command unanimously and with uncharacteristic emotion rejected and condemned a ten-volume history of World War II edited by one of its own, Col. Gen. Dmitri Volkogonov.

Volkogonov, who headed the Defense Ministry's Institute of Military History, had been commissioned to produce the history in time for the fiftieth anniversary of the Nazi German attack on the USSR in June 1941. He was coincidentally a military adviser to Russian president Boris Yeltsin. In discussing the early days of the war, Volkogonov apparently revised previous official histories by showing that there was little dedication to socialism and the Great October Revolution on the part of Soviet citizens, civilian and military, who lay in the path of the Nazi invasion. This was considered little short of blasphemous by the minister of defense, chief of the general staff, chief of the main political directorate, and various other military notables, who promptly fired Volkogonov from his institute, accusing him of "anti-Sovietism." The literary "trial" by his peers took place on March 7, but a shortened version of their denunciations was only published on June 18. Four days later, on the anniversary of the attack, Gorbachev formally decreed an end to CPSU control over the military.[37]

As more and more previously classified information found its way into open print, the Soviet public began to learn about such matters as the military crime rate, including a 1990 revelation that in 1989 59 officers had been murdered and thefts of arms and ammunition had jumped by 55 percent over 1988. The murder rate went up to at least 101 in 1990, with desertion rates that year at a record high of more than forty-three hundred, "practically all" of whom had seen service in Afghanistan.[38] In 1991 it was revealed that some seven thousand Soviet soldiers died every year from noncombat causes, 18 percent of them by suicide. An army officer privately acknowledged that the other causes listed—crimes (5.5 percent), accidents (13.5 percent), safety violations (17 percent), illness (21 percent), traffic accidents (15 percent), and misuse of firearms (9.5 percent)—actually concealed a large number of intraservice murders.[39]

A telling indicator of the public's disenchantment with the army was revealed in piecemeal draft-dodging statistics that were released from 1989 to 1991. The following numbers of eligible recruits failed to report for duty from 1985 onward:

TABLE 1
Draft Dodging in the Soviet Union, 1985–91

	1985	1986	1987	1988	1989	1990	1991*
Number	600	—	1,000	1,044	7,500	35,000	86,000
Convictions	280	—	250	—	—	30	—

*January to May only.

In vain did Yazov and other generals (including Boris Gromov, the last commanding general of Soviet forces in Afghanistan) rail against the growing criticisms and warn that the new liberalism was undercutting public respect for their service. General Moyseyev declared that public opinion had been "tainted by incompetent, naive, and self-serving reporting on military issues," which was undermining patriotism and the general moral character of Soviet youth.[40]

In June 1989, speeches reflecting hypernationalism and a Nazi-like hysteria and paranoia began to be heard from hard-line members of the Congress of Peoples Deputies.[41] In 1990 the hopeless rearguard action continued, with a long tirade by a Colonel Kulichkin against the alleged antimilitary prejudices of the popular weekly *Ogonek*.[42] And in July 1990 the newly appointed chief of the armed forces Political Directorate, Col. Gen. Nikolay Shlyaga, denounced "antiarmy hysteria" and efforts by unspecified dark forces to "diminish faith in our people's holy feelings of patriotism and internationalism."[43] But the media, far from leading public opinion, were merely reflecting it.

A *Pravda* reporter on May 16, 1990, wrote nostalgically about how the soldier had been viewed until the most recent times: "In the eyes of the population, he was the country's defender, was the very epitome of nobility, dignity, and courage. Only recently the military man was the boy's idol." But now, he went on, military prestige and military authority were in decline, in part reflecting the problems of the rest of society, but also because "actions carried out during the stagnation years and condemned by the country's legislators did not help strengthen the army's authority."[44]

Of those unspecified actions, Afghanistan was unquestionably the most devastating to the army's image.

NOTES

1. Fukuyama and Korbonski, *Soviet Union and the Third World*, 24–45.
2. Azrael, "Civil-Military Relations," 552, 554.
3. Avtorkhanov, "Andropov: God na postu genseka," 21–23.
4. Azrael, "Civil-Military Relations," 557.
5. Quoted in Isby, *War in a Distant Country*, 88.
6. Roy, "Origins," 43.
7. *Christian Science Monitor*, January 20, 1981, 1.
8. Collins, *Soviet Invasion of Afghanistan*, 139, 145.
9. *Ibid.*, 147–48.
10. See U.S. Department of State, *Chemical Warfare*; *Washington Post*, September 9, 1985, A-1. See also George Carver, "Common Sense and Yellow Rain," *Baltimore Sun*, April 15, 1982, C-17 and April 16, 1982, C-15.
11. Malhuret, "Report from Afghanistan," 429.
12. Radio Vienna, December 29, 1981 (FBIS-VIII, December 31, 1981, C-3).
13. Isby, 28; Collins, 149; *San Francisco Chronicle*, June 29, 1981, 16.
14. Isby, 28.
15. *San Francisco Chronicle*, June 29, 1981, 16.
16. *Christian Science Monitor*, July 23, 1981, 1.
17. *Ibid.*, April 13, 1984, 1, 3.
18. Isby, 32–33.
19. *New York Times*, May 2, 1984, 3.
20. Isby, 32; conversations with Olivier Roy.
21. Isby, 32; *New York Times*, May 27, 1984, 6.
22. See Borovik, "Chto my natvorili?"
23. *San Francisco Chronicle*, April 4, 1983, 1.
24. *Voyenno-istoricheskiy zhurnal*, no. 8 (August 1984): 72.
25. Arnold, "Soviet Threat to Pakistan," 10.
26. Kennan Institute, *Meeting Report* ("Jack F. Matlock on U.S.-Soviet Relations"), March 24, 1988.
27. *San Francisco Chronicle*, April 9, 1981, 14; *London Times*, July 30, 1986, 7.
28. For periodic assessments of Soviet involvement, see U.S. Department of State, *Afghanistan: 18 Months* (August 1981); *Afghani-*

stan: Three Years (December 1982); *Afghan Resistance* (December 1984); *Afghanistan: Six Years* (December 1985).

29. *Financial Times*, October 1, 1985, 6.
30. Parker, *Kremlin in Transition*, vol. 2, p. 85. Parker cites Don Oberdorfer's *Washington Post* April 17, 1988 "Afghanistan: The Soviet Decision to Pull Out" as the source for this statement (which he dismisses, incidentally), but the article does not mention Zaytsev. This author finds the allegation eminently believable.
31. Sliwinski, "Afghanistan 1978–87," 5.
32. Isby, 38, 44.
33. Alexiev, "Inside the Soviet Army," 42–43.
34. *New York Times*, June 17, 1988, A-1; November 29, 1989, A-6.
35. Foye, "Maintaining the Union," 6.
36. *Krasnaya Zvezda,* May 24, 1991, 1.
37. *Christian Science Monitor*, June 28, 1991, 8; Foye, "Gorbachev's Return," 7.
38. TASS International Service in Russian, December 5, 1990 (FBIS-SOV-90-235, December 6, 1990, 53); *Sobesednik*, no. 8. (February 1990), 4.
39. New York Times News Service (Moscow), February 9, 1991.
40. See Foye, "Chief of General Staff"
41. See "Congress Discusses Afghan War," FBIS-SOV-89-106-S, June 5, 1989, 18.
42. *Literaturnaya Rossiya*, no. 15 (April 13, 1990): 8–9.
43. Reuters (Moscow), "Hardliner Becomes Soviet Armed Forces Political Chief," July 13, 1990.
44. *Pravda*, May 16, 1990, 2.

CHAPTER 8

THE KGB'S TURN (1985–91)

Falsehood has been the principal ailment of Russian politics along with its usual companions, hypocrisy and cynicism. They run through our whole history.
Sergey Volkonskiy, *The Decembrists—Family Recollections*

Part I: In Afghanistan

The detectable direct impact of the Afghan experience is easiest to identify in the Soviet military, difficult in the CPSU, and virtually impossible in the KGB. For the Soviet military, the war was of unique importance as the only place where regular field units had been in combat since the end of World War II, and it drew correspondingly high attention both inside and outside the service. The party's role by definition was less noisy than the army's, and Afghanistan, being only one of several Third World countries with struggling Marxist-Leninist parties under siege, was not so uniquely important for the CPSU. For the professionally secret KGB, with its unacknowledged role in Afghanistan kept under careful wraps even within the service, Afghanistan was only one relatively minor responsibility among a growing mass of security problems.

Thus, few Soviet citizens knew of the KGB's role in Afghanistan, and those who did were not inclined to deplore it. Still, the KGB failure to solve the Afghan problem meant that the problem itself could grow to the point of undermining Soviet institutions in general, including the KGB.

"Afghanization" and the Afghan Political Course Change[1]

Just as the Americans had been driven in 1969 to "Vietnamize" the war in Indochina (i.e., turn it over to their local allies), so Mikhail Gorbachev had reached a parallel decision in Afghanistan by the fall of 1985. As was said of President Johnson in 1968, he no longer wanted to win the war, he wanted to end it. And just like the Americans before them, the Soviets, evidently with little confidence that their Afghan comrades could win a military victory alone, pinned their hopes on some kind of peace settlement that would leave their clients in power.

Unlike their American counterparts, however, the Soviets had in the KGB a uniquely endowed and qualified organization. As the most sturdy of the three pillars at this time, it enjoyed top priority for state resources. It was also eminently qualified and experienced in clandestine political operations both at home and abroad.*

Not only did the KGB have the experience, but it could wield nearly absolute power in Afghanistan because of its connections with the Afghan secret police (KHAD, soon to be renamed WAD and later SIS) and its multiple agents throughout the rest of the Afghan military and PDPA apparatuses. Far more than either the CPSU or the Soviet military, the KGB had the informational base and the operational flexibility to "save Afghanistan for socialism." Later, many of the same maneuvers introduced there would be employed in a vain attempt to save the Soviet Empire itself, but ironically, the parent regime in Moscow would collapse before its test-tube offspring in Kabul.

The basic task before the KGB in Afghanistan was twofold: to establish the Kabul regime's legitimacy at home and abroad, and, while retaining secret Soviet control over the PDPA, to turn it into a reunited, effective master of Afghanistan's fate, able to survive without end-

---

*Here, some try to equate the KGB with the CIA. In this writer's opinion, the CIA, though often tarred with the brush of clandestine political action, never deserved most of the rare credit and frequent blame it got for such activity. It was *not* active politically at home, and abroad such action was almost invariably the doing of individuals and masses proceeding on their own volition and at their own pace, with or without consultation with agency representatives and generally heedless of outside advice. To some extent the latter phenomenon was also true of the KGB (especially when dealing with Afghans), but it is scarcely necessary to state that the CIA's relative weight in Washington was minimal compared to the KGB's in Moscow.

less expenditures of Soviet blood and treasure. The two goals were contradictory, for in the eyes of most Afghans the PDPA, as Moscow's designated surrogate, was unacceptably illegitimate. The only way of reconciling the two was via another KGB talent: deception and informational sleight-of-hand.

Afghan *Glasnost* and *Perestroyka*

In late 1985, signs of the change in Afghanistan were clear and abrupt, though at first they passed unnoticed in the West. As late as September, the Soviet-installed Afghan leader, Babrak Karmal, had asserted in traditional Marxist-Leninist terms that the state apparatus's sole duty was to carry out party orders, but in November he suddenly reverted to the 1980–81 broadened-base concept of government and declared that the DRA must be prepared to survive independently. The renewed attempt to win popular approval for the DRA was the first clear but still largely unrecognized indication that the Soviets intended to withdraw militarily.

Karmal also engaged in unprecedented criticism of PDPA theories and practices. The party's failure to defeat outnumbered resistance forces, its bombast and ostentation, nepotism, involvement in corruption and embezzlement, disunity, and unpopularity among the peasants were some of the more serious charges he leveled. In what was then a shocking departure from conventional ideology, he even stated that in the future the PDPA would not have a monopoly on political power, although he ruled out having the PDPA ever share power with "murderers," (i.e., the resistance). Although the self-criticism reflected Gorbachev's campaign of *glasnost,* it went far further than anything expressed or even remotely contemplated in the CPSU at that time. So did Karmal's call for promotion of private enterprise, including the startling statement in January 1986 that party and state authorities who sought to hinder the growth and protection of the private sector would be investigated and taken to court.

Various propaganda touchwords suddenly dropped from the DRA propaganda lexicon. No longer was the revolution "irreversible." The PDPA itself was no longer a vanguard party. Heralding what later would become his successor's (and Gorbachev's) policy of "national reconciliation," Karmal voiced a breathtaking ten-point program that made concessions to, among others, several distinctly bourgeois groups:

landowners, businessmen, the clergy, and traders, all of whose support he solicited. Interestingly, the last (and hence presumably lowest priority) of the nine occupational and social groups to which he appealed was the very institution that was maintaining him physically in power: the army. Conspicuous by its total absence from the list was his one and only political bulwark: the PDPA.

To the doctrinaire Khalqis, this was yet another example of Parchami right-wing opportunism, and during the last weeks of 1985 Karmal had to maneuver some of them out of important positions in the state apparatus while promoting others in party ranks. This move was designed to restrict their Marxist-Leninist vehemence to the party (where they would come under control of party discipline) while he proceeded with a reorganization to make the state appear to be the dominant institution. Thus, the rubber-stamp Revolutionary Council was suddenly expanded from 69 to 148 members, and its nonparty component jumped from 2 to 58. Of twenty-one newly appointed ministers, fifteen were billed as nonparty. Just as with *glasnost,* the Afghans were moving rapidly ahead of the Soviets in *perestroyka* (restructuring); the same emphasis on state over party would not be seen in the USSR for several years.

The urgency of his demands for reform and reorientation of the government were reflected in Karmal's insistence in December 1985 that DRA power be established throughout the country in "two stages, in the course of two and four months." He was spurred by the knowledge that the KGB was grooming a powerful rival, ex–secret-police chief Najib, to take his place. Like Andropov in June 1982, Najib had just quit his job as secret police chief in November 1985 to become a member of the party Secretariat; like Andropov, he was clearly preparing himself for something better.

Karmal's concerns were well founded: his two-month deadline for the first stage of establishing DRA power coincided with the twenty-sixth CPSU party congress (where Gorbachev snubbed him and referred to Afghanistan as a "bleeding wound"), and his four-month deadline with his own removal in favor of Najib, in May 1986. KGB responsibility for Afghanistan, inaugurated in 1985 but until 1986 successfully concealed, had become unmistakable.

The KGB and Najib (Najibullah)[2]

The choice of the single-named Najib as the Soviets' new viceroy in Afghanistan was in itself a revealing indication of both the strength and weakness of KGB vision. On the one hand, the KGB correctly perceived the need for a new, skillful orator and charismatic politician to take the place of the jaded Karmal. In Najib they found both, for Najib has the flowery extravagance of Pashtun public speaking down to a fine art. He is also a superb actor; intolerant and belligerently rude in private to those he considers his inferiors, he can switch in an instant to sweet reason, proud but gentle authority, emotional patriotism, or whatever other personality suits the need of the moment when he is before a camera or important audience.[3]

His first eighteen months in office were marked by elaborate public fawning on the Soviets. On a July 1987 trip to Moscow he referred to Gorbachev in terms reminiscent of Stalin's personality cult: a man "all aspects of whose life teach one the essence of work, action, and courage and guide a person [to] love the people and human beings [*sic*]," a man with "philosophical depth . . . farsightedness . . . benevolent ideals" who was also "an outstanding personality, peace fighter, prominent internationalist." Later in the year, he was just as extravagant in his panegyrics to Lenin and the October Revolution, pledging the Afghan people's "inseparable link" to both.[4]

Born Najibullah, as a Communist he was "embarrassed by the reference to Allah in his name [and] asked to be known as 'Comrade Najib.'"[5] Later, after learning that the Soviet forces really would be withdrawn, he reattached the religious ending to his name in an attempt to distance himself from his former mentors and sell himself as a true Moslem. (In this book he goes by the atheist version of his name as reflecting more accurately his true convictions.)

Unlike his Tajik predecessor, Najib was a Pashtun and hence more acceptable to Afghanistan's traditional ruling ethnic group in both the pro- and anti-Communist camps. In particular, it was logical to assume that the predominantly Pashtun Khalqis within the party would find it easier to reach accommodation with him than with Karmal, the ethnic and ideological personification of all they hated in Parcham. Previously held in fairly low regard even in party circles for his brawling, nonintellectual approach to politics, Najib's very absence of commitment to one line of ideology gave him more flexibility in intraparty politics and made him more amenable to KGB direction. Also, the absence of comradely respect within the PDPA meant that he had to rely more on the Soviets for support, thus increasing his dependency. Finally, he had been a brutally effective secret police chief.

It was this last attribute that effectively undid all the others, and the KGB inability to perceive its importance as a negative factor is a testimony to their arrogance and self-delusion. As chief of KHAD, Najib was accused by many witnesses of personally torturing many of his countrymen on behalf—and with the assistance—of the KGB. He was even less acceptable to most Afghans than Vidkun Quisling was to most Norwegians after World War II.

Nevertheless, there was logic in the KGB's choice. It could point to its experience in promoting the image of Andropov, who, objectively, was scarcely a more lovable figure than Najib, yet for whom they had successfully crafted the image of the reforming intellectual, an image that would continue to be cultivated long after Andropov died. Najib, too, as his police role receded, overcame part of the tarnish of his past in the eyes of many outsiders and even some Afghans, leading some observers to underestimate the cordial hatred with which he continued to be regarded by most of his long-memoried countrymen.

Najib's rise to power can also be seen as a partial reflection of a much broader and more critical problem stemming from a peculiar double role of the KGB, both in Afghanistan and later at home. So long as it did not have operational responsibility for the Kabul regime, the KGB probably fulfilled its mission of reporting more-or-less objectively on Afghan developments. But once it took that responsibility, objectivity must have disappeared; like all other bureaucratic hierarchies, the KGB stifled bad news within its own assigned areas. Unlike more open societies, the Soviet Union had no independent channel to keep the KGB honest; as the only organization trusted to report to Kremlin leaders with true objectivity, it had nothing to fear from rival organizations or investigative journalists.

Najib's Initial Tactics

After Najib took power, his first move was to consolidate his position within the PDPA. This took two forms: an expansion of the Central Committee, which in two sessions (July and November) he more than doubled in size and loaded with his own partisans (most previously unknown); and an attempt to smooth over differences with the Khalqis by promoting some of their better-known figures to important party and state positions. (The de facto head of the faction, then–Minister of Interior Sayed Mohammed Gulabzoy, became an alternate member of the Politburo, for example.) Party unity was clearly a first-priority matter, though it was as doomed to defeat as ever; instead of healing the split with the Khalqis and consolidating the party, the installation of Najib merely split the Parchamis into pro-Karmal and pro-Najib factions, dividing the PDPA into yet-finer splinters and possibly fostering Khalqi hopes for eventual victory in the intraparty battle.

Najib also immediately took up and outdid Karmal's *glasnost* campaign, not only repeating all the charges his predecessor had leveled against the party and state, but adding such previously unmentionable topics as the alienation of the masses from the PDPA, military draft dodging (with or without the connivance of family relations in high party posts), desertion, and cowardice. Interestingly, these charges were then replayed in the press in the Soviet Union, where the use of family influence to avoid conscription would become an issue sometime later. Perhaps the most intriguing aspect of Najib's hyper*glasnost* was the inescapable inference that it could not have taken place without the blessing of his KGB mentors if, indeed, it was not at their instigation.

Again with the presumed assistance of his KGB mentors, Najib undertook some peculiar experiments in pseudodemocracy. Just three years before (July 1983), Najib's own secret police had jailed a group of Kabul University professors who had had the audacity to advocate a "national unity" government that would include opposition figures. Now Najib was suggesting cooperation with anyone who would "obey DRA laws."

In the last months of 1986, some four or five small, ostensibly independent political groups suddenly made a brief appearance, each of their overlapping names rendered in several different ways to produce utter confusion. Najib termed these "leftist and democratic organizations" and almost immediately incorporated them into the PDPA, where they disappeared from public view. Only a very few individuals, almost all previously unknown, were named as belonging to them.

In late 1987, two of these "parties" reemerged as supposedly independent entities. They were followed by the three others and a newcomer in 1988, but the odd, intermittent way they got publicity as a pseudo loyal opposition can only be interpreted as unsuccessful efforts by Najib and the KGB to craft credible democratic decoys. None attracted a significant following, and by their very willingness to join in a PDPA-controlled government they automatically discredited them-

selves. Since 1985 first Karmal and then Najib had been promising
that the PDPA would share power with other parties, but four years
after these groups first made their appearance they remained as
unconvincing as ever: although twenty-four of thirty-six government
ministers in late 1990 claimed not to be members of the renamed PDPA,
only one of them claimed membership in a different party; the rest called
themselves simply "nonparty," though most, in fact, were identified
PDPA collaborators. At that time Najib himself ingenuously commented
that the PDPA's new incarnation, the Homeland party (HP), had "not
yet succeeded" in sharing power.

Parallel to the power-sharing theme was the main PDPA propaganda
line, dominant since 1986, of "national reconciliation," designed to
promote the return of Afghan refugees from Pakistan and Iran and to
establish working relationships between the regime and various resistance
groups. It seems unlikely, however, that the very concept of true power
sharing ever penetrated the PDPA/HP mental armor. Even as Najib was
regretting its absence in 1990, he made clear that the HP, in its "vanguard role" (the first time the term had been used since 1985) had reserved
the "determining share" of government posts for itself. Power sharing, he seemed to imply, was admirable providing it did not entail the
loss of single-party control.*

Finally, from 1987 onward Najib followed through on Karmal's "Ten
Theses" by promoting private enterprise in industry, agriculture, and
trade. He also made heavy and well-publicized government investments
in Islam, rebuilding mosques destroyed in the war and emphasizing
his own personal commitment to religion.

Gorbachev's Puzzling Miscue

One may infer that the KGB somehow misled Gorbachev shortly
after Najib came to power, for the CPSU general secretary then com-

---

*Najib's (and the KGB's) real plans for Afghanistan's political structure probably
drew on old precedents. Wolfgang Leonhard, a former East German Communist who
just after World War II had the responsibility for setting up local government in Berlin's
twenty districts, put it thus: "For each district we had to set up a little government of
12 different officials, only a very few of whom should be communists: the vice mayor
of the district, the head of personnel, and the head of police. Everyone else was nonparty . . . [Party boss Walter] Ulbricht gave his famous statement that it should 'look
democratic but we have to have everything in our hands.' " (*Christian Science Monitor*,
August 4, 1987, p. 8.)

mitted a serious and unnecessary political error. Since about the end of 1980 there had been a steady diminution of high-level CPSU-PDPA contacts, and an increasingly emphatic denial by the PDPA that it was socialist. (It was, said its ideologues, in the "national democratic" stage of development, with socialism only as an ultimate and rarely mentioned goal.) Nevertheless, in December 1986 Gorbachev and his ranking party colleagues invited seven of the eleven PDPA Politburo members to be their guests in Moscow, leaving the newly installed non-Communist false-front chief of state (Haji Mohammed Chamkani) behind. It was an unmistakable party-to-party summit meeting, one that explicitly equated their common ideological base.

It was not only an ideological blunder. Until that point, the Afghan adventure was not Gorbachev's responsibility. He had inherited it as an unwanted bequest from his predecessors, and there was no reason for him or his partially revamped top party organs to become personally associated with it. By inviting the PDPA's leaders to Moscow, he became politically linked with them and to some degree committed to their survival. The move is even harder to understand in the light of the deteriorating military situation in late 1986 following the resistance's deployment of Stinger antiaircraft missiles, and the ever-stronger indications that Moscow planned a military withdrawal.

One may only speculate why Gorbachev became involved. A possible explanation is that his KGB advisers wanted him to be committed to their cause of saving Afghanistan so that he would find it hard to refuse their future requests for support for that goal. As a possible selling point they had only to appeal to a politician's ego, suggesting that the reforms they were pushing through in Afghanistan would rouse so much opposition within the PDPA (especially from the Khalqis) that only a demonstrative show of CPSU ideological support would allow Najib to squeak through. In fact, of course, so hated was the Soviet Union among non-PDPA Afghans—the vast majority of the country—that a blessing from Gorbachev was likely to be the political kiss of death. As developments would show, the KGB soon came to hold this opinion if it did not already secretly believe it.

Shedding the Communist Image

Before the end of 1987, it became clear that the admission of the Moscow-Kabul association was something the KGB did not consider beneficial for the continued survival of the Kabul regime. This was reflected in an odd semantic revolution that swept over the country from 1987 to 1990 and purged the nation's institutions of most of their Marxist-Leninist outward trappings. Although two front organizations were retitled in May 1986 and January 1987 (the Democratic Organization of Afghan Women to the All-Afghanistan Women's Council, and the umbrella National Fatherland Front to the National Front, respectively), they may not have been part of this program; the "newspeak" only picked up momentum and became clearly a policy matter toward the end of 1987.

In October, coyly asserting he was acting at the behest of the Revolutionary Council, Najib himself set the pace by revising his own name to its more religious version, Najibullah, in conjunction with his campaign to present himself as a born-again Moslem. Soon he was being referred to in Afghan media as "Esteemed," not "Comrade," and by his state title of president, not PDPA general secretary. (The practice would spread more slowly among lesser officials, but by 1991 only Najmuddin Akhgar Kawiani, chief of the PDPA's International Department, was still being called "Comrade." His duties as liaison man for other Communist parties required the debased title.) The DRA itself became simply the Republic of Afghanistan (RA) in November 1987.

In the years that followed, the renaming of Afghan Communist institutions and the ostentatious turn away from traditional Marxism-Leninism gathered force. Newspapers, journals, front organizations, government branches, and even most of the make-believe opposition parties all received new labels, many of them reverting to pre-1978 names. Gone was the Revolutionary Council in 1988, to be replaced by a bicameral National Assembly. Political indoctrination courses at Kabul University were abruptly canceled in October 1988. Finally, in June 1990 the very PDPA itself, having held its first congress in 1965 to establish itself, held its second to commit formal suicide—at least in name. It became the Homeland party and its various branches, from cell through Central Committee, Secretariat, and Politburo—even general secretary—all received new, untainted tags.*

*The renaming phenomenon in countries that wish to shed the burden of their past without actually changing single-party rule can also be seen in such places as Burma, now called Myanmar, whose Burmese Socialist Programme party became the State Law and Order Restoration Council (SLORC).

While the renaming proceeded, official denials of the PDPA's socialist aspirations became more and more explicit. In 1988 Radio Kabul denied that the party was Marxist, and in 1990 Najib blandly asserted that "our party never pursued socialist or Communist objectives in the past," thus contradicting the original party constitution's proclaimed goal of carrying out "the practical experience of Marxism-Leninism." In general, however, the party preferred to go into eclipse plumage, releasing minimal information about its own doings and concentrating media coverage instead on the various branches of the state bureaucracy.

In line with this downplaying of the party's significance, there were also tentative experiments with installing various non-Communist chiefs of state (a relatively meaningless, figurehead position unless accompanied by a powerful party rank) following Karmal's departure from that office in late 1986. At first, as with Karmal, the title went with the chairmanship of the Revolutionary Council. Haji Mohammed Chamkani, a colorless front official, was Karmal's replacement, but within a year Najib demoted him and briefly took the position as his own. Later, in 1988, the job carried the title of prime minister and was held first by PDPA stalwart Sultan Ali Keshtmand, then by Hassan Sharq (notorious for his alleged collaboration with the KGB even before 1978 but never openly associated with the PDPA), again by Keshtmand, and finally by Fazl Haq Khaleqyar, an apparently genuine but undistinguished non-Communist who took over in May 1990. Like the renaming of institutions, however, the inauguration of non-Communist prime ministers failed to strengthen the regime's legitimacy.

Neither did Najib's exhortations to party activists to go forth and build contacts among the people so as to gain enough favor to win some possible future election. Those holding real power, first and foremost Najib himself, remained the same. Afghanistan had acquired a kind of Potemkin-village non-Communist false front, but except to the most politically blind the underlying red still showed through.

Oddly, there would be one last rejuvenation of the party image in the press. This occurred suddenly in May and June 1991, touched off by a Najib speech to Kabul city and province party activists (the very term *activist* had fallen into disuse until revived in this coverage). From that point until at least July, there was almost daily mention of the party and/or its youth group in the media. In mid-May a CPSU dclegation headed by Central Committee secretary Yury A. Manayenkov—the most prestigious CPSU visitation to Kabul since Najib came to power—arrived in Kabul amid media fanfare.

Though often repeating his supposed dedication to political pluralism, a free press, and other democratic ideals, Najib began laying renewed emphasis on party unity and discipline, "political vigilance," and other terms associated with a Stalinist approach. In the middle of this campaign, on June 20, Babrak Karmal was returned from his involuntary exile in the Soviet Union, where he had been sent in early 1987. Another exile, Sultan Ali Keshtmand (a former PDPA Politburo member and secretary, as well as a former prime minister), returned at about the same time. Neither, however, would play any political role for at least the balance of 1991.

It is most probable that this renewed emphasis on party loyalty and the return of the exiles was connected with the knowledge that Soviet military and financial aid to the Kabul regime was coming to an end, and that a final battle with the resistance might be looming. In such a case, all party resources had to be mobilized for the desperate struggle ahead. It is not impossible, however, that the Moscow coup already in preparation to unseat Gorbachev in August had some bearing on Afghanistan's muted re-Stalinization: Manayenkov would soon be one of those indicted for complicity in the failed plot, whose aim was to turn the Soviet clock back to 1984.

Party Disunity

If the KGB's efforts to increase the Kabul regime's legitimacy by shedding Communist labels had proven ineffective, they were no more successful in restoring party unity. Here again, the two goals were contradictory. For the rigidly Marxist-Leninist Khalqis, any resort to even pseudodemocracy was typically Parchamist right-wing deviationism, unworthy of any true believer. Moreover, by demoting and then exiling Karmal, the new regime had opened up a split within the Parchami ranks, with Karmalists now feuding with Najibists.

Against this backdrop, Najib's efforts to restore unity were futile. In 1986 and 1987, in addition to repeatedly trumpeting the need for closing ranks, he quietly freed some of the seventeen ranking Khalqis held incommunicado and under house arrest since 1980. The de facto chief of the Khalqi wing, Minister of Interior Gulabzoy, was promoted to alternate Politburo status in 1986 and a year later to full membership. Another Khalqi was given control of the party's Central Control Commission. But Najib moved cautiously, being sure not to cede too much power.

He obviously did not provide enough promotions to mollify the Khalqis nor display enough partisanship to satisfy hard-line Parchamis. Once the Soviet troops began their withdrawal in 1988, there were muffled indications that political crisis was following political crisis. In October 1988, Gulabzoy was unceremoniously bundled off to Moscow (some said at gunpoint) to be ambassador, apparently in the wake of a failed coup.

Coup Attempts in 1989–90

His removal did not solve the problem. There was one rumored coup attempt in the spring of 1989 and a second, sponsored by Minister of Defense Shahnawaz Tanai, followed in August. Najib at first tried conciliation, issuing four Central Committee memberships to previously arrested Khalqis in October. But Tanai tried again in December, and this time Najib responded with force, arresting 127 conspirators, among them 11 generals—but not Tanai. The stick, however, proved no more effective than the carrot, and in March 1990 Najib narrowly escaped death when Tanai launched the last and most determined Khalqi attempt, including an air attack on the presidential palace and an attempt by ground forces to seize the Ministry of Defense headquarters in Kabul.

The plot, which eventually resulted in the arrests of 623 acknowledged conspirators, included five of the fourteen Politburo members, five of the nineteen Supreme Defense Council members, and at least twenty-four PDPA Central Committee members. Like the two that preceded it, the coup attempt also involved the active connivance of the most radically religious, Pakistan-based resistance leader, Gulbuddin Hekmatyar, an alliance as outwardly unlikely as that between Hitler and Stalin a half century before. So improbable did Hekmatyar's association with Tanai seem that most observers did not credit the rumors of their cooperation that flew after the August and December 1989 attempts; only when Tanai escaped to join Hekmatyar and both acknowledged their prior association were all doubts removed.

Perhaps more peculiar than the Hekmatyar-Tanai link was the failure of Najib to visit any retribution on the Khalqis after the August attempt, and his failure to go for Tanai's jugular at least after the December

attempt. In both cases there was never any question about the Khalqis'—
and specifically Tanai's—responsibility; as recognized leader of the
Khalqi faction, he had to answer for all Khalqi behavior. Even in societies
with less dedication to revenge than the Afghan, unsuccessful efforts
to overthrow an existing government almost invariably turn out badly
for the conspirators. In old Afghan history, the least punishment a coup
plotter could expect was to have his eyes put out; into the third decade of this century, the more usual punishment was to be tied across
the mouth of Kabul's Noon Gun, whose daily boom signaled the midday
and, on occasion, the demise of some unfortunate who had taken
unsuccessful issue with the existing administration.

Possible KGB Link with Coups

Improbable as it might seem on the surface, there are reasons to consider the possibility that the KGB was promoting the Hekmatyar-Khalqi
alliance while restraining Najib's justifiable impulse to take vengeance
on his rivals.

Circumstantial evidence linking Hekmatyar to the KGB has mounted
over the years. In almost every report of internecine fighting among
resistance groups, Hekmatyar's Hezb-e-Islami is one of the participants.
Other resistance groups have accused him of deliberately avoiding combat
with Soviet forces; although one purported motivation for this was to
hoard arms for a final fight with other groups for power, there was
also an obvious benefit to the Soviets as well. In 1988, as the Soviets
were beginning their withdrawal, Hekmatyar's group invited the seven
leading subcommanders under resistance leader Ahmad Shah Massoud
to a parley on joint action, then ambushed and murdered them all. The
blow set back Massoud's strategic plans for destroying the central
government by at least two years.

It is probably an exaggeration to call Hekmatyar a KGB agent (he
is too much the loose cannon to take orders from anything but his own
ego), but he has proven himself capable of collaborating with anyone
who can further his dictatorial ambitions. Consistently anti-American,
he could be relied on to keep all Western influence out of Afghanistan if he were in power.

Looking at Afghanistan from Moscow's viewpoint in 1989, there
could have been few remaining hopes that the regime left behind by
the last departing Soviet troops in February would remain viable for

long. True, Najib had survived for the first few months and, thanks to an ongoing massive Soviet weapons airlift, including hundreds of Scud surface-to-surface missiles, had barely succeeded in defending Jalalabad against a combined resistance assault in the spring of that year. But the expenditure of Scuds could not be maintained (annual production in the USSR at that time was only four hundred, less than a third the number launched against the resistance from April to December 1989 alone), and the flow of other arms could not be maintained indefinitely.[6] Eventually Moscow would have to give up its expensive holding action.

When Najib and the PDPA went, as it seemed they must, the chances for some regime under heavy American influence being established seemed excellent. This was obviously a development Moscow wished to avoid. The best the USSR might hope for was some government that could appear anti-Soviet enough to satisfy the average Afghan, yet was under some degree of covert Soviet influence. Most importantly, it had to be genuinely and vehemently anti-American, dedicated to insulating Afghanistan from Western influence.

The unholy alliance of Hekmatyar and Tanai would have answered all these conditions, especially because the Khalqis, despite their socialist convictions, could have been portrayed as hating the Soviets for their partiality to the Parchamis. To bring Tanai and Hekmatyar together would have posed no problem for the KGB. Deterring Najib from taking revenge on Tanai after the August and December attempts would have been much harder but could have been justified to him on the grounds that the PDPA could not afford an open schism, which executing Tanai would surely have provoked.

Only after the failure of the March 1990 attempt, which had involved the Khalqis' open resort to arms and purposeful efforts to kill Najib, would there have been no longer any possibility of pursuing this approach. At that point the only recourse for the Soviets was to fall back on their existing relationship with Najib, weak though he must have seemed to them at that time.

Aftermath of the Coup

The successful rebuff of the Tanai attempt thinned out top-level Khalqi ranks as no other preceding event had. It enabled Najib to push through the renaming of the PDPA (until then bitterly opposed by Khalqis), and it gave at least some temporary surface calm to the normally seething subsurface strife among Afghan Communists. But nowhere in the world is the Maoist dictum that power grows out of a gun barrel truer than in Afghanistan, and the Khalqis, though deprived of their most important state and party positions, still controlled an impressive armory in their traditional strongholds of the army and uniformed police.

At the dawn of 1992, stability was as remote as ever from Afghan politics. Though the KGB's traditional cloak of secrecy had preserved it from praise or blame for propping up Najib's tottery political redoubt, the KGB had kept its clients in power for longer than almost anyone had thought possible. To the extent the redoubt was still standing, the KGB in Afghanistan had succeeded in preserving what the party and military had been on the point of losing. But in the writhing segments of Moscow's by-then dissected empire, that fact was no longer of any great consequence, for thanks in part to Afghanistan the KGB, like the CPSU and the military, had failed signally where it counted most, at home.

Part II: Inside the USSR

Afghan Echoes in the KGB

The cumulative indirect impact on the KGB of its failure in Afghanistan was devastating because of one internal and two external factors. The external factors were the rearrangement of alliances within the ruling oligarchy on the one hand and the slow evolution of Soviet society as a whole on the other. The internal factor was the eventual collapse of internal KGB discipline. Of these, the evolution of society, spurred on by the worldwide communications revolution, was the most critical, just as it was with the CPSU at the same time.

In opposition to these forces, the survival strength of the KGB was impressive. It had a guaranteed place of privilege in the highest councils; the inherited aura of merciless terror, omniscience, and omnipotence that still remained from Stalin's day; the experience in controlling and warping information at home and abroad in the broader interests of the empire but also for its own institutional interests; and the physical means to enforce its will.

Gorbachev and the KGB

As Andropov's protégé, Gorbachev had had a close and long-standing association with the KGB, and it was unquestionably with that organization's assistance that he was able to beat back the military challenge when vying with Romanov for the general secretary's post in 1984–85. The KGB did not go unrewarded for its support. Within a month of Gorbachev's accession to power, KGB chief Viktor Chebrikov became a full Politburo member. A year later he delivered an aggressive, propolice speech at the twenty-seventh party congress, the first time since 1961 that a KGB chief had addressed such a body, and the party program adopted at the congress for the first time made pointed references to safeguarding state security.[7]

This should have been interpreted, however, as a sign not only of KGB strength but of KGB concern. In 1961 the twenty-second party congress had revealed even more damning information about Stalin (and by implication about the secret police) than had come out in the better-known twentieth party congress of 1956, where Khrushchev gave his famous "secret speech." The KGB show of force at that time was doubtless intended to make sure everyone understood there would be no lessening of the institution's importance. Probably the same considerations, prompted by the destabilizing potential of Gorbachev's revolutionary reforms, led to Chebrikov's being given the honor in 1986.

It was also at that congress, moreover, that Gorbachev made headlines by referring to Afghanistan as a "bleeding wound." The term clearly implied a need for healing, and the KGB, as the institution to which responsibility for Afghanistan was being transferred, was the designated doctor. Unlike the military in 1982, it most likely did not welcome the task of curing a patient who by then was probably considered terminal.

The Soviet public during this stage was largely quiescent. The KGB's relentless persecution of the small, courageous dissident movement during the 1960s and 1970s had taken a quantum jump after the invasion of Afghanistan. Andrei Sakharov had been sent into internal exile at Gorky for criticizing the invasion, and human rights groups in various major cities had disbanded. Nevertheless, as we have seen, dissent was still there, and it was still active, but in the odd ways dictated by the odd environment.

In a public relations campaign of self-glorification that had begun
in the 1920s, the KGB, often sonorously called the "organs of state
security" (or simply "organs" for short) by 1977 could point to some
2,000 books and countless shorter works extolling the service and its
officers. Between 1984 and 1987 alone, 250 new books were published,
and prizes continued to be offered for the best creative arts produc-
tions centered on the organs. (Some authors went to Orwellian extremes
to sell the message: in one fictional work from the 1970s a KGB officer,
asked his opinion of the most important quality for a Chekist, replies
after serious thought, "the most important thing—is to love people."[8])

The previous outpouring of literature was clearly inadequate, however, for in November 1987, in response to a KGB memorandum setting
forth a plan to improve its image, the Politburo passed a resolution
recommending *glasnost* for the agency. By 1990, more than five thousand
articles on the history of the police were being written annually.[9]

Within the KGB, there were no obvious signs of dissent through
the mid-1980s, although there were indirect signs aplenty. In 1983,
France's President Mitterrand had expelled forty-seven Soviet offi-
cers from various diplomatic and trade establishments in his country.
He did not reveal how these had been identified, but it was later re-
vealed that the French external intelligence service had doubled a ranking
KGB officer engaged in scientific and technical operations, Vladimir
I. Vetrov, code-named Farewell, who was subsequently shot.[10] In August
1985, Vitaly Yurchenko, the supposedly fifth-ranked officer in the whole
KGB service, defected to the Americans in Rome. The following month
Oleg Gordievskiy, the top KGB man in England, defected to the British,
who revealed he had been working for their service for many years.

For the new Soviet leadership, the defectors were not the only
embarrassment. In 1985 about fifty Soviet diplomats were expelled from
various countries around the world for spying, and in 1986 the United
States alone expelled eighty. For all the valuable data that the spies
were gathering, they were posing a serious image problem for a traditionally prestige-hungry Soviet Union. Gorbachev's initial reaction
was to stonewall the West by expelling exactly as many diplomats from
each country as that country had expelled Soviet officers, but this soon
proved impractical as there were too few diplomats from some of the
smaller countries to match their expulsions of Soviets. As Gorbachev
staked more and more of his personal prestige on settling problems

with the West, his sensitivity to KGB misdeeds—at least to those that blundered into the open—must have sharpened, although he did not reveal any such thoughts to the outside world.

The Soviet Union's broad masses also held their opinions to themselves at this time. Popular fear and loathing were far more prevalent than the in-house doubts or the leadership embarrassment, but were so carefully camouflaged that only a few foolhardy dissidents dared to express them, and these were silenced with increasing severity.

Cracks Appear—1987

By the end of 1986, a clear conflict was developing between Gorbachev and Chebrikov. The former's reform programs, especially *glasnost,* were undercutting the KGB's mission of maintaining political control over the country. Like many of his ranking party colleagues, Chebrikov, whose KGB background was in domestic operations and personnel, was not a man inclined to liberal thinking.

This alone would have soured relations between the two men, but it is also possible that the visit of the Afghan Communist notables to Moscow in December 1986 had left Gorbachev unhappy with the diminished prospects of a positive solution to his Afghan problem. Expert politician that he was, he may have seen through Najib's crude bombast and felt he had been misled by the high assessment of the Afghan leader that his KGB advisers had doubtless given him.

December 1986 also saw Gorbachev's release of Andrei Sakharov and his wife from their internal exile in Gorky. In one respect this was a public relations plus for the KGB, which was finally freed of the unceasing international rebukes over its persecution of the famous physicist. But domestically the Sakharovs' liberation was also perceived as a loss of police authority and thus a most serious development. For the KGB, popular contempt was a much more dangerous adversary than popular hatred.

Almost immediately, the KGB image suffered another jolt. In January 1987, following revelations that its Ukraine office had arrested a muckraking journalist on false charges, Chebrikov released an unprecedented announcement in *Pravda* that the responsible officials had been disciplined. One can only speculate how much pressure Gorbachev (for only he could have done it) had to exert on the hard-bitten old Chekist to make him destroy the myth of KGB infallibility by such an act.

Over succeeding months the gap between Chebrikov and other conservatives on the one hand and Gorbachev and his liberals on the other continued to widen. In September and again in December 1987 Chebrikov gave rousing speeches to senior party, police, and security officials in which he laid out his concern with the pace and extent of reform. He made it clear that he agreed with *perestroyka*—how else could the Soviet Union remain competitive if it did not reform—but in unbridled *glasnost* he correctly perceived a threat to the very structure of the state.

Chebrikov did not confine himself to words. In December 1987, plainclothes KGB officers disguised as "peace demonstrators" broke up a Jewish rally in Moscow. Others, making no secret of their police role, used strong-arm methods in apprehending U.S. newsmen covering the demonstration. This was just before a Gorbachev summit meeting with President Reagan. The attack on the newsmen provoked the expected U.S. protest, but if summit sabotage had been the intent, it failed; Gorbachev came home with solid success to report.

Cracking the Information Monopoly—1988

On return, he had more than one reason to call Chebrikov on the carpet. In August 1987 Gorbachev had angrily demanded that U.S. Secretary of State George Schultz retract an "unfriendly" State Department booklet that gave details about the wild stories and forged documents that the KGB was creating and spreading to discredit the United States—disinformation, to use the KGB's own term. At the time, Gorbachev obviously believed the booklet itself was disinformation, but between August and his December meeting with Reagan he must have learned that it was accurate. He informed the president that he had given orders for "no more lies, no more disinformation." Nevertheless, beginning in January and on into 1988 several old stories (e.g., that the United States was working on an "ethnic" weapon that would kill only those with dark skins, and that the AIDS virus had been developed in U.S. bacteriological warfare laboratories) were again being busily played in Soviet official and secret outlets.

This apparent disobedience of Gorbachev's orders was one of several signs that the KGB lacked the flexibility to accept the loss of their informational monopoly. In April, Chebrikov made himself and his service look foolish by accusing "Western secret services" of causing ethnic unrest in the Soviet Union, a charge reminiscent of Stalin-era paranoia. The release during the summer of a promotional film hailing KGB activities was ludicrously ineffectual.

Meanwhile, the informational dam was leaking on all sides. In June, written history examinations were canceled in Soviet high schools with the frank acknowledgment that the courses and texts that went with them had been based largely on lies. The USSR's chief cartographer wrote openly that the KGB had falsified virtually all public maps for the past fifty years in a vain attempt to mislead the West. Economists and scholars complained that excessive secrecy had crippled their ability to develop sensible policies. In September, the KGB role in unseating Khrushchev, who was now being posthumously rehabilitated for his 1950s reform efforts, was revealed for the first time in *Literaturnaya Gazeta,* formerly a frequent outlet for hard-line propaganda.

The key to the informational hemorrhage was the dawning realization among Soviet citizens that they were no longer subject to arrest for expressing themselves, at least in the larger cities; in 1987–88 there were no such arrests reported in Moscow or Leningrad. The KGB might use other methods, as revealed by the anti-Semitic "peace demonstrators," but the playing field was becoming more level, and the inner dissidence that fear had repressed for so many years in so many people gradually became a conscious if still undemonstrative opposition.

An important sign of the times in 1988 was the destruction of the Pavlik Morozov myth. Ever since the 1930s, young children had been required to honor the thirteen-year-old Pavlik for having informed the authorities that his father was helping rich peasants (kulaks), and for the youth's subsequent martyrdom at the hands of those who sympathized with his father. In a long overdue reevaluation, the March issue of the magazine *Yunost* (Youth) described the boy as a "symbol of . . . legalized and romanticized treachery." In destroying Pavlik's aura of virtue, the magazine also undercut the main moral justification for informing, traditionally the mainstay of KGB domestic operations.

No sooner had the Morozov myth been destroyed than a much more important idol was threatened. In June, the mass-circulation *Novy Mir* revealed to the Soviet public for the first time that the previously untouchable Lenin had personally authorized and encouraged the use of terror, and that his precedent had set the stage for Felix Dzerzhinskiy, founder of the Cheka (KGB) to expand terror in all directions. The article did more than destroy Lenin's aura of total virtue and infallibility. If the philosophical import of the Morozov debunking had been to undercut the informant system, that of *Novy Mir*'s revelations was to challenge Lenin's contemptuous rejection of legal processes as the foundation of society. The rule of law would be fatal for the KGB's unacknowledged but consistent and rarely challenged practice of ignoring the law whenever its purposes required—which was most of the time. (Some years before, confronted by an unusual dissident who demanded his legal rights, a KGB interrogator is supposed to have replied with a look of pain, "Please—we're having a serious conversation."[11])

But pending the imposition of legal restraints, the most ominous threat to the KGB was the first open critique from within its own ranks. In September 1988 Vladimir Rubanov, then described merely as a "department head of a KGB institute," bluntly stated that the KGB's obsessive secrecy and control of information served only to preserve the myth of the infallibility of the bureaucracy and was being used "irresponsibly and uncontrollably in the narrow interests of small groups of people." The KGB reputation for internal discipline was so firm that those reporting the story in the West postulated that Rubanov was acting on orders, and that the KGB was possibly using an unconventional means of revealing a new policy.[12] Nothing could have been further from the truth; as the West learned only later, Rubanov was fired outright for his criticism.

Paradoxically, however, the KGB as an institution continued to enjoy silent support from a perhaps unexpected quarter. Although Chebrikov openly censured his leader's policies (and hence, by implication, their author), Gorbachev himself did not join in the rising anti-KGB chorus. He never criticized the KGB publicly. It may not have been his ideal pillar, but he still recognized it as a valuable if not crucial one for maintaining himself in power.

The KGB was especially needed to control the virulent epidemic of minority nationalism that was sweeping through the borderland republics. But even if the service as a whole was a vital element in keeping things under control in the republics—and here there were no restraints on the use of force—their chief was expendable. Following Gorbachev's 1988 late-summer vacation, Chebrikov was transferred out of the KGB, but without losing his Politburo seat. In strictly party terms, his new appointment was a promotion because he now became a member of the exclusive CPSU Central Committee Secretariat as well. Moreover, his new duties were not calculated to inspire confidence among reformers; Gorbachev made him chief of a newly established party commission on legal reform, thus in effect setting the fox to watch the henhouse.

In retrospect, however, a case can be made that Gorbachev was acting just as Babrak Karmal had when he promoted Khalqis in the party apparat while simultaneously downgrading them in the newly important state apparat. Gorbachev, too, was outflanking his conservative party opposition by increasing the relative importance of state organs, and it would be logical to promote Chebrikov to the pinnacles of party power while simultaneously undermining that pinnacle's base. If this interpretation is correct, it was a rich irony, for Chebrikov was thereby made a victim of the strategem invented by his own service to sidetrack potential Afghan troublemakers.

Within ten days of Chebrikov's ouster from the KGB in September 1988, there was a new Soviet–United States agreement to stop the spread of Soviet-inspired disinformation. Like its predecessor, however, this agreement would soon be honored in the breach, a breach that should not have been too surprising, for the man who had overseen the disinformation program for many years was Vladimir Kryuchkov, Chebrikov's replacement as KGB chief.

The Kryuchkov Period—1988–91

Another longtime KGB professional, Kryuchkov was chief of the First Chief Directorate, responsible for foreign operations, including "active measures," a part of which is disinformation. According to Oleg Gordievskiy, England's top-ranking double agent in the KGB, Kryuchkov was "an enthusiastic supporter of active measures, with . . . an exaggerated faith in their effectiveness."[13] Gorbachev appointed Kryuchkov head of the KGB over two more-senior deputies, apparently in an effort to steer internal security away from its traditional, now discredited focus on ideological deviation, while at the same time maintaining the flow of valuable intelligence from abroad. He also wanted to install someone whom he personally trusted.

In 1956, Kryuchkov had been an embassy third secretary under Ambassador Andropov in Hungary and had taken part in the false negotiations that led to the arrest and execution of Imre Nagy. Almost as suave, deceptive, ruthless, and ambitious as Andropov himself, Kryuchkov became another Andropov protégé, and when Andropov took over the KGB in 1967, he brought Kryuchkov with him. Given Gorbachev's own close relation with Andropov, the two men had probably known each other for years. In the end, Gorbachev would pay the penalty for trusting him too far.

When Kryuchkov took over the KGB, the Soviet retreat from Afghanistan was half completed as the world looked on approvingly. But even as Moscow's image abroad improved, domestically the Afghan albatross still hung heavy around the Soviet neck. The cost of keeping Najib in power with arms, fuel, and food would continue at the equivalent of several hundred million dollars per month, money the staggering Soviet economy could ill afford. It was not a burden that Moscow could carry indefinitely, but the KGB, like the CPSU and the military before it, failed to find a face-saving solution.

Had it been able to solve the Afghan problem, the KGB would have emerged with a stronger mandate at home. As it was, Gorbachev still did not turn on the service, but neither did he endorse it openly. Behind the scenes, the organs had solid support. Their massive program of building new installations in most big cities continued unabated, Kryuchkov was given more deputies than any of his predecessors, and all KGB personnel would receive a fat pay raise in January 1990. Nevertheless, the organizational image was suffering.[14]

Faced with a public that in the first two months of 1989 was not merely criticizing but ridiculing the KGB and demanding cuts in its personnel, Kryuchkov responded by publishing a monthly journal, *Informatsionnyi Byulleten KGB SSSR* (Information Bulletin of the USSR KGB), a limited-circulation but unclassified periodical that seemed intended to promote *glasnost* both inside and outside the service. This supplemented regular KGB columns in other journals and frequent speeches and interviews by ranking KGB officers, measures Kryuchkov had also introduced. But the basic aim was still *controlled* candor, as shown by the renewed jamming of Radio Liberty in March 1989, a form of information quarantine that had been lifted shortly after Kryuchkov became KGB chief.

In April Kryuchkov's public standing shrank again when special troops believed to be under KGB command attacked nationalist demonstrators in the Georgian capital of Tbilisi with sharpened entrenching tools and toxic agents, causing numerous casualties and at least sixteen fatalities. Although no proof was forthcoming, there was widespread suspicion, later confirmed, that the riot control forces were under the command of the KGB.

At this point the former director of disinformation widened his own version of *glasnost*. Using the tame "dissident" historian Roy Medvedev,* he released new statistics on Stalin's crimes against the people: some thirty-six million were said to have been "repressed," a term that encompassed both those executed and those sent to prison or labor camps (but did not include the millions who perished from the artificially induced famines of the early 1930s). By not listing deaths specifically, this admission was probably designed to leave the door open for a later, milder reinterpretation of the term if necessary.

In May 1989 Kryuchkov, under the headline "The KGB and Glasnost" in the government paper *Izvestiya,* promised to inform the people about "all important operations carried out by our service," a promise so transparently false as to be ludicrous. This announcement followed closely on the heels of the published results of an alleged poll showing that the KGB was favored by the public ahead of twenty-two other selected Soviet institutions, outpacing not only the CPSU Central Committee but even the prestigious Academy of Sciences.[15] Articles attributed to KGB officers began to appear, lauding the service and darkly hinting that the proreform Democratic Union then gaining momentum in parliament was all a conspiracy hatched by imperialist intelligence services.[16]

The alleged poll itself may well have been a piece of internal KGB disinformation. Public feeling against the organs was running high, not only because of the widely held belief that the KGB had been involved

---

*Medvedev is a quasi liberal who only after the conclusive defeat of communism became an outright critic of the system. While criticizing Stalin and secret police excesses under Beria, for example, he defended collectivization and other harsh measures taken by the state. He would occasionally receive a figurative slap on the hand from the authorities, but these looked suspiciously like gestures designed merely to improve his credibility as a dissident. He was probably chosen to release the KGB victim figures both because he could be trusted not to ask embarrassing follow-up questions and to reinforce his credibility.

in the Tbilisi atrocity but because of documentary reports of the organization's previous misdeeds. These included March reports that mass graves of 1930s victims had been discovered in Byelorussia with the unmistakable KGB signature, a single bullet hole in the back of the skull.[17]

A better indication of what people thought of the KGB was provided in a speech by an elected member of the Congress of Peoples Deputies in the Kremlin on May 31. In a blistering indictment of the secret police, Yury P. Vlasov stated that "in conflicts with the KGB the truth cannot be found, and it is dangerous to look for it . . . Alleged psychiatric abnormality can still threaten people who are dangerous for the apparatus" and "the KGB is not a service but a real underground empire."[18]

At the end of the summer, Chebrikov was replaced on the Politburo by Kryuchkov, and another old-time KGB collaborator, Nikolay Talyzin (who as minister of communications helped pave the way for the invasion of Afghanistan—see chapter 6), was also dropped. Public criticism of the service now began to trace its misbehavior back to the time of the heretofore idealized Andropov, who was accused of corruption and other shortcomings by another ex-KGB chief, Vladimir Y. Semichastnyy.

The autumn and early winter of 1989 was a time of vast upheaval as the Soviet Empire in Eastern Europe crumbled and imploded. Within the USSR contradictory currents swirled. In late October, following Moscow's admission that its invasion of Afghanistan had been illegal and immoral and its confession of deliberate violations of the antiballistic missile treaty, a war powers act was drafted to prevent further commitment of military forces without parliamentary approval. In November, a 10 percent cut in KGB personnel keeping watch over the army was announced.

But at the same time, the government forcibly canceled a live television broadcast of a show about Afghanistan, featuring Andrei Sakharov and using taped interviews with Afghan resistance leaders. Just hours before show time, police descended on the studio to enforce the ban. The right of party leaders to fire editors (as Gorbachev had just done with an individual who displeased him) was reaffirmed. In December, a journalist in Sverdlovsk (now restored to its prerevolutionary name of Yekaterinburg) was arrested for "slandering" the KGB.

In 1990, the party/state apparatus, and particularly the KGB, resorted to threats and political maneuvering and to such less-blatant informational weapons as deception and public relations. Already in August 1989, in a vintage piece of Kryuchkov deception, the old Fifth Chief Directorate (responsible for monitoring and controlling ideological dissidence) was abolished and replaced with a "Directorate for the Protection of the Constitution," which in effect had precisely the same duties, though it was described as designed to protect human rights.

The agency also made intensive efforts to divert public attention from its less acceptable activities by focusing on its fight against organized crime, corruption, industrial polluters, and drug traffickers instead of ideological offenders. (Even here, however, the old Stalinist paranoia died hard; one Chekist, speaking of those in high places responsible for pollution, wrote, "Somebody made these decisions. And who can prove to me that this someone made these decisions without intending to harm Soviet power, to discredit socialism? No one will prove this to me.")[19]

It was about this time that Kryuchkov is reported to have set up his own private disinformation service, the "Information and Analysis Directorate" (IAU), ostensibly designed to monitor grass-roots public opinion via the KGB's mammoth domestic network of agents and informants. Instituted at Kryuchkov's direction by Valery Lebedev, a former member of the Fifth Chief Directorate, the IAU was supposed to condense the avalanche of information that came in daily through KGB channels, and from it to derive a picture of public opinion that could then be used by policymakers.[20] The more probable reason for the IAU's existence, however, was to counteract the ever more widely publicized product of such independent organizations as the Institute of Public Opinion, whose findings were proving so devastating to many Soviet institutions, not least the KGB.

Given Lebedev's background in antidissident operations—not a field conducive to liberal thinking—there was a built-in incentive from the lowest to the highest level to slant information in a manner pleasing to the conservative view. With Lebedev and Kryuchkov as the final lenses through which the information had to pass before being viewed by Gorbachev, the already remote likelihood of the president receiving an objective picture from this source was reduced still further. The disgruntled KGB officer who described the IAU noted Gorbachev's use of such key KGB buzzwords as "extremists," "antisocial groups," and "nationalists" as evidence of his reliance on KGB materials.[21]*

In the spring of 1990, recognizing the growing role of the state, the KGB launched a massive campaign to get its own officers elected at all levels in the countrywide elections. It not only created special task forces to influence public opinion but set up special training courses for the candidates. As a result, some 2,756 KGB candidates won seats in the republican and local soviets. Although no figures were released on the total number who ran, the indications were that the sophisticated campaign paid off with better than 50 percent success in most areas and over 90 percent in the central Asian republics of Uzbekistan and Kirghizia.[22]

In April 1990, after formal control of the KGB was vested in the Soviet parliament, Kryuchkov paid lip service to the power of the state system when he asserted that "day-to-day direction of KGB activities" was the responsibility of the USSR president and government. This claim was probably designed to make more palatable a draft law to be put before the Supreme Soviet on the KGB's future responsibilities, but it was scarcely credible. The proposed law, which the KGB itself had written, included the right to coordinate and control the activities of the armed forces, MVD troops, and other armed units in matters of state security, and it specified that the service would supervise itself.

The Supreme Soviet was not impressed with these suggestions, which would have put into law many of the powers the KGB already enjoyed, and added a few more. Those delegates who were not party members recalled that in January the KGB had issued dire warnings about its readiness to step in and save socialism at whatever cost, again raising the specter that unnamed foreign intelligence services were exploiting *glasnost* and *perestroyka* in an effort to bring down the Soviet system. These same delegates became even less comfortable when Kryuchkov gave a speech in June saying that he was all for multiparty democracy in the USSR, but the KGB would remain committed to commu-

---

*Interestingly, these were also the standard negative terms that Najib employed frequently during this time to describe the resistance.

nism. A week after his speech, striking miners echoed a demand of most other democratic groups that the KGB and armed forces be depoliticized.[23]

Possibly anticipating these negative reactions, a renewed and intensified public relations campaign in favor of the KGB and denigrating opposing security services got under way in May. In multiple items in major media outlets that month, the hero image of the Chekist, his moral purity, the absence of nepotism in the service, and other alleged KGB virtues were extolled, sometimes set against the contrasting alleged villainies of Western intelligence services. As part of its face-lift, the KGB opened a public relations office on the third floor of its notorious Lyubyanka headquarters on Moscow's Dzerzhinskiy Square.

Whatever success the public relations campaign might have had, it was undercut by an authoritative source before it was fairly launched. On June 20, Gen. Oleg Kalugin, formerly second in command in the KGB's Washington office and former chief of its foreign counterintelligence branch, blew the whistle on high-level KGB corruption, abuse of power, and deliberate falsification of intelligence that amounted to betrayal of its basic mission. He derided the "new face" that Kryuchkov had crafted for the agency, asserting that it only masked a reality that had not changed in the past fifty years.

Thrown on the defensive, the KGB reeled as other "internal defectors" from its ranks stepped forward with their own stories. One, an anonymous colonel, gave a most comprehensive indictment of the organization as a whole and of Andropov personally, blaming him as the main instigator of the Soviet invasions of Hungary, Czechoslovakia, and Afghanistan. Both he and Kalugin accused Andropov of having blocked key intelligence reports that might have deterred the invasions of Czechoslovakia and Afghanistan. The colonel then detailed many of the charges of corruption, nepotism, and embezzlement that the May public relations campaign had gone to such pains to deny.[24]

Another renegade, retired Col. Yaroslav V. Karpovich, who had been a KGB plant in a Russian anti-Soviet émigré group called the National Labor Alliance (NTS), had an interview with a Soviet journalist that showed he had fallen victim to his opponents' democratic principles. Again accusing the KGB of warping reporting to suit the political needs of the moment, Karpovich put his finger on a fundamental KGB vulnerability. "By exerting colossal efforts to protect ideology and not the state, the KGB even today is failing to fulfill its basic function," he asserted.[25]

The loss of KGB face was alarming even to Gorbachev. At the June party plenum meeting, he gave a rare, indirect endorsement of the service by deploring the public's "lack of confidence" in law-enforcement organs and asking the party to help rebuff pressures against them. He even spoke of having increased their strength and pay, moves he said had met with public understanding.[26]

Like other leading government figures (except Gorbachev himself), Kryuchkov lost his Politburo seat at this meeting. In previous eras this probably would have indicated a politically fatal fall from grace, but such were the times that the move said more for the decline of the party than for the decline of Mr. Kryuchkov or his organization. He kept his seat on the presidential council, which had become the key locus of power.

In October, by hailing KGB border troops' heroics in Afghanistan and boasting that they had not suffered a single desertion, the KGB seemed to be resurrecting a Kiplingesque approach that other Soviet propagandists had long since abandoned. Meanwhile, it also opened a museum at KGB headquarters, but the effectiveness of this ploy could only be described as marginal. The main figure in a film shown to those attending the grand opening was a Colonel Prelin, who confessed shyly to being a poet in his spare time, and who marveled that the prison porridge was superior even to his wife's. Neither claim added much luster or dignity to the KGB image. The museum also had to vie for public attention with a large stone from a prison camp that citizens left outside the headquarters building in memory of prisoners who had perished at the hands of the organs.

The public relations campaign, which continued through 1990, reached its farcical peak when a curvaceous brunette, her torso fetchingly twisted, was pictured in *Komsomolskaya Pravda* donning a bulletproof vest after being crowned Miss KGB of 1990. The ghost of the ascetic Felix Dzerzhinskiy must have writhed.[27]

In 1991, there were new revelations of KGB misdeeds, including a Bulgarian charge that the KGB had provided the murder weapon for a successful Bulgarian intelligence service assassination of an émigré propagandist (Georgy Markov) in London in 1978. Although KGB complicity in this murder had been widely assumed in the West, its confirmation by the Bulgarians was particularly upsetting to the KGB, which reacted by floating the story that it had really been Western counterintelligence that had killed Markov.

The public relations campaign might have been going badly, but as Gorbachev swung more and more toward the conservatives at the end of 1990, the KGB's real power was slated to increase. Television censorship, last seen with the cancelation of the Afghanistan program in 1989, was resumed when Eduard Shevardnadze was banned from explaining why he had resigned as foreign minister. (His warning at that time that the Soviet Union was headed toward a reactionary coup was prophetic.)

The KGB also appeared to be involved in internal political action, in the form of support for a so-called Centrist Bloc of Political Parties and Movements, a vague organization made up of minuscule or nonexistent parties and groups, whose two leaders were known mainly as eccentrics. Courtesy of its access to the main CPSU press center, its meetings with Kryuchkov and other hard-liners, and its frequent mentions in party-controlled media outlets, the bloc was quickly pegged as a KGB false-front operation. It was suspiciously reminiscent of an Afghan development, Najib's bloc of "leftist and democratic organizations" that first appeared in 1986.

More ominously, the subordination of some army units returning from Germany was reported to have shifted from the general staff to the KGB, among them the 103d Guards Airborne Division. In January 1991, Gorbachev decreed new sweeping powers for the KGB to combat economic sabotage and control domestic and foreign private businesses. The suppression of nationalism in the Baltic states became murderous, with bloody attacks on the Lithuanian television studio and Latvian Ministry of the Interior headquarters. The attacks were rationalized in part on the basis of documents allegedly authored by ultra-nationalist Lithuanians (but written for some odd reason in Russian) that threatened CPSU members with extermination. Later, a faked documentary of the attack was produced to put the blame on the victims. Domestic disinformation was back in style.

Boris Pugo, the former chief of the KGB in Latvia, was made USSR minister of interior, replacing the reformer Vadim V. Bakatin. In January 1991, a Kremlin decree authorized joint military-police street patrols in major cities. The KGB was not mentioned, but it almost certainly had ultimate responsibility for this activity, even though the draft law of the previous year was still stalled in parliament. In February, the uniformed police and KGB were ordered to collaborate to fight organized crime, drug dealing, and corruption, and Pugo was promoted to colonel general. His contemptuous dismissal of the Moscow police chief, who in January had been elected by a city council vote of 281 to 5, was indicative of the increasingly centralized police power.

The KGB's increased authority was accompanied by a sudden spurt in propaganda about alien menaces. In December 1990, a hard-line activist told the army journal *Red Star* that the CIA was conspiring with dissidents to dismember the USSR by forming a Baltic–Black Sea confederation. Kryuchkov accused the United States of delivering "impure and sometimes infected grain, as well as products with an above-average level of radioactivity or containing harmful chemical mixtures."[28] A spy mania took hold, with the West accused of trying to steal Soviet economic (!) and technological secrets. The Germans were allegedly trying to subvert labor unions in Leningrad. Kryuchkov announced in March that seven out of sixteen KGB defectors since 1975 had been apprehended, and of these six had been shot. Western arms control inspectors were accused of conducting espionage. By June, Kryuchkov was asserting that U.S. promises of aid were partly illusion, partly a devilish plot to break up Soviet society and disorganize the Soviet economy, a line that continued to be played through July.

Nevertheless, the spring of 1991 still saw a great deal of free expression. The KGB law was finally passed on May 16, and *Novoye Vremya*, while lauding the legalization of what the service was doing anyway, deplored the broadness of the powers it was given. Two weeks later, the journal demanded that Kryuchkov resign. This boldness of expression was a reflection of Gorbachev's own swing away from the hard-liners and his renewed support for the liberals. Thus, the paranoid KGB propaganda lines could have been interpreted in part as a somewhat panicky reaction as the organs saw their power slipping away.

The real significance of the antiforeign theme, however, would only become clear in August, when the ill-fated coup against Gorbachev briefly brought the leading party and state old guard to power. The line had been designed to mobilize advance public support for the plotters by exploiting traditional Russian fears of external aggression, the same kind of xenophobia that had proven so effective in justifying Stalin's purges of the 1930s. By laying all the nation's woes at the doorstep of the external enemy, the plotters absolved themselves of responsibility for the nation's ills and set the stage for a return to complete despotism. In the process, however, they also destroyed their own credibility, not only among outspoken liberals outside their control but, more fatefully, within the ranks of their own organizations.

The false propaganda widened the rift between the upper levels of the military and KGB and their middle-level subordinates. This became clear when, in the aftermath of the coup, the new minister of defense, Marshal Yevgeniy Shaposhnikov, announced that 80 percent of the ministry's top brass (including all first deputy and deputy ministers) would be replaced. This implied that the coup had had 80 percent support at that level, but it obviously enjoyed no such popularity at subordinate levels, where key units, such as the Taman Motorized Rifle Division, the 106th Airborne Division, and the Kantemirov Tank Division all reportedly refused orders to attack Boris Yeltsin in the Russian White House. Shaposhnikov himself, who was then an air force general, threatened to scramble his fighters to down the army helicopters the coup leaders were planning to use in the attack.[29]

Within the KGB ranks discipline was also dissolving; according to one disgruntled officer, from October 1990 onward the service was losing young officers at the rate of up to six hundred per month. The critically important Group A (also known as Group Alpha), the same unit that under Colonel Boyarinov had assassinated Hafizullah Amin in 1979 and in January 1991 had been the key unit in the lethal attack on the Lithuanian television station, was ordered to storm the White House. Its commander refused to do so, less from humanitarian motives as he later claimed (they had not been in evidence in the Vilnius assault) than because he had only 30 men of his 150-man unit available in Moscow. In the absence of army units to spearhead the assault and faced with the angry crowds defending the White House, he had powerful disincentives for the action. Nevertheless, this was the first time that Group A had ever refused an order since the unit was formed in 1974.[30]

For the military, the mutinous refusal by key commanders to obey orders was the most critical development of all. But for the KGB, important though Group A's disobedience had been, something even more significant was at stake. The IAU, as an intelligence unit, always cooperated closely with the operational unit in Department Z (formerly the Fifth Chief Directorate) responsible for clandestine aspects of molding public opinion. Just as had happened in Afghanistan, the mixture of operational responsibility proved fatally contaminating for intelligence objectivity.

Vladimir Kryuchkov would eventually stand accused—probably correctly—of having masterminded the whole coup plot. He certainly must have had responsibility for informing his coplotters about how the citizenry at large would react to the coup and about their willingness or unwillingness to act on the basis of their convictions. He also had responsibility for assessing the reliability of both his own and the military's units. He was hopelessly wrong on all counts.

And herein lay the ultimate poetic justice. Kryuchkov, the man with the final responsibility for protecting and promoting the official lie and simultaneously for knowing and hoarding the objective truth, must have fallen victim to his own disinformation. Just as the IAU, under Kryuchkov's guidance, had misinformed Gorbachev concerning grassroots support for a hard ideological line (did they use the term *silent majority?*), so it must have continued with the same slanted reporting when what its leader needed above all else was truly objective reporting.

The debacle of the August coup brought down the Soviet Union. As a minor sideshow it also led to the final unmasking of Vladimir Kryuchkov, whose only regret, as he would subsequently frankly admit, was not having arranged things better. For once, the devotee of disinformation could be taken at his word.

NOTES

1. For an expansion of this and the following section, see Arnold, "Parallels and Divergences," 123. For detailed, year-by-year developments in the PDPA, see the Afghanistan chapters in Richard F. Staar, ed., *Yearbook*, 1981–82 and 1984–91, and Robert Wesson, ed., *Yearbook*, 1983.
2. For an expansion of this and the next two sections, see Arnold, "Soviet Relations with Afghanistan," 198–204.
3. Conversation with Stephane Thiollier, a Frenchman fluent in both Dari and Pushtu who conducted several interviews with Najib as well as with resistance leaders in late 1989 and early 1990 for a documentary on the war.
4. *Kabul New Times*, July 26, 1987 and November 5, 1987.
5. Andrew and Gordievsky, *KGB: The Inside Story*, 577.
6. Bermudez, "Ballistic Missiles," 51–58.
7. Knight, "KGB and Civil-Military Relations," 106–7.
8. Knight, *KGB: Police and Politics*, 3.
9. Knight, "The Future of Communism," 24.
10. Andrew and Gordievsky, 622.
11. *Washington Post*, December 10, 1989, C-1.
12. *New York Times*, September 8, 1988, A-12.
13. Andrew and Gordievsky, 628.
14. Yasmann, "KGB and Party Congress," 13.
15. *New York Times*, May 7, 1989, A-1.
16. See A. Vasilkov, "Operatsiya 'Demsoyuz'," (Operation Democratic Union), 1. Vasilkov's byline is "responsible worker of the USSR KGB."
17. *New York Times*, March 6, 1989 A-1.
18. Moscow Television Service, May 31, 1989, (FBIS-SOV-89-104-S, June 1, 1989, 31–34). The speech was broadcast live.
19. Quoted from *Rabochaya Tribuna*, March 10, 1990 in Mikhail Tsypkin, "A Split in the KGB?" 6–9.
20. Kichikhin, "The KGB Knew Everything," 14–17.
21. *Ibid.*, 15.
22. Rahr, "New Evidence," 3–4.
23. Yasmann, "KGB and the Party Congress," 12–13.

24. *Sobesednik*, no. 36 (September 1990), 6–7.
25. *Literaturnaya Gazeta*, December 5, 1990, 13.
26. Yasmann, "KGB and the Party Congress," 12.
27. *Washington Post*, October 31, 1990, C-1.
28. Schoenfeld, "Red Inc.," 16–17.
29. Radio Liberty, *Report on the USSR* 3, no. 35, August 30, 1991, 42; no. 38, September 20 1991, 27; no. 39, September 27, 1991, 1.
30. Kichikhin, 17.

CHAPTER 9

THE PRICE OF WAR

The war made the good better—and the bad worse.
Soviet wildlife biologist to the author, January 1992

The preceding chapters have discussed the direct and indirect corrosive effects of the Afghan war on the three pillars that supported Kremlin rule over its vast empire. But these pillars were not floating in some kind of political ether; they stood on a bedrock of society, a bedrock that had been compacted and glazed over into seeming solidity by generations of oppression. The solidity was only on the surface, but it took the war in Afghanistan to flake off the glaze and expose the cracks that lay beneath.

Establishing the Parameters

It is not easy to set a price on a war. The conventional yardsticks of financial drain and human loss at best give only approximations and at worst are misleading. At Stalingrad, for example, in a period of less than six months (August 1942–January 1943), the Soviet high command spent many times the munitions, supplies, and lives than it would lose in the entire Afghan war, yet few in the USSR, then or later, would argue that the price was too high.

The essential ingredient on the balance sheet is not even victory or defeat: in our own history, Wake Island and the Alamo were losing fights whose cost we do not grudge. In fighting the Soviet invaders the Afghans suffered more than a million dead, a ruined economy, and such political disintegration that the very future survival of the Afghan nation is problematical, yet it is hard to imagine that, if the war had to be fought all over again, most Afghans would choose to give in without a fight.

More important than the tangible gains or losses are the intangibles: the effect the war has had on individual and collective aspirations, self-esteem, political activism, world image, patriotism, and a host of other psychosocial dimensions (some of them hidden for years after the fighting) that are hard enough to identify, much less to assess. It is how a society emerges from a war that provides the war's most important measure, and the bottom line is: Was the war worth fighting?

For the former Soviet Union the answer to that question in relation to the Afghan war is an unconditional no. If one accepts the basic argument of this book, the war meant nothing less than national suicide. Even if it is regarded in this larger sense as merely a catalyst that hastened the end of a terminally sick empire, its narrower social consequences were unacceptably costly.

In the discussion that follows, we will start with the known and estimated tangible costs. First, however, we must look at one separate factor that affects all of our measurements: time. The USSR was engaged in Afghanistan for more than nine years—well over twice as long as it fought in World War II. Like the droplets of a Chinese water torture, costs that were initially ignorable became bothersome, the bothersome in turn became agonizing, and the agonizing—ultimately—intolerable. Losses that the Soviets could and did brush aside as negligible in 1980 had become unsustainable in 1988. That the war dragged on to this crucial stage is thanks almost solely to the indomitable spirit of the Afghan resistance, the *mujahidin*, who refused to admit defeat.*

---

*An Englishman wrote as follows of another war waged by Russians against mountain Muslims in another era: "Such, in brief, was the country; and such were the peoples who, with no outside assistance, with no artillery but what they could capture from the enemy, with no trust but in Allah and His Prophet, their own right hands and flashing blades, defied the might of Russia for more than half a century; defeating her armies, raiding her settlements, and laughing to scorn her wealth, her pride, and her numbers." (John Baddeley, *The Russian Conquest*, pp. xxxvii–xxxviii.) Fortunately for all concerned, Moscow's rulers in the twentieth century did not have the luxury of a half century enjoyed by the tsars in the nineteenth.

Economic Costs

In the 1980s, some analysts assessed the direct economic costs of the war to the USSR as negligible, or at worst bearable. Most, however, agreed that the country paid heavily, especially in view of the deteriorating Soviet economy. The U.S. State Department gave a figure of about $3 billion per year in the early 1980s, but in May 1989 unidentified Soviet economists told a Western reporter the occupation had cost 5 billion rubles annually, or about $8.2 billion at the official rate of exchange. They added that just transporting the massive postoccupation weapons resupply ($300 million to $400 million worth per month, according to U.S. government estimates) was costing Moscow more than 300 million rubles ($490 million) per year. Other observers estimated the annual costs of Soviet support after withdrawal at $4 billion. The level of military hardware support was reportedly greater in the first four months of 1989 than in all of 1988, and was running at a one-third higher rate in early 1990 than during 1989.[1]*

An extraordinarily high figure for 1989 was provided by a Soviet specialist on Afghanistan who had served as a consultant for the Soviet government, including the KGB. He told a Western opposite number in 1990 that the cost of maintaining the Kabul regime for the first nine months of 1989 had been 6.5 billion rubles. This figure included aid of all kinds, arms as well as consumer goods.[2] If prorated for the year, this would mean that Afghanistan cost the USSR 8.7 billion rubles ($14.2 billion) in 1989, a third of the entire estimated Soviet foreign aid budget for that year. These figures contrasted sharply with the much more modest *declared* foreign aid budget, as indicated below.

On the nonmilitary side, there were three unique attributes of the declared Soviet aid program for Afghanistan. The first was its larger

---

*During the 1980s, the USSR reportedly exported 25 percent of its arms production; in 1988 alone, arms exports to Third World countries amounted to $9.9 billion. It has been argued that the Soviet arms aid to Afghanistan came from obsolete supplies that had already been paid for and needed replacing with modern weapons anyway, and thus did not represent an economic drain. There is some strength in this argument, though a parallel contention that the cost of sending them to Afghanistan was less than scrapping them seems specious.

slice of the overall foreign aid pie in 1991. Out of a much-reduced Soviet foreign aid budget of 400 million rubles, the Afghans were to get 280 million, or 70 percent. Second-place Cuba was to receive only 55.7 million (about 20 percent), and twenty-eight other countries were supposed to share the remainder. The Afghan share in 1991 showed a huge relative gain over its modest portion in earlier years; in 1983–84, for example, it received less than 10 percent of a foreign aid budget that devoted 28 percent to Vietnam ($1 billion), 20 percent to Cuba, and 17 percent to Mongolia.[3]

The second unique attribute was the decentralization of much of the aid, a trend that grew during the 1980s decade: individual Soviet cities, regions, oblasts, and republics established direct links with Afghan towns and provinces, rather than having the aid funnel through central bodies. The dual goal was to integrate the Afghan economy more bindingly with the USSR's, while at the same time diffusing the image of *Russian* colonization; much of the aid and trade came from the central Asian republics, with direct cross-border links to neighboring Afghan provinces.

The third attribute was Soviet concentration on the private sector of the economy, a sudden refocusing that became apparent in 1987, after Kabul itself had begun to promote private enterprise, with the signing of the first Soviet loan to an Afghan private company. In less than a year, there were one hundred more such applications, resulting in twenty-eight contracts. A credit line for private enterprise of fifty million rubles was established in early 1988.[4] It seemed clear that Moscow had decided that private enterprise was the way to go in Afghanistan, a decision it would only reach for itself sometime later.

Despite the seemingly precise figures we have cited about the estimated cost of the war, it is improbable that even the best-informed Soviet official (much less any Western analyst) knew how much the Afghan albatross weighed either during or after the occupation. Even in the unlikely event that he had an exact ruble figure, the real cost in dollar terms would have remained a mystery, because the fickle ruble was an essentially meaningless unit of currency, a variable whose value for weaponry was quite different from its value for consumer goods.

Moreover, the expense was not only in directly attributable rubles and kopecks but in the insidious side effects that a losing war has on an economy, especially the Soviet economy. In the West, any kind of national failure is often accompanied by conscious and deliberate demonstrations, strikes, and other protest activity, whose economic cost can at least be estimated. In old Russia and the USSR, however, until the 1990s protest was forced into more subtle channels.

Faced with a succession of all-powerful autocratic regimes, the Russian man in the street found Western-style open expressions of dissent to be painful if not suicidal, and he adopted his own, mostly subconscious alternatives. These included absenteeism, laziness, drunkenness, corruption, pilfering of government property, and indiscipline—all attributes of Russian and Soviet society long before Afghanistan became an issue, but especially prevalent as the 1980s war wore on. The effect of these on labor productivity and production quality was unmistakable.

Andropov's concentrated but vain efforts to impose a work ethic, discipline, and enthusiasm were indicative of the depth of the problem. He sent roving patrols into public bathhouses and cinemas to spot and punish malingering bureaucrats, more than doubled the price of vodka while cutting back on hours of sale, tried to tie workers' pay to their individual productivity, declared war on corruption, and brought new, younger faces into the top party ranks. After the one-year moratorium of Chernenko's rule, Gorbachev started off with more of the same medicine.

But with bored cynicism the Soviet peoples disregarded his calls for more discipline and faster work ("acceleration" was the propaganda watchword), and the growth curves for gross national product and worker productivity became flatter than ever. No matter what the methods, one does not inspire responsibility, enthusiasm, and a healthy work ethic in a work force whose sons are called on to die in an unpopular, losing cause. To revive the economy, Gorbachev needed peace in Afghanistan, whether by victory or retreat.

Both in direct and indirect costs, the bottom economic line for the Soviet Union in Afghanistan was written in large red numbers, an immense if not ruinous expense at a time when the Soviet economy was in an ever-steeper decline. The Kremlin's dogged willingness to persevere in trying to keep its foothold in Afghanistan, even after the August 1991 coup attempt presaged the collapse of the economy and the end of the empire, is witness to the durability of this last, dying imperial dream.

Casualties

Measuring the full economic costs of the war will never be better than guesswork, but some close approximation of the Soviet human losses, the most sensitive issue of the war to most citizens of the former Soviet Union, should emerge eventually. If the following discussion seems over-detailed, it is because the author felt an obligation to compile the conflicting statistics as they were known in 1991, both as raw material for possible future studies and as an illustration of Soviet domestic disinformation.

For the first several years of the war Moscow all but denied there had been any casualties at all. "Not a single Soviet unit has taken part in suppressing counterrevolutionary bands," TASS stated blandly in March 1980. In 1981, with deaths mounting, the practice of sending enlisted men's bodies home in zinc coffins was abruptly suspended, and grieving relatives were actively discouraged from holding funeral ceremonies for the fallen. With one apparently accidental exception, there were no mentions of war deaths in Soviet media until late 1983, after the USSR by its own later admission had already lost more than five thousand killed. When it did begin to release such information, it was in minor rural newspapers, on an individual basis, and with no mention of Afghanistan; the deceased had merely "died doing their international duty." By October 1985, the Soviets had admitted to only twenty specific fatalities. The belief spread that the conscripts sent to Afghanistan were deliberately selected from rural parts of the Soviet Union to diffuse the social impact of casualties.[5]

Later, when casualties were admitted, censors carefully metered the release of information. When a Soviet journalist wrote an article about an enlisted man who had lost both legs in saving the life of an officer, the military censor tossed it aside without reading it, on the grounds that the same journalist had already written one report about a wounded soldier. The journalist protested, "But there are lots of wounded— thousands of them!" "And my limit for the number of pieces about them is four in the next six months. Four mentions of wounded. And nothing at all about anyone being killed. Got that?"[6]

If the human losses could no longer be totally denied or stifled, it was judged best, apparently, to make them heroic, to Kiplingize the war into something dramatic, exciting, and historically necessary. A suspiciously repetitive scenario of different wounded Soviet soldiers blowing themselves up with grenades so as to take up to thirty guerrillas with them appeared in the press in the mid-1980s. Expressing a broader view—one closer to that of Adolf Hitler than to that of Rudyard Kipling—the Soviet propagandist Alexander Prokhanov in 1985 referred to the war as a nationally purifying, disciplining, rejuvenating experience, something to set right the demoralizing, stagnating effects of peace; in a phrase reminiscent of Hitler's desire for "Lebensraum," he added that it would help secure the USSR's "balance of global space."[7]

Even as he was writing in this vein, Prokhanov knew that the message was not getting through. In early 1988, abandoning his effort to sway public opinion, the former prowar enthusiast angrily denounced the invasion as a ghastly mistake and pointed the finger of blame in all directions but his own. Two months later, he conceded to a Western journalist that by 1984 "casualties had become a problem," and that by the end of 1986 Afghanistan had become "an extremely acute internal problem" for the USSR.[8]

Unlike economic difficulties, the losses could not be shrugged aside with bored cynicism. In the discussion below, we go into some statistical detail because of the political impact that the casualties had and are still having in what used to be the Soviet Union.

The Soviets published the first "exact" casualty figures on May 25, 1988, shortly after the withdrawal began. General Lizichev, chief of the armed forces political department, said that 13,310 Soviet soldiers had died in the war, 35,478 had been wounded, and 311 were missing. Just before the last troops pulled out, in February 1989, a Soviet news feature syndicate said that an additional 1,700 soldiers had died, bringing the total to just over 15,000. Later, however, in August 1989, seemingly even more precise figures on casualties were released (Table 2). Finally, in May 1991 General of the Army V. I. Varennikov stated that "18,826 Soviet citizens placed their lives on the altar of the Fatherland—more than 50,000 were wounded."[9]*

*This figure, given before a conference of "soldier-internationalists" who had served worldwide, may inadvertently have included casualties from other theaters. Note the

The inconsistencies in these figures are apparent. The initial release in May 1988 was obviously too low and suspiciously precise for an ongoing conflict. It may have been intended to match approximately with a U.S. State Department estimate, given shortly before, that 15,000 soldiers had died *in combat* during the war. Later, by including *noncombat* deaths in the total, the Soviets in effect lowered the U.S. estimate.

This was a much lower figure than popularly believed. In January 1988, when a Western reporter asked an unnamed specialist in Moscow whether another Western estimate of 35,000 Soviet fatalities was accurate, the answer was, "That may be very close." Shortly before, the same journalist had reported the wide perception among many Soviet citizens that 280,000 Soviet soldiers had died in Afghanistan.[10] Though obviously an exaggeration, this number is generally consistent with the stated beliefs of various soldiers: 20,000 to 25,000 by the end of 1981 (students in a Soviet sergeants' school), 50,000 by the end of 1983 (an enlisted deserter's estimate), and 10,000 to 20,000 per year from 1980 to 1987 (the opinion of officers in a combat unit in Afghanistan).[11]

Skepticism about the official tally was also found among virtually all educated Soviets, and most Westerners, who had studied the war. In 1990–91, most had come to a generally consistent estimate of between 40,000 and 50,000 dead. Both Soviets and Americans agreed that the Soviet official figures appeared to be grossly understated and that the deaths from accidents, disease, and suicide more than matched those on the battlefield; in late 1984, Western intelligence estimates held that twice as many perished from these causes as did from bullets. This contrasted with the official breakdown of casualties announced in August 1989, which indicated a consistently low ratio of noncombat to total deaths, averaging 12.9 percent for the years 1980–88.[12]

Leaving out the partial years of 1979 and 1989, the lowest casualties appear to have occurred in 1987 and 1988, during the withdrawal. The highest were registered in 1984. The year Gorbachev came to power, 1985, had the third-highest Soviet death rate.[13]

---

implied inclusion of civilians in the "citizens"—a high toll of more than three thousand if this figure indeed applies only to Afghanistan, and if the original military mortality figures are accurate.

TABLE 2

Officially Acknowledged Soviet Fatalities in Afghanistan, 1979–89
(Source: *Pravda*, August 17, 1989)

Year	Total	Officers	Other ranks[a]	Combat	Noncombat
1979	**86**	10	76	70	9
1980	**1,484**	199	1,285	1,229	170
1981	**1,298**	189	1,109	1,033	155
1982	**1,948**	238	1,710	1,623	215
1983	**1,446**	210	1,236	1,057	179
1984	**2,343**	305	2,038	2,060	285
1985	**1,868**	273	1,595	1,552	240
1986	**1,333**	216	1,117	1,068	198
1987	**1,215**	212	1,003	1,004	189
1988	**759**	117	642	639	106
1989	**53**	10	43	46	9
TOTAL	**13,833**	1,979	11,854[a]	11,381[b]	1,755[b]

a. Derived figures, not given in the *Pravda* article.

b. There is no explanation of why the sum of combat and noncombat fatalities does not equal total fatalities.

In 1988, responding to public calls for full revelation of the death toll, the Soviet Ministry of Defense promised to produce a book with the names of all the war dead by 1990 or 1991. This was not done, nor was there any answer to a demand that a war memorial with the names of all the dead "in one place" be constructed.[14]

Social Costs

We have listed the flagging work ethic as an economic cost, but its component parts (especially amorality, drunkenness, irresponsibility, and pilfering) could equally well have been termed a social cost. One corruption indicator specifically tied to the war was the going price in 1987 for a medical exemption from service in Afghanistan (one thousand rubles) versus one to avoid cleaning up the Chernobyl nuclear disaster (five hundred rubles).[15]

Among the most obvious war-attributable social costs has been the spread of drug abuse. According to General Varennikov, 546,200 Soviet citizens served in troop units in Afghanistan from 1979 to 1989. Virtually all of them had the chance to experiment with drugs for the first time.

Cheaper and easier to come by than alcohol in Afghan bazaars, drugs often changed hands in exchange for military materiel, including guns and ammunition. Some captured and deserting Soviet soldiers believed that more than 50 percent of their comrades used hashish, heroin, or opium, and there is no question that drug use became an ever greater and more publicized problem in the USSR in the late 1980s and early 1990s. According to one veteran, every soldier tried drugs, every other one was an occasional user, and every tenth was a regular user.[16]

By official count, in 1987 there were 46,000 registered addicts in the USSR, a figure that had climbed to 60,000 by 1990. Another 130,000 had been caught using drugs at least once by 1990. These figures were deemed far too low by one Western analyst, who said that perhaps 15 million Soviet citizens had experimented at least once with drugs and that narcotics use in the USSR was a snowballing problem.[17]

Although the growing drug problem attracted attention in both the Soviet and Western press, it paled beside the Russian abuse substance of choice, alcohol.* In this area of social malaise, however, the Afghan war played only a minor direct role. Some officers had access to liquor, but not the average soldier. It was usually enlisted men who experimented with such extraordinary substitutes as shoe polish left to melt in the sun and filter through a piece of bread. But those who returned home psychologically scarred tended to join the swelling ranks of domestic alcoholics, despite the temperance drives first of Yury Andropov and then of Mikhail Gorbachev.

Another indirect social impact came from Afghan veterans, the so-called *afgantsy*. Returning to an uncaring society that did not recognize their sacrifices, some of the *afgantsy* managed to deal successfully

*Legend has it that in the tenth century St. Vladimir, in trying to choose a world-class religion for Russia, accepted Christianity over Islam mainly because, in the words of the British historian Bernard Pares, "it was quite impossible to be happy in Russia without strong drink."

with the transition to civilian life, but many others either suffered psychological problems from the war's horrors (there were at least six thousand invalids according to Varennikov) or turned to a life of sanctioned or unsanctioned violence. The psychoses suffered by the *afgantsy* are carbon copies of those suffered by American soldiers in Vietnam, with the added disadvantage that almost nothing is being done to treat them.[18]

The "legally" violence-prone included many Afghan veterans rehired by their former commanding officer, General Gromov, who became deputy minister of interior in 1990 and in early 1991 used them as riot-control troops in the murderous attacks on Lithuanian and Latvian peaceful demonstrators. The "illegal" category included not only those who beat up and murdered their compatriots in flashes of uncontrollable rage, but those who ran protection rackets or acted as bodyguards for native Mafia "godfathers."[19]

Others, in the name of revolutionary purity, physically attacked punk rockers, officials believed to be cheating the state, or any other social element they deemed undesirable. These last received ambivalent coverage in the conservative Soviet press. On the one hand they were chided for taking the law into their own hands, but on the other they were clearly admired for their forthright solutions to perceived social problems.[20]

Political Costs

The ultimate political cost to the Soviet rulers was the destruction of the surface glaze that had hidden society's underlying fissures and averted their spread. A key to preventing that development was control of information, and at first the traditional means succeeded, both inside and outside the USSR.

The Soviet public first heard of the invasion through its own media on December 30, 1979, three days after it had made banner headlines elsewhere in the world. The action was described as a response to "numerous" requests for help from the Kabul government, to involve a "limited contingent" of Soviet forces that would remain in the country only "temporarily." This line would be repeated with few variations for the next eight years.

For the first month, the majority (about two-thirds) of Soviet media coverage was in foreign languages, directed at the outside world in an effort to contain the surge of international anti-Soviet emotion that the invasion had provoked. Before long, however, the coverage became divided about evenly between domestic and foreign languages. It must be emphasized, however, that the absolute volume of coverage was extremely low: the U.S. Foreign Broadcasting Information Service (FBIS), which publishes English-language translations of radio, television, newspapers, and other frequent periodicals in all the Soviet languages, registered an average weekly total of fewer than ten items for the internal audience in 1980, and fewer than five per week in 1981 and 1982. In September 1984, when there was more coverage than in any single month since early 1980, the entire month's coverage in *Pravda* and Moscow television was only nine articles each. (Although FBIS translations are usually selective, government and public interest in Afghanistan in the 1980s prompted virtually complete coverage of this topic.)[21]

For Soviet intellectuals, according to one view, Afghanistan in 1980–81 was tenth on their list of concerns, while Poland was first.[22] In January 1980, the exiling to Gorky of the famous Soviet physicist and human-rights advocate, Andrei Sakharov, was greeted with outrage by the dissident community, yet few of his followers seemed to recall that it was Sakharov's condemnation of the Afghanistan adventure that had triggered his banishment. Fewer still adopted this issue as their own main antigovernment platform.

There are several explanations for the lack of public furor. One is certainly the relative success of the Soviet news blackout on remote, isolated, Soviet-dominated Afghanistan compared to the failure to keep a lid on reporting about mainstream-European, relatively free Poland. Another is the fact that demonstrating against military involvement was viewed by both the authorities and the demonstrators as uncomfortably close to treason. It was thus a potentially life-threatening, not merely a freedom-threatening, risk for the objector to take. There are doubtless other explanations as well.

But if the intellectual class and the population at large seemed at first relatively unmoved by the conflict, the same could not be said of the leadership. From the outset, the official measures taken to stifle discussion of the war and its costs reflected extreme sensitivity. So did the other policies designed to clamp down on dissent.

The emigration of Jewish and German minorities, which had peaked in 1979, was sharply curtailed in the early 1980s. Although lip-service encouragement to authors to tackle controversial problems remained in vogue at this time, it was probably less a genuine policy than a KGB tactic to flush out dissidents and expose them to ever-increasing repression. In any case, the policy on dissidents had changed greatly by 1984, when writers were told to stop writing about "loose and whining" heroes, and concentrate instead on those with "noble goals, ideological convictions, industry, and fortitude."[23]

Starting with Andropov's rule, random identity checks on the streets of Moscow became frequent, and citizens without proper residence permits went to jail. As described above, the campaign was partly to improve economic performance, but it had other dimensions as well. There was an all-out effort to quash the "petit bourgeois virus" in youth and to eliminate social apathy. The few hardy pacifists who dared challenge the CPSU's propaganda monopoly of the peace theme by demonstrating independently received especially harsh treatment, including street beatings. Militia patrols raked in "hooligans" on the basis of their outward appearance. For *druzhiniki* (volunteer junior policemen from the CPSU's Komsomol youth group), there was no longer a day off for each evening's patrol. Repression of dissidents, from religious believers to independent peace groups, became more severe, with thirteen-year sentences the norm, and the widespread incarceration of political dissidents in "psychiatric hospitals of a special type," normally reserved for the criminally insane. There were numerous cases of guards' beatings that led to the crippling or death of prisoners, and camp commanders were given the power to extend prisoners' sentences almost at will.

But overall, the state's demands for sociopolitical conformity were met with the same quiet, absorptive, passive resistance as its demands for economic progress. When it came to Afghanistan, however, the efforts to stifle information about the war failed, and public resentment slowly built up as it continued to drag on. It will be recalled that the Battle of the Panjshir in the spring of 1984 was a key military turning point (chapter 7); perhaps coincidentally, 1984 may one day be hailed as a political watershed as well.

Civil Disobedience—and Its Significance

In George Orwell's *1984,* totalitarian states have moved by that year to a stage where they can successfully impose total, genuine conformity on their citizens, abolishing not only dissident actions but even dissident thoughts. Andropov, even if he had wanted to, could not afford that luxury. True, he believed he had to do all in his power to curb open dissent, but he also needed people to think creatively in the interests of the state. In the appropriate year of 1984, the contradiction between these two judgments showed signs of approaching a crisis.

From January to December 1984, a Radio Liberty poll of twenty-six hundred Soviet travelers to Western Europe revealed that only about 25 percent were in favor of the war, 25 percent were more or less actively opposed to it, and 50 percent refused to voice an opinion. A similar poll taken during 1985–86 showed an average of 42 percent disapproval, 31 percent approval, and the remaining 27 percent with no opinion.[24] But the samples polled were heavily weighted in favor of the government; about a quarter of the respondents were party members (well over twice the national average), and at that time permission to travel abroad was only given after more-or-less rigorous checks on the loyalty of the applicants. Obviously, no open opponent of government policy would have been allowed out.* Moreover, as noted in the studies, a large portion of those who declared "no opinion"—especially among party members—were signaling disapproval without wanting to say so openly.

Perhaps the most startling aspect of the Radio Liberty poll was the fact that so many Soviet respondents were willing to answer questions of such a sensitive nature put by an unknown foreigner. Only about 10 percent of those approached refused to answer the pollsters' questions in 1984 and 1985–86 surveys, compared to 23 percent when a similar sampling was attempted in 1980. Even more startling, the percentage of party members who disapproved jumped from 8 percent in 1984 to 22 percent in 1985–86. This represented defiance of party discipline at the grass-roots level, and though it was not noisily demonstrative, it set the stage for the slow emergence of real public opinion about the war in the years that followed.

---

*The author has used the raw data in the cited references. For some inexplicable reason, that data was weighted by a computer simulation to indicate in the later report that approval, disapproval, and nonopinion were equally divided at about one-third each. If anything, the data should have been weighted the other way.

The importance of this development cannot be overstated. Until people were willing to *act,* the disaffection that had been smothered in all but the bravest by a varying blend of raw terror, social stigma, and economic discrimination was of no consequence.

True, there had been isolated exceptions in the first years of the war. Twenty-one courageous Balts signed a January 17, 1980, letter addressed to the chairman of the USSR Supreme Soviet, the secretary general of the UN, and "the Afghan nation," pointing out the illogic of the Soviet rationalization for its aggression, drawing a parallel with the Soviet invasion of their own countries in 1939, and demanding a Soviet withdrawal. In August that year some feminists briefly urged young men to burn their draft cards. In 1983, a heretofore-conforming radio announcer, Vladimir Danchev, in five broadcasts about Afghanistan over the span of a week, succeeded in switching obligatory negative and positive propaganda terms, applying the former to the Soviet occupation troops (e.g., "invaders," "criminal bands") and the latter to the resistance. Also in 1983, stickers protesting the war appeared on walls and in telephone booths all around the Soviet Union. None of these acts occasioned more than passing international comment.[25]

Yet these expressions of popular dissent, brief and swiftly repressed as most were, carried a profound significance. A new activism was gradually taking hold, even though it was only partly detectable and almost totally ignored outside the USSR until 1988. When the topic was raised at all, the prevailing view was that public opinion in the USSR did not really matter anyway. (Only a few analysts contended otherwise, among them Dr. Ronald R. Pope of Illinois State University, who in 1981 predicted that an aroused Soviet public would eventually prove to be the Achilles' heel of the invasion and occupation.[26])

Until the Afghan war, dissidence in general had been largely the private preserve of intellectuals. There had been isolated outbreaks of popular rage, such as the 1953 Vorkuta labor-camp uprising and the 1962 Novocherkassk food riots, but they had been unconnected rarities. Now, the Afghan war was provoking small spots of trouble, like measles spreading through the body politic.

By the end of 1985, there had been a protest demonstration in Armenia by parents of conscripts, Lithuanian underground papers had reported anti-Russian demonstrations at soldiers' funerals, similar Ukrainian papers railed against fighting "Russia's war," Chechen conscripts in the northern

Caucasus had mutinied when told they were to go to Afghanistan to fight their co-religionists, and five Tajiks reportedly had been arrested for distributing antiwar leaflets in Dushanbe. There was other minor protest activity as well, constituting "an important political factor" that reflected "shifts . . . in the mood of the masses."[27]

Although there was also a small but active peace group in Moscow, it is interesting that most of the reported incidents had occurred in minority nationality areas, where they took on anti-Russian as well as anti-Soviet overtones. Nevertheless, in December 1986 the most authoritative voice of conscience in the USSR, that of the Russian Andrei Sakharov, was again raised against the occupation of Afghanistan immediately after he was released from internal exile.

The Chernobyl Factor

Not related to Afghanistan but profoundly affecting the public's willingness to speak up was the April 1986 Chernobyl disaster and the spotlight of international attention that it threw on official Soviet lying. The world's focused horror, ridicule, and contempt were much harder for the Kremlin to live down than such previous incidents as the 1983 shooting down of the Korean Airlines jumbo jet. For Gorbachev, the exposure of his administration as unmitigated liars during their initial efforts to conceal the catastrophe was an anguishing humiliation. It conclusively proved that the original concept of *glasnost* as a kind of controlled candor was inadequate in a world where information technology had completely outpaced information control. Neither at home nor abroad could the instruments of the Soviet state stifle or dictate what people knew.

In 1987 more popular grievances about Afghanistan were beginning to be heard. There was grumbling in the Soviet media about the sale of "footwear and clothing destined for poor people . . . Soviet army vests and all sorts of ammunition" in Kabul bazaars. During the year, three-quarters of all the letters to the editor received by the leading state newspaper, *Izvestiya*, concerned Afghanistan, most from mothers asking about their sons. No breakdown of writer opinions about the war in these letters was reported, but it is safe to say that most were negative: in November, 53 percent of those polled in Moscow favored a total withdrawal of Soviet troops.[28]

In 1988, protests took on a mass nature and involved far more than just the Afghanistan issue. That year there were twenty-six hundred demonstrations and other mass actions that involved sixteen million people in 170 Soviet cities, 60 percent of which were linked to ethnic problems.[29] The dimensions of dissent were beyond anything seen in the Soviet Union for generations. In February 1990, more than one hundred thousand citizens gathered on Red Square in Moscow to demand repeal of Article 6 of the Soviet constitution, which gave a monopoly of power to the CPSU, and within days the appeal was granted. That autumn, a whole small village of makeshift shacks sprang up next to Red Square, pointing up the problem of the homeless.

These gatherings were a legal—or at least semilegal—form of political action; a year later the population at large and even its security forces showed their willingness to disobey the orders of their appointed chiefs. The refusal of key military and KGB subordinate commanders to follow the orders of Dmitri Yazov and Vladimir Kryuchkov in the fateful days of August 1991 would signal the end of the Soviet Empire. It was fitting that the KGB Group A (Alpha), so important in disposing of Hafizullah Amin in Afghanistan in 1979, refused orders to storm the Russian parliament where Boris Yeltsin held out against the conspirators. It is also significant that among those civilians who manned the barricades around that same building and defied the tanks was a sizable contingent of Afghan veterans. At least one of them paid with his life there.[30]

The Impact of Truth

During the last years of the 1980s, Gorbachev began peeling back the layers of secrecy that had been the traditional cloak behind which the Soviet state had operated, revealing more and more of the general public revulsion against the war. But that very policy itself was in good part a result of the war. Confronted with the spread of wild rumors as to the extent of casualties, with a work force that through sloth and indifference was sabotaging economic progress, with a corrupt and stagnant bureaucracy that used secrecy as an essential weapon to fight reform, and with an ever-more-obvious public contempt for the basic institutions of Soviet power, Gorbachev, like Alexander II before him, made the fateful decision to relax censorship. He even chose the same word that Alexander had used—*glasnost*—a term that attempted to reconcile authoritarianism and freedom, by retaining the autocracy but making the restrictions on freedom a matter of law rather than bureaucratic whim.[31]

Attempting to marry freedom and autocracy worked no better for Gorbachev than for Alexander. In the ensuing struggle, a modified form of autocracy won out in the nineteenth century, just as it almost did again in August 1991. The key difference between the 1860s and the 1990s was that the Soviet peoples were far better educated and more politically alive than their ancestors. They were also equipped with modern means of mass communication. And they had just passed through a unique and painful psychological trauma: the shock of realizing that at the command of party and state they had been parroting bald-faced lies for a lifetime.

Most of them understood as individuals that things within their ken were not as they should be; what they did not realize until the bonds of information control were at last loosened was how common and widespread the evils of the system were. When they at last could share their experiences and true beliefs without fear of reprisal for anti-Soviet activity, the regime was doomed.*

In the failed 1991 coup, the social base dissolved from underneath the three pillars. But more important than the fall of any one of them was the destruction of the elaborate structure of lies that had upheld each individually and the Soviet Union as a whole.

The USSR had been one gigantic Potemkin village, a structure whose principal brace had been its false front. When that false front was seen for what it was and demolished, not only did the sad reality that lay behind become revealed, but the cohesive force that had held that reality together was fatally weakened. To the extent that the Afghan war contributed to letting truth into the USSR, it was responsible for this final, lethal blow to the world's last imperial superpower and its supposedly universal dogma, Marxism-Leninism.

---

*In the fall of 1990, speaking of her lifelong party membership, a retired Soviet school-teacher told the author's wife, "I believed—I really *believed*," as if shocked at her own naiveté. "They said we were the happiest people in the world," said a visiting Russian biologist in early 1992. "How were we to know differently?"

NOTES

1. *Wall Street Journal*, January 17, 1984, 6; *New York Times*, May 24, 1989, A-8, and June 25, 1989, A-8; *Christian Science Monitor*, June 6, 1989, 8, and April 16, 1990, 2.
2. Personal contact of the author in the USSR.
3. Tedstrom, "The 1991 Budget," 8; *Background Brief* ("Soviet Aid to Special Friends"), June 1986.
4. Bakhtar News Agency (Kabul), January 2, 1988 (FBIS-NES-88-002, January 5, 1988, 45.)
5. Arnold, "Situation in Afghanistan," 740; *The Economist*, October 26, 1985, 48; personal conversations with Soviet citizens in 1990.
6. Bocharov, *Russian Roulette*, 53.
7. *Literaturnaya Gazeta*, August 28, 1985, 14. The article was devastatingly reviewed and dissected in Khovanski, "Afghanistan: The Bleeding Wound."
8. *Literaturnaya Gazeta*, February 17, 1988, 9; *Christian Science Monitor*, April 13, 1988, 1.
9. *New York Times*, February 10, 1989, A-6; *Krasnaya Zvezda*, May 24, 1991, 2.
10. *Christian Science Monitor*, January 8, 1988, 7, and January 22, 1988, 1.
11. *Posev* 39, no. 6 (June 1983): 15; "A Soviet Soldier Opts Out in Afghanistan," Radio Liberty Research Bulletin RL 121/84, March 19, 1984; *Christian Science Monitor*, October 7, 1987, 1.
12. *San Francisco Chronicle,* December 26, 1984, 4. See also Table 1. According to Radio Liberty, *Argumenty i Fakty* of November 4, 1988, and the Estonian Komsomol publication *Noorte Heal* of January 24, 1989, quoted figures of 40,000 and 50,000, respectively. The former figure had come from Eduard Gams, a people's deputy. See Radio Liberty, *Report on the USSR* 1, no. 46, January 17, 1989.
13. *New York Times*, May 26, 1988, A-6.
14. *Komsomolskaya Pravda*, May 27, 1989, 2; *Izvestiya*, January 2, 1989, 1.
15. As told to the author by a Soviet expert on Afghanistan.
16. *New York Times*, October 3, 1988, A-6.

17. *New York Times*, November 2, 1985, 1; *Pravda*, January 6, 1987, 3; Reuters (United Nations, New York), February 22, 1990; Kennan Institute, *Meeting Report* (Dr. Renselaer Lee), January 17, 1991.
18. See Tamarov, *Afghanistan: Soviet Vietnam* for a moving firsthand account by a badly traumatized Soviet soldier.
19. *Krasnaya Zvezda*, May 24, 1991, 2.
20. Nahaylo, "When Ivan Comes Marching Home," 16.
21. Arnold, "Situation in Afghanistan," 734–44.
22. Nagorski, *Reluctant Farewell*, 51.
23. Private conversation with Soviet émigré.
24. See Radio Liberty, AR-4-85 and AR-1-87.
25. *London Times*, January 27, 1983, 12; *Washington Post*, May 27, 1983, A-24; *Posev* 39, no. 7 (July 1983): 3.
26. Pope, "Afghanistan," 347.
27. Khovanski, 3, 4; Nahaylo, 15; Radio Liberty Research Bulletin RL 97/80, March 6, 1980.
28. *Literaturnaya Gazeta*, October 14, 1987, 14; *Financial Times*, May 14, 1988, 3.
29. Yasmann, "The Internal Situation," 8–14.
30. *London Times*, August 31, 1989, 8.
31. Ulam, *Russia's Failed Revolutions*, 115.

EPILOGUE

The tears of strangers are only water.
Russian saying

By the summer of 1991, the Soviet Union's three pillars of support, each of them weakened to varying degrees, were ceasing to be mutually supportive. In July, Boris Yeltsin decreed that the party, shorn of its monopoly of power, should no longer maintain offices in state institutions, including the military and KGB. The KGB had cut its Third Chief Directorate (military security) by 10 percent and was already acting within the state framework rather than the party's. And the military, faced with a cutback of five hundred thousand troops, plummeting morale, and growing demands by the peripheral republics for their own home-guard forces, was in no shape to support anyone.

The August coup attempt totally destroyed whatever remaining prestige each of the three institutions' leaders still had. Their disgrace and arrest on charges of high treason opened the door for dismemberment of the empire and reform within its constituent parts. In early 1992, that reform is still in its painful birthing stage, a stage whose duration and final outcome are still in question.

In Russia (for we must now confine ourselves only to this largest surviving remnant of the Soviet Union), the Communist party appears to be shattered and incapable of reviving. Its noisiest fragment, the Bolshevik (Majority) party led by Nina Andreyeva, a sturdy Stalinist from Leningrad (better death than to call it St. Petersburg), carries on a lonely fight to reinstate the old system, but few take her or her small, inappropriately named party very seriously. Despite the Communist-led demonstrations against rising prices and deteriorating living conditions in Moscow and elsewhere in February 1992, the chances for a CPSU comeback are judged by most observers to be essentially zero.

This is not to say, however, that some other authoritarian or even totalitarian government could not take the CPSU's place, or that unemployed Communist apparatchiks might not become born-again fascists. Democracy is still a feeble baby in Russia, vulnerable to infanticide by the same burly bureaucrats who still exist and have administered the country for so long.

By contrast the Russian army, though temporarily in disarray, is sure to revive. It has been too elemental a part of Russian society down through the centuries to allow itself to be relegated to permanent secondary status. Armies may not be the best tools for establishing or maintaining democracy; but properly and responsibly led, they can be a stabilizing force when anarchy threatens. It was a healthy sign when the new, postcoup minister of defense, Marshal Shaposhnikov, called for revival of honor in the officer corps, asserting that officers must refuse to either issue or obey an illegal order, or to become the tool of any individual's ambition. But Shaposhnikov's emphasis on internal priorities for the Russian army's mission (serving the people, implementing the constitution, and only then defending the homeland) reflect the unhappy reality that the army cannot avoid playing a political role in these troubled times.

To keep the army from becoming a tool of repression, however, more is needed than a declaration of principles. The key to its standards will be the integrity of those who run it, and some of them in power today gave accounts of themselves in Afghanistan that should be troubling.

As just one example, General Gromov, former commanding general of Soviet forces in Afghanistan, in early 1992 is commander of all Russian army ground troops. Between the time he left Afghanistan and the August coup, he was briefly deputy minister of interior, in which capacity he enlisted a good many veterans of the Afghan campaign into the dreaded OMON troops, tasked with riot control. Gromov accompanied these troops to Lithuania in January 1991, where they took part in the bloody attack on the Lithuanian television studio. He also participated in combat operations in the Nagorno-Karabakh dispute between Armenia and Azerbaijan in 1990. A charismatic figure who puts one in mind of the late Gen. Douglas MacArthur, Gromov is also an elected delegate to the Russian parliament. Although he denied complicity in the August 1991 plot (he was on vacation at the time), there are enough other indications of questionable character traits to warrant concern about his continued command over armed units.*

The future of the KGB and its role in Russian life is a key unknown. After the coup attempt, the service was split into four large pieces: external intelligence, internal security, border guards, and a cryptography-communications service. Each of these is probably considerably larger than its nearest Western counterpart, and Russia is assured of remaining an intelligence superpower.[1] Again, there is a Russian heritage to consider—and it is not one to encourage optimism. Unlike the army, the KGB is not heir to a proud tradition and an honored place in society. From Peter the Great's *fiscals* down through the nineteenth-century *okhrana* to the various "organs" that served as Soviet watchdogs, Russian security services have richly deserved the fear and hatred of succeeding generations.

After the coup, the worst of the KGB offenders were removed; Kryuchkov awaits trial on charges of treason, and four out of five of his main deputies, including Valery Lebedev of IAU notoriety, have

---

*The CPSU Politburo decision to withdraw from Afghanistan was taken no later than November 20, 1986, and was passed to Najib during his mid-December visit to Moscow that year. (Khan, *Untying the Afghan Knot,* p. 182.) Gromov, who must have been aware of the decision, launched two major offensives in 1987, against Jadji in June and Khost in November-December. The first resulted in a defeat for the Soviet forces as the resistance stood and fought. In the second, Gromov undertook a month-long offensive to relieve a besieged DRA garrison, now unable (because of Stingers) to receive supplies by air. Committing 20,000 troops to the battle, he finally broke through, but before the end of January 1988 the outposts along the relieving Gardez-Khost road, won at such cost, were abandoned and the resistance siege was resumed. The purpose of these needless and costly offensives presumably was to experiment with new tactics that might compensate for the Stinger-caused loss of air supremacy. They undoubtedly accounted for a significant percentage of the 1,004 Soviet combat deaths acknowledged for 1987.

Claiming to be the last Soviet soldier out of Afghanistan in February 1989 (although actually there were still KGB border guards units deployed there at the time), Gromov informed the media in advance that he would deliver a private soliloquy when he reached the middle of the bridge crossing the Amu Darya River, and, indeed, he paused when he reached that point. But neither then nor later has he revealed what he said there. This leaves him with a remarkable opportunity for creative recall whenever the time might come for a politically appropriate statement backdated to his departure.

been fired. But many senior KGB officials remain in place after the coup, says one former KGB officer, who detects in the postcoup statements of some KGB officials an effort to escape retribution by heaping all blame on Kryuchkov.[2]

By 1992 KGB officials were supposed to have been separated from the many media jobs they once held, thus presumably removing any direct KGB input into the molding of Russian public opinion. Still unknown, however, is the fate of Lebedev's IAU subordinates. It is KGB remnants such as these who pose one dangerous threat to the future of responsible government in Russia, for it is they who are the most experienced in handling, restricting, and manipulating information in their own institutional and personal interests.

"Our country," mused the philosophically inclined Vladimir Rubanov (the KGB whistle-blower who first decried the KGB cult of secrecy in 1988), "regrettably lacks any kind of information culture," and he went on to confirm implicitly KGB Lieutenant Colonel Kichikhin's public charge that Gorbachev's perceptions about domestic and foreign affairs had been deliberately warped by the skewed information the IAU had fed him.[3]

Another residual KGB threat lies in the officials who in 1990 were elected to local soviets thanks to KGB training and campaigning. Just as Western politicians are obliged to pay off campaign debts of various kinds, so these elected officials have an implicit obligation to their old employers. How those debts might be called in is still unknown in 1992.

In short, in the last decade of the twentieth century the latest Russian revolution still has to confront not only the residue of the Communist era but some basic problems inherited from the tsars. Will the Russian people, with or without Boris Yeltsin, succeed in establishing a nonimperial, peaceful Russia? Or will the ex-Communist philosopher/historian Tibor Szamuely's gloomy dictum that "of all the burdens Russia has had to bear, the heaviest and most relentless of them all has been the weight of her past" prevail? It is still far too early to tell.

The destroyed pillars, bad as they were and dangerous as their resurgence might become, were not only flawed in their own right but symptomatic of an even more basic social weakness. The character of the nation that arises from the ashes of Russian communism—and the emergence of some powerful Russian state seems inevitable in the long term—will depend to a large extent on the ability of its people to rekindle within themselves a virtue that Soviet rule had systematically destroyed: inner discipline and the moral commitment to individual accountability. The habit of expressing dissent by simple nonperformance, best expressed by the bitter observation that "they pretend to pay us and we pretend to work," must be rooted out and replaced by a true social conscience. If individual inner discipline cannot be revived, the Russian nation is doomed to despotism or anarchy.

The old Soviet system collapsed thanks in large part to the weaknesses in its supporting pillars that the war in Afghanistan revealed. By exposing those weaknesses and helping trigger the collapse of the system, the Afghans opened the way to fundamental reform and thus did the Russians a huge service. If now in rebuilding their society the Russians can inspire the same kind of inner strength in themselves that individual Afghans (for all their inability to cooperate in large groups) showed during the war, their chances for success are good.

But the irony and tragedy of Afghanistan is that its immense sacrifices are not recognized internationally. In the course of warfare that is about to enter its fifteenth year, a million and a half lives have been lost, 50 percent of the people have been displaced from their homes (a third of the population into foreign exile), an agricultural infrastructure of orchards, vineyards, and irrigation systems has been largely destroyed, much of the formerly tilled land has turned to virtual cement from neglect, and the deserted farms that await the return of their owners are sowed with twenty to thirty million unexploded land mines, most of them undetectable by even the most modern technology. The age-old social fabric of a stable, pastoral society has been strained and ripped beyond repair.

These sacrifices were not made in the name of world peace; still less were they intended to promote reform in Russia. They were made because millions of Afghans reacted with visceral outrage to the invasion first of an alien culture (the PDPA coup) and then of an alien army. But their effect in the end has been to defuse the bipolar superpower competition that had continued to grow and threaten all human life for more than four decades.

It is because the Afghans deserve better recognition for what their sacrifices have given the world that this book has been written.

NOTES

1. See Yasmann, "KGB and Internal Security," 19–21.
2. Kichikhin, "The KGB Knew Everything," 14.
3. *Komsomolskaya Pravda*, September 20, 1991, 2.

GLOSSARY

afganets (afgantsy)   Soviet veteran(s) of the Afghan war

AIG   Afghan Interim Government (government in exile)

AVHI/AVO   Hungarian secret police in the 1950s

basmachi   Soviet term for anti-Soviet Afghan and central Asian guerrillas

Cheka   Acronym for original Soviet secret police

Chekist   Secret police officer under Cheka and later security organizations

CPSU   Communist Party of the Soviet Union

Decembrists   Russian military revolutionaries of the 1820s

disinformation   False propaganda

ERW   Enhanced radiation weapon ("neutron bomb")

FBIS   Foreign Broadcast Information Service

glasnost   Gorbachev reform permitting candid criticism of Soviet shortcomings

GLCM   Ground-launched cruise missile

HP   Homeland party—see PDPA

IAU   The KGB's Information and Analysis Directorate

ID   International Department of the CPSU Central Committee

jihad   Holy war

jirga/loya jirga   Assembly/grand assembly (Afghan decision-making forum)

KHAD (WAD)   Afghan secret police since 1980

Khalq/Khalqi   Rigidly Marxist/Leninist branch of the PDPA/HP

kray   Soviet administrative district

mujahidin   "Holy warriors," i.e., Afghan resistance fighters

MVD   Soviet Ministry of Internal Affairs

NTS   National Labor Alliance—Russian political exile group

okhrana   Secret police under the tsars

organs   Short for Organs of State Security, customary Soviet term for the KGB and its predecessor organizations

Parcham/Parchami   PDPA/HP faction, less outspokenly Marxist than the Khalqis

Pashtunistan   Pakistani area inhabited by Pashtuns and defined by Afghans as wishing independence; source of Afghan/Pakistani friction

PCI   Partito Comunista Italiano—Italian Communist party

PDPA   People's Democratic Party of Afghanistan—the Afghan Communist party, renamed the Homeland party (HP) in 1990

perestroyka   Restructuring—name given to sweeping reforms initiated by Mikhail Gorbachev in the old Soviet Union

Potemkin village   Any false-front effort to make things look better than they are

Radio Liberty   U.S.-government-financed radio station broadcasting to the USSR

rezident   Chief of a KGB unit abroad

rezidentsiya   KGB unit abroad

Russian, Great   The main group of eastern Slavs, whose other branches were the Ukrainians and Byelorussians (sometimes called "Little Russians")

SS-20   Soviet intermediate range surface-to-surface missile

TASS   Telegraphic Agency of the Soviet Union (official Soviet wire service)

WAD   See KHAD

BIBLIOGRAPHY

Books and Journals

Adams, Jan S. "Incremental Activism in Soviet Third-World Policy: The Role of the International Department of the CPSU Central Committee." *Slavic Review* 48, no. 4 (Winter 1989): 614–30.

Albright, David. "The Vanguard Parties of the Third World." In Walter Laqueur, ed., *The Pattern of Soviet Conduct in the Third World*. New York: Praeger, 1983.

Alexiev, Alexander R. "Inside the Soviet Army in Afghanistan." Santa Monica, Calif.: Rand Corporation R-3627A (May 1988).

———. "The Soviet Stake in Angola: Origin, Evolution, Prospects." In Dennis L. Bark, ed., *The Red Orchestra*. Stanford: Hoover Institution Press, 1988.

Andrew, Christopher, and Oleg Gordievsky. *KGB: The Inside Story*. New York: Harper Perennial, 1990.

Anwar, Raja. *The Tragedy of Afghanistan: A First-Hand Account*. London: Verso Press, 1988.

Arnold, Anthony. *Afghanistan's Two-Party Communism: Parcham and Khalq*. Stanford: Hoover Institution Press, 1983.

———. *Afghanistan: The Soviet Invasion in Perspective*. Stanford: Hoover Institution Press, 1985.

———. "The Soviet Threat to Pakistan." In Theodore L. Eliot, Jr. and Robert L. Pfaltzgraff, eds., *The Red Army on Pakistan's Border: Policy Implications for the United States*. Washington, D.C.: Pergamon-Brassey, 1986.

———. "Parallels and Divergences between the US Experience in Vietnam and the Soviet Experience in Afghanistan." *Central Asian Survey* 7, no. 2/3 (1988): 111–32.

———. "The Situation in Afghanistan: How Much of a Threat to the Soviet State?" In Alexander Shtromas and Morton A. Kaplan, eds., *The Soviet Union and the Challenge of the Future*, vol. 3, *Ideology, Culture, and Nationality*. New York: Paragon House, 1989: 725–60.

———. "Soviet Relations with Afghanistan: The Current Dynamic." In Hafeez Malik, ed., *Domestic Determinants of Soviet Foreign Policy towards South Asia and the Middle East*. London: Macmillan, 1990.

Arnold, Ruth L., and Anthony Arnold. "Afghanistan." In Robert Wesson, ed., *1983 Yearbook on International Communist Affairs*. Stanford: Hoover Institution Press, 1983: 139–47.

Avtorkhanov, Abdurrahman. *Sila i bessiliye Brezhneva*. Frankfurt: Possev Verlag, 1979.

———. "Andropov i ego pravleniye." *Posev* 39, no. 8 (August 1983): 26–29.

———. "Andropov: God na postu genseka." *Posev* 40, no. 1 (January 1984): 21–23.

Azreal, Jeremy R. *The Soviet Civilian Leadership and the Military High Command 1976–1986*. Santa Monica, Calif.: Rand Corporation R-3251-AF (June 1987).

———. "Civil-Military Relations in the USSR." In Alexander Shtromas and Morton A. Kaplan, eds., *The Soviet Union and the Challenge of the Future*, vol. 2, *Economics and Society*. New York: Paragon House, 1989: 549–65.

Background Briefs. London: United Kingdom Foreign and Commonwealth Office. (Ad hoc publications on matters of international interest.)

Baddeley, John. *The Russian Conquest of the Caucasus*. London: Longmans, Green, 1908.

Bark, Dennis L., ed., *The Red Orchestra*. Stanford: Hoover Institution Press, 1988.

Berdyayev, Nikolay. *The Origins of Russian Communism*. Ann Arbor: University of Michigan Press, 1960.

Bermudez, Joseph S. "Ballistic Missiles in the Third World—Afghanistan 1979–1992." *Jane's Intelligence Review* (February 1992): 51–58.

Bialer, Seweryn. *The Soviet Paradox*. New York: Vintage Books, 1987.

Billington, James. *The [Ikon] and the Axe: An Interpretive History of Russian Culture*. New York: Vintage Books, 1970.

Bittman, Ladislav. *The Deception Game*. New York: Ballantine Books,1972.

Bocharov, Gennady. *Russian Roulette: Afghanistan through Russian Eyes*. New York: Harper Collins, 1990.

Borovik, Artem. "Chto my natvorili?" *Sobesednik*, no. 37 (September 1989): 2,10.

Bradsher, Henry S. *Afghanistan and the Soviet Union*. Durham, N.C.: Duke University Press, 1983.

Carrott, Bruce. "Political Change in Civilian-Military Relations." In Timothy J. Colton and Thane Gustafson, eds., *Soldiers and the Soviet*

State: Civilian-Military Relations from Brezhnev to Gorbachev. Princeton: Princeton University Press, 1990.

Collins, Maj. Joseph J. *The Soviet Invasion of Afghanistan: A Study in the Use of Force in Soviet Foreign Policy.* Lexington, Mass.: Lexington Books, 1986.

Colton, Timothy J. *Commissars, Commanders, and Civilian Authority: The Structure of Soviet Military Politics.* Cambridge: Harvard University Press, 1979.

———. "Perspectives on Civilian-Military Relations." In Timothy J. Colton and Thane Gustafson, eds., *Soldiers and the Soviet State: Civilian-Military Relations from Brezhnev to Gorbachev.* Princeton: Princeton University Press, 1990.

Conquest, Robert. *The Great Terror: Stalin's Purges of the Thirties.* New York: Macmillan, 1968.

———. *The Harvest of Sorrow: Soviet Collectivization and the Terror-Famine.* New York: Oxford University Press, 1986.

Daglish, R. K., et al. *Russko-angliyskiy slovar.* Moscow: Sovetskaya Entsiklopediya, 1965.

Dorronsoro, Gilles, and Chantal Lobato. "The Militia in Afghanistan." *Central Asian Survey* 8, no. 4 (1989): 1–8.

Dupree, Louis. *Afghanistan.* Princeton: Princeton University Press, 1978.

Eliot, Theodore L., Jr., and Robert L. Pfaltzgraff, eds. *The Red Army on Pakistan's Border: Policy Implications for the United States.* Washington, D.C.: Pergamon-Brassey, 1986.

Foreign and Commonwealth Office. "Soviet Aid to Special Friends." *Background Brief* (June 1986).

Foye, Stephen. "Chief of General Staff Responds to Criticism of Military Reform." Radio Liberty *Report on the USSR* 1, no. 35 (August 31, 1989): 22–24.

———. "Maintaining the Union: The CPSU and the Soviet Armed Forces." Radio Liberty *Report on the USSR* 3, no. 23 (June 7, 1991): 1–8.

———. "The Soviet High Command and the Politics of Military Reform." Radio Liberty *Report on the USSR* 3, no. 27 (July 5, 1991): 9–14.

———. "Gorbachev's Return to Reform: What Does it Mean for the Armed Forces?" Radio Liberty *Report on the USSR* 3, no. 28 (July 12, 1991): 5–9.

Fukuyama, Francis. "Patterns of Soviet Third-World Diplomacy." *Problems of Communism* (September-October 1987): 1–13.

Fukuyama, Francis, and Andrzej Korbonski. *The Soviet Union and the Third World: The Last Three Decades*. Ithaca: Cornell University Press, 1987.

Girardet, Edward R. *Afghanistan: The Soviet War*. New York: St. Martin's Press, 1985.

Goodman, Melvin A. "Foreign Policy and Decision-Making Process in the Soviet Union" In Hafeez Malik, ed., *Domestic Determinants of Soviet Foreign Policy towards South Asia and the Middle East*. London: Macmillan, 1990.

Gregorian, Vartan. *The Emergence of Modern Afghanistan*. Stanford: Stanford University Press, 1969.

Hingley, J. Ronald. *The Russian Mind*. London: Bodley Head, 1977.

Isby, David. *War in a Distant Country—Afghanistan: Invasion and Resistance*. London: Arms and Armour Press, 1989.

Ivanov, Nikolay. "'Shtorm 333'." *Nash Sovremennik*, no. 9 (September 1991) 148–54.

Jarintzov, Nadine. *The Russians and Their Language*. London: M. Kennerley; 1916.

Karpovich, Michael. "Russian Imperialism or Communist Aggression?" *The New Leader*, June 4 and 11, 1951.

Kenez, Peter. *The Birth of the Propaganda State: Soviet Methods of Mass Mobilization, 1917–1929*. Cambridge: Cambridge University Press, 1985.

Kennan Institute. *Meeting Reports*. (Periodic accounts of lectures given at the Kennan Institute for Advanced Russian Studies at the Woodrow Wilson Center in Washington, D.C.)

Khan, Riaz M. *Untying the Afghan Knot: Negotiating Soviet Withdrawal*. Durham: Duke University Press, 1991.

Khovanski, Sergey. "Afghanistan: The Bleeding Wound." *Détente* 6 (Spring 1986): 2–4.

Khrushchev, Nikita. *Khrushchev Remembers*. New York: Little Brown, 1970.

Kichikhin, Alexander. "The KGB Knew Everything and Acted Accordingly." *New Times* 30–91 (September 3–9,1991): 14–17.

Knight, Amy W. *The KGB: Police and Politics in the Soviet Union*. Boston: Unwin Hyman, 1988.

————. "The KGB and Civil-Military Relations." In Timothy J. Colton and Thane Gustafson, eds., *Soldiers and the Soviet State: Civilian-*

Military Relations from Brezhnev to Gorbachev. Princeton: Princeton University Press, 1990.

———. "The Future of Communism." *Problems of Communism* (November/December 1990): 20–33

Kulichkin, Colonel S. "Desecration of Banners—Perusing the 'Military' pages of *Ogonek*." (In Russian.) *Literaturnaya Rossiya*, no. 15 (13 April 1990): 8–9.

Laquer, Walter, ed., *The Pattern of Soviet Conduct in the Third World*. New York: Praeger, 1983.

Lasky, Melvin J., ed. *The Hungarian Revolution: The Story of the October Uprising as Recorded in Documents, Dispatches, Eye-Witness Accounts, and World-Wide Reactions*. New York: Praeger, 1957.

MccGwire, Michael. *Military Objectives in Soviet Foreign Policy*. Washington, D.C.: The Brookings Institution, 1987.

Malhuret, Claude. "Report from Afghanistan." *Foreign Affairs* (Winter 1983–84): 426–35.

Malik, Hafeez. *Domestic Determinants of Soviet Foreign Policy towards South Asia and the Middle East*. London: Macmillan, 1990.

Malyshev, Venyamin. "Kak my brali dvorets Amina." *Stolitsa* 1 (September 1990): 58–59.

Morozov, Aleksandr. "Kabulskiy Rezident." *Novoye Vremya*, no. 38 (pt. 1—September 1991): 36–39; no. 39 (pt. 2—September 1991): 32–33; no. 40 (pt. 3—October 1991): 36–37; no. 41 (pt. 4—October 1991): 28–31.

Mosse, W. E. *Alexander II and the Modernization of Russia*. New York: Collier Books, 1958.

Nagorski, Andrew. *Reluctant Farewell*. New York: Holt, Rinehart & Winston, 1985.

Nahaylo, Bohdan. "When Ivan Comes Marching Home: The Domestic Impact of the War in Afghanistan." *American Spectator* (July 1987): 15–18.

Nollau, Guenther, and Hans Juergen Wiehe. *Russia's South Flank*. New York: Praeger, 1963.

Ozhegov, S. I. *Slovar russkogo yazyka*. Moscow: Sovetskaya Entsiklopediya, 1973.

Paloczi-Horvath, George. *Khrushchev: The Road to Power*. London: Secker & Warburg, 1960.

Pares, Bernard. *A History of Russia*. New York: Alfred Knopf, 1948.

Parker, John W. *The Kremlin in Transition*, vol. 2, *Gorbachev 1985– 1989*. Boston: Unwin Hyman, 1991.

Pennar, Jaan. *The USSR and the Arabs: The Ideological Dimension*. New York: Crane Russack, 1973.

Pfeiffer, George. "Russian Disorders: The Sick Man of Europe." *Harpers* (February 1981): 41–55.

Polyakov, Yu. A., and A. I. Chugunov. *Konets basmachestva*. Moscow: Nauka, 1976.

Pope, Ronald R. "Afghanistan and the Influence of Public Opinion on Soviet Foreign Policy." *Asian Affairs* (July-August 1981): 346–52.

Radio Liberty. *The Soviet Public and the War in Afghanistan: Perceptions, Prognoses, Information Sources*. Soviet Area Audience and Opinion Research AR-4-85 (June 1985).

———. *The Soviet Public and the War in Afghanistan: A Trend toward Polarization*. Soviet Area Audience and Opinion Research AR-1-87 (March 1987).

Radu, Michael, ed. *The New Insurgencies: Anticommunist Guerrillas in the Third World*. New Brunswick, N.J.: Transaction Publishers, 1990.

Rahr, Alexander. "New Evidence of the KGB's Political Complexion Published." Radio Liberty *Report on the USSR* (January 18,1991): 3 3–4.

Rees, David. "Afghanistan's Role in Soviet Strategy." *Conflict Studies* 118 (May 1990): 1–10.

Roy, Olivier. *Islam and Resistance in Afghanistan*. Cambridge: Cambridge University Press, 1986.

———. "The Origins of the Afghan Communist Party." *Central Asian Survey* 7, nos. 2/3 (1988): 41–57.

Saikal, Amin, and William Maley. *Regime Change in Afghanistan: Foreign Intervention and the Politics of Legitimacy*. Boulder, Colo.: Westview Press, 1991.

Sakharov, Andrei. *Memoirs*. New York: Alfred Knopf, 1990.

Sakwa, Richard. *Soviet Politics: An Introduction*. New York: Routledge, 1989.

Schoenfeld, Gabriel. "Red Inc." *The New Republic* (April 15, 1991): 15–17.

Schultz, Richard. H., and Roy Godson. *Dezinformatsia: Active Mea-*

sures in Soviet Strategy. Washington, D.C.: Pergamon-Brassey's, 1984.

Seabury, Paul, and Walter McDougall, eds. *The Grenada Papers*. San Francisco: Institute for Contemporary Studies Press, 1984.

Shevchenko, Arkady. *Breaking with Moscow*. New York: Alfred A. Knopf, 1985.

Shtromas, Alexander and Morton A. Kaplan, eds. *The Soviet Union and the Challenge of the Future*, vol. 2, *Economics and Society*. New York: Paragon House, 1989.

———. *The Soviet Union and the Challenge of the Future*, vol. 3, *Ideology, Culture, and Nationality*. New York: Paragon House, 1989.

Sinyavskiy, Andrei. *Soviet Civilization: A Cultural History*. New York: Arcade Publishing, 1990.

Sliwinski, Marek. "Afghanistan 1978–87: War, Demography, and Society." Central Asian Survey Incidental Papers Series, no. 6 (London, May 1988).

Smolar, Aleksandr. "Afghanistan et Pologne." *Esprit* (January 1981): 91–95.

Solzhenitsyn, Alexander. *The Gulag Archipelago*, vols. 1–3. New York: Harper and Row, 1974, 1975, 1978.

Staar, Richard F., ed. *Yearbook on International Communist Affairs*. Stanford: Hoover Institution Press, 1981–82, 1984–91.

———. *USSR Foreign Policies after Détente*. Stanford: Hoover Institution Press, 1987.

Szamuely, Tibor. *The Russian Tradition*. New York: McGraw-Hill, 1974.

Tamarov, Vladislav. *Afghanistan: Soviet Vietnam*. San Francisco: Mercury Press, 1992.

Teague, Elizabeth. "Is the Party Over?" Radio Liberty *Report on the USSR*, no. 193/90 (April 24, 1990):1–8.

Teague, Elizabeth, and Vera Tolz. "CPSU R.I.P." Radio Liberty *Report on the USSR* 3, no. 47 (November 22, 1991): 1–8.

Tedstrom, John. "The 1991 Budget." Radio Liberty *Report on the USSR* 1, no. 8 (February 22, 1991): 5–9.

Troyat, Henri. *Catherine The Great*. Translated by Joan Pinkham. New York: Dorset Press, 1991.

Tsypkin, Mikhail. "A Split in the KGB?" Radio Liberty *Report on the USSR* 2, no. 39(September 28, 1990): 6–9.

Ulam, Adam. *Russia's Failed Revolutions*. New York: Basic Books, 1981.

U.S. Department of State. Bureau of Public Affairs. *Tales of Afghanistan, Moscow Style*. Current Policy paper no. 143. Washington, D.C., March 1980.

―――. *Afghanistan: 18 Months of Occupation*. Special Report no. 86 (August 1981).

―――. *Chemical Warfare in Southeast Asia and Afghanistan: Special Report to the Congress from Secretary of State Alexander M. Haig Jr., March 22, 1982*. Special Report no. 98, March 1982.

―――. *Afghanistan: Three Years of Occupation*. Special Report no. 106 (December 1982).

―――. *Afghan Resistance and Soviet Occupation*. Special Report no. 118 (December 1984).

―――. *Afghanistan: Six Years of Occupation*. Special Report no. 135 (December 1985).

Vance, Cyrus. *Hard Choices: Critical Years in America's Foreign Policy*. New York: Simon & Schuster, 1983.

Vasilkov, A. "Operatsiya 'Demsoyuz'." *Novgorodskiy Komsomolets*. (April 30, 1989): 1.

Wesson, Robert, ed. *1983 Yearbook on International Communist Affairs*. Stanford: Hoover Institution Press, 1983.

Yasmann, Viktor. "The Internal Situation in the USSR and the Defense Council." Radio Liberty *Report on the USSR* (September 1, 1989): 8–14.

―――. "The KGB and the Party Congress." Radio Liberty *Report on the USSR* 332/90 (August 3, 1990).

―――. "The KGB and Internal Security." Radio Free Europe/Radio Liberty, *RFE/RL Research Report* 1, no. 1 (January 3, 1992): 19–21.

Newspapers and Periodicals (1978–92)

Afghan Realities (1981–87).
Afghanistan Forum (1984–92).
Afghanistan Forum Newsletter (1979–83).
Christian Science Monitor.
Financial Times.

Foreign Broadcast Information Service (FBIS) *Daily Report*. (Selected translations of foreign media releases.)

Independent. London.

Izvestiya.

Kabul Times (1978–79 and 1988–92).

Kabul New Times (1980–88).

Komsomolskaya Pravda.

Krasnaya Zvezda.

Literaturnaya Gazeta.

Literaturnaya Rossiya.

Moscow News.

New Times.

New York Times.

Novoye Vremya.

Posev.

Pravda.

Radio Liberty *Report on the USSR*. (Weekly publication. Individual articles are cited here by author and title; descriptions of chronological developments are cited only by the issue number and date.)

San Francisco Chronicle.

San Francisco Examiner.

Voenno-istoricheskiy zhurnal.

Wall Street Journal.

Washington Post.

INDEX

103d Airborne Division, 177
106th Airborne Division, 179

Abdur Rahman Khan, 34–35, 40
Advisers, Soviet, 41, 90, 93, 99, 105–6
Afgantsy, 192–93, 199
Afghan Interim Government, 3
Afghanistan, pre-1978: foreign aid to, 34,
  37, 40–43; Russian aims in, 33, 34;
  Soviet influence in, 36–39, 42–44, 89-
  90; wars with England, 5, 33–36, 37.
Afghanistan Commission, 92
Afro-Asian Peoples' Solidarity Organi-
  zation, 94
Ahmadzai, Mohammed Najibullah. *See*
  Najib(ullah)
Aid to Afghanistan: British, 34, 37; Soviet
  diplomatic 47; Soviet economic, 37,
  40, 41; Soviet military, 40–43, 161,
  170, 185–86; U.S., 40–41
Albania, 110
Alexander I, 22
Alexander II, 23–25, 29, 30, 199–200
Alexander III, 25
All-Afghan Women's Council, 156
Amalrik, Andrey, 71
Amanullah, 36–39, 40
Amin, Hafizullah, 52, 91, 99–104, 179,
  199
Amnesty (for Soviet forces), 141
Andreyeva, Nina, 203
Andropov, Yury, 58, 92; and Najib, 150,
  152; as CPSU leader, 114, 121–23, 187,
  195; death of, 134; in Hungary, 77–
  78, 169–70; KGB career, 74, 84, 85,
  172, 175
Anglo-Russian border accords, 34, 35
Angola, 55
Arkhipov, Ivan V., 92
Armenia, 197, 204
Australia (Communist) party, 54-55
Azerbaijan, 204

Bacha-e-Saqao, 38
Bagram air base, 92, 131
Bakatin, Vadim V., 177
Basmachi, 38–39
Beria, Lavrenty, 73–74, 75, 76
Berlinguer, Enrico, 114
Bishop, Maurice, 57n
Borovik, Artem, 28, 134
Boyarinov, Colonel, 103–4, 179
Brezhnev, Leonid, 69, 92, 112, 121; and
  Afghan invasion, 58, 101n; leadership
  style of, 80–82; corruption under, 114
Bukhara, 38
Bulgaria, 110, 176–77

Cambodia, 55, 110
Carter, Jimmy, 56, 109, 110, 111
Carter Doctrine, 109
Casualties: Afghan, 138; Soviet, 99, 127,
  128, 135, 188–91, 199
Catherine the Great, 10–11, 20–22, 25,
  29
Censorship, 23, 24, 25, 29–30, 177
Central Asia, 33, 37–38, 40, 41
Central Asian Confederation, 37
Central Committee (of the CPSU), 78–
  79, 171; International Department of,
  50, 54, 93–94; KGB link broken, 116;
  Ruling Communist Parties Department
  of, 113
Central Intelligence Agency, 90, 103,
  148n, 178
Central Intelligence Service, 70n
Centrist Bloc of Political Parties and
  Movements, 177
Chamkani, Haji Mohammed, 155, 157
Charles XII, 18, 20
Chebrikov, Viktor, 163–69 passim
Chechens, 197–98
Cheka, Chekist. See KGB; Secret police
Chernenko, Konstantin, 121, 134
Chernobyl, 191, 198

220